SIENA

A City and its History

JUDITH HOOK

SIENA

A City and its History

HAMISH HAMILTON
LONDON

British Library Cataloguing in Publication Data
Hook, Judith
Siena
1. Siena – History
I. Title
945′.58   DG975.S5

ISBN 0–241–10297–9

Printed in Great Britain by
Ebenezer Baylis and Son Limited
The Trinity Press, Worcester, and London

For Nathaniel
who gave me a child's-eye view
of Siena

CONTENTS

ILLUSTRATIONS

1*

PREFACE

THE FAME of Siena once rivalled that of any city in Italy. But year by year it is the bookshelves devoted to Florence and Venice that seem in need of constant extension. Siena's particular appeal to visitors from northern Europe has long been recognized so its comparative neglect by writers and publishers is all the more surprising. The last major account of Sienese history written in English, that of Ferdinand Schevill, was first published as long ago as 1909. Although Schevill's fine work still makes rewarding reading there is no doubt that it is now out of date. Since it was written, new manuscript materials have become available and the Archivio di Stato of Siena has been completely reorganized. Changes in public taste have led to a new and more just understanding of the nature of Sienese art and architecture, and much important historical work, most notably that of Professor William Bowsky, has led to a total reassessment of medieval Sienese history. More recently a number of scholars have begun to interest themselves in the forgotten years—the period after the loss of the city's independence in 1555.

The purpose of this book is to take account of these advances in knowledge and to present a reassessment of the history of the city in relation to the great works of Sienese art and architecture which the majority of visitors come to see. The emphasis throughout has therefore been on explaining the peculiar nature of Sienese civilization and why the city we see today is as it is. My concern, in fact, has largely been with urban and cultural history.

Much of the research for this book was undertaken in Italy over a period of several years. This was only made possible by generous research grants from the British Academy, the Carnegie Trust for the Universities of Scotland and from my own University of Aberdeen. I am deeply grateful for this generous assistance. I also owe a large debt to the staff of the Archivio di Stato of Siena, which must be one of the most pleasant places in which to study in the whole world. I should particularly like to acknowledge the kind assistance of the Archivist, Dr. Sonia Fineschi. In my researches I have also been helped and stimulated by many conversations with Professor Giuliano Catoni, whose own work on Sienese history deserves an audience wider than one restricted to those able to read Italian.

Many libraries and their staffs have given me help over the years. In particular I would like to thank the Biblioteca Comunale of Siena, the Biblioteca Nazionale Centrale of Florence and the Library of the University of Aberdeen. For obvious reasons, I owe the staff of the Inter-Library Loan counter of the Aberdeen Library a particular debt. It can truly be said that, without their hard work on my behalf, this book could never had been written.

My particular personal thanks are due to Miss Freda Booth for producing a flawless typescript of my manuscript at a difficult period of the academic year, and to my family who have accepted, without complaint, both my absences in Italy and the necessity of spending their summer holidays in Siena. To my husband, above all, I am indebted for his constant and unflagging interest, for the many insights into Sienese civilization that we have shared, and for his having read the manuscript of this book so carefully.

1

Introduction

'For the sake of all these things men live in peace and harmony with one another.'—San Bernardino

EACH YEAR thousands of visitors come to the prosperous little hill-town of Siena which lies at the very heart of Tuscany. Unless they are attending a course at the University, or studying at the Accademia Chigiana, they do not usually stay very long; Siena, after all, is less famous, less grand, less romantic than Rome, Florence or Venice, and Sienese art is something of an acquired taste. But most visitors will at least go to the Palazzo Pubblico and pause to look at one of the more familiar of late medieval works of art, Ambrogio Lorenzetti's *Allegory of Good and Bad Government* painted in about 1340. Frequently reproduced, almost an obligatory inclusion in any work dealing with medieval or renaissance Italy or medieval town-life, these frescoes have a tantalizing effect, seeming both to resurrect medieval Siena, to make it tangible and populated with familiar figures, and paradoxically, to emphasize the remoteness of an age and a world we no longer share.

In the following account of the history of Siena that remoteness will be reiterated in the discovery of a city whose values are often as particular as they are universal. To understand those values it will be necessary to concentrate more upon a community than upon individuals, and, in consequence, I have chosen to call this study a cultural history. In doing so, I have clearly made a number of assumptions both about Siena and about its civilization. I have, for instance, assumed that there is something unique about Siena and that much of that uniqueness finds expression in its art, architecture, town-planning and urban life. I have assumed, in fact, that the city itself—its buildings, artefacts, institutions, and customs—has been a means by which certain central traditions, whose origins may be so remote that they cannot now be traced, have been handed down from generation to generation,

moulding the life of each individual Sienese, and influencing his attitudes inside and outside his city-walls. The words of the tragic Pia dei
Tolomei—'Siena mi fe—Siena made me'[1]—with their insistence that
the physical and social environment of the Siena in which she grew up
determined her personality and outlook on life, would thus be entirely
comprehensible to every Sienese since Pia's day.

Such assumptions about the uniqueness of the particular urban
experience are, perhaps, essential to the study of the evolution of any
town or city. Certainly, similar assumptions would have to be made
in considering any Italian city, for, in Italy, *campanilismo*—attachment
to one's local church-tower—has remained one of the primary human
experiences. Each Italian city has its own essential character which it is
the task of the urban historian to identify and explain. What are the
distinctive elements that make Florence, Florence, or Siena, Siena?
Such a question is clearly not easy to answer, but it can be approached
by studying the mixture of economic, social, political and cultural
forces which, interacting together, created each individual city and
community.

Clues to the particular nature of Siena's civic identity are to be
found in the Lorenzetti frescoes of *Good and Bad Government*, for they
date from a period when, out of the context of the Italian city-state,
there had emerged a new and exciting view of the place and the function of the city within human society. For the first time since the fall
of the Roman Empire, a positive value was placed on the communal
life of the city, which was seen as the ultimate source of all culture and
civilization. Dante's *Divine Comedy* is one expression of this new view
of the world. In Siena, the Lorenzetti frescoes are another. They are,
in fact, a peculiarly Sienese celebration of life in the city or, as Lorenzetti's contemporaries called it, the *vita civile*, a phrase combining the
concepts of civic life and civilization.

In the creation of the *vita civile* in Siena the visual arts and urban
development played a prominent part. Citizens came to care about
what was said of their city, and hence, about its public image. As the
Sienese Franciscans reminded the magistrates in 1286 when they
wanted help in building the façade of their new church:

> When cardinals and bishops visit our convent, or prelates or ambas-
> sadors from other cities in Tuscany, they see that the façade of our
> church is incomplete and this does not redound to the honour of the
> city of Siena.[2]

The Franciscans would have found an ally in the Sienese chronicler for the year 1309 who thought it as important to record the completion of Duccio's *Maestà*—'the most beautiful picture that anyone had ever seen'—and its installation in the cathedral, as to record a famine, riot or war. An identical concern for the value of their city has since been manifested by Sienese citizens in every century.

Such views are always expressions of what became the most enduring features of Sienese urban civilization: its understanding that the ability of men to live together in cities is itself a work of art, and, equally, its capacity to place a proper value upon that achievement. It is the means by which the Sienese created and maintained such urban values, in a Siena which was always their outward manifestation, that provides the principal theme of this book.

In the process of Siena's civic development different forces were at work and the succeeding chapters select and analyse only those events and influences which had the greatest impact at different periods. In earlier centuries, for instance, when the gravest problems facing Siena seemed to be those making for disintegration and collapse, what appears to have been most important in the creation of Sienese civilization was the conscious imposition of a political and civic framework upon a feudal and frequently disordered world. An account is thus given of this period in which the Sienese genius found its most characteristic expression in the conquest of the Sienese *contado*, in the creation of the city's constitution and the organs of government which were to serve throughout the period of the city's independent existence, and in the development of the great corporate institutions, like the Cathedral, the Hospital of Santa Maria della Scala, and the University or Studio, which are so characteristic of Sienese urban life. This lengthy process of urban consolidation was to reach its apogee under the rule of the Nine in the thirteenth and early fourteenth centuries, a secular regime remarkable as one of the first to make a lavish patronage of the arts into an essential arm of government. The manner in which the Nine were effectively to inaugurate a new period in the urban history of Siena, after the essential political, social and economic structures of the city had been delineated, and when the main and most enduring lines of an urban framework had been drawn, is examined in some detail.

For the succeeding century and a half Sienese civilization was to develop according to a pattern established in the earlier middle ages, just as the Sienese citizen was to live his life largely within an urban fabric which had been created before 1355. Whenever he happened to live within this century and a half, the citizen's concerns would have been the same—and instantly comprehensible—to his thirteenth-century counterpart: the maintenance of justice and order in the urban community, the supremacy of the common good over the rights of the individual, the value of the corporate experience, the threat to the Sienese community from internal faction and from external hostile forces, and the just reconciliation of sacred and secular concerns.

The first major change in this overall framework came in the later fifteenth and early sixteenth centuries, partly through internal shifts in the social and economic structures of the city which found expression in the art of the Sienese Renaissance—here reassessed—but also with the loss of independence after a protracted and particularly bitter struggle. That struggle, in turn, created a series of myths which ever since have dominated and nourished Sienese culture. Walking about Siena today, one is constantly made aware that the heroic if tragic days of the last siege of the city are but a matter of yesterday, that the events of the war that accompanied that siege are still a matter of debate, and that the bitterness of the final surrender in 1555 can never really be assuaged. So important is that struggle to an understanding of present-day Siena and, indeed, to an understanding of the significance of the Sienese Palio, that a chapter has been devoted to an episode which, while it has been seen to represent a special chapter in the history of the struggle for Italian independence from foreign rule, has rarely received the attention it deserves from non-Italian historians.

All subsequent developments in the urban civilization of Siena have, to some extent, been a comment upon the events of 1552–59. But those events, in turn, inaugurated a new phase in the development of Sienese civilization in which the Sienese had to come to terms, not, as previously, with themselves, but with outsiders. They had to learn to preserve and maintain their unique Sienese identity in the context first of the Grand Duchy of Tuscany, in which they frequently appeared to play but an insignificant role, and subsequently of that greater Italy which was brought into being by the Risorgimento. This was to be achieved by a careful balance of the preservation of the old, the introduction of the new, and the perpetual nourishing of myths which find their truest expression in the Palio. Thus the subject-matter of the last chapter is the Palio itself which today is as true an expression of Sienese urban values as the Lorenzetti frescoes of *Good and Bad Government* were of those values in the fourteenth century.

The Palazzo Pubblico seen across the Campo

The City of Siena from Orlando Malavolti, *Dell 'Historia di Siena*

The Sienese State from ibid.

Model of Siena in the fourteenth century, based upon Lorenzetti's *Good and Bad Government*, and now housed in the Palazzo Pubblico

Duccio, *The Healing of the Blind Man*

The Fontebranda

San Domenico and the Cathedral from the Lizza

2

Medieval Siena

The government of the communes was never like the majority imagine it. There are many who, like Dante, lament the past at every opportunity, just as if there was once a time without passions and without crime; all they praise are the works left by our ancestors.—C. Falletti-Fossati

I

SIENA IS a typical Tuscan hill-top town. At 322 metres, perched on the hills which separate the basin of the Arbia from that of the Elsa, the city's elevated site, from which it dominates the surrounding countryside, was determined by the centuries of disorder which followed the barbarian invasions and the collapse of the Roman empire. A hill-site was more easily defended than a lowland one, so Siena is built along the curves of three ranges of hills separated by characteristic ravines and valleys. From one of these ridges, one can look across to another area of the city, separate, but still a part of the whole, enclosed within the circuit of Siena's fourteenth- and fifteenth-century walls. On the highest ground in the city—the Castelvecchio—stands the Duomo or cathedral. It would seem the natural centre of Siena were that role not disputed by the Campo, the public square which slopes downwards in a graceful curve to the Palazzo Pubblico, where a slender tower—the Mangia—rises to the same height as the cathedral. Siena, then, like the majority of medieval towns, was built around not one but several focal points.

Siena is a beautiful city. In medieval Italy, there were, no doubt, other towns and cities quite as beautiful, but, by an accident of history, it is Siena which has survived unspoilt. One of the most important commercial and banking centres of Europe between the twelfth and the fourteenth centuries, it subsequently suffered economic and political eclipse and entered a period of relative obscurity. This meant that little was added to the city's essential fabric between the late-sixteenth and the twentieth centuries and, as a result, the greater part of its medieval inheritance has been preserved. Siena, therefore, is still to a considerable extent the expression in physical form of the cultural values of the medieval urban mind; the articulation in stone, brick and marble of a medieval view of the world.

An important and powerful ingredient in that view of the world was the whole corpus of myths, beliefs and legends about Siena's past history which became woven into the fabric of urban life. Myths and dreams, for instance, were part and parcel of the stories concerning her origin in a Roman past. That the city once had such a Roman and, indeed, an Etruscan past, there is no doubt, but the actualities of Siena's classical experience have little to do with the city's subsequent development. City-life in medieval Europe had virtually nothing in common with city-life in antiquity, and the cities themselves existed for purposes and were based upon social structures which were completely different in the two eras. It was, therefore, neither the Roman city-state, nor the Roman city's function, nor the Roman city's structures that contributed to the subsequent development of Siena, but Roman myth and Roman symbolism.

Of such myths, the most picturesque was that which described how Siena was founded by Senius and Ascius, the sons of Remus, who gave to the city the symbol of the she-wolf suckling her twins, which can be observed in manifold different guises and materials all over the city. The she-wolf and her twins are still the badge of Siena and in the past were so important that in 1264 a painter was fined for decorating a shield with the image of a wolf overcome by a lion.

According to this legend of the foundation of Siena, when Senius offered sacrifice to the gods, a dense black smoke arose from the altar of Apollo and a pure white smoke from that of Diana. Alternatively it is said that Senius rode a white horse, Ascius a black. This gave to the Sienese their enduring symbol of the *balzana*, the black and white communal shield which decorates the city's gates and all her public buildings. Two other shields often accompany it: a blue shield with the word *Libertas* in gold letters, and a red shield with a white lion rampant. These also are symbols of the commune, and, about them, as about the *balzana*, legends were inevitably woven. Reputedly they were gifts to Siena from the Emperors Charlemagne and Otto respectively.

Emperors were accorded peculiar respect in Sienese mythology for Siena was one of the more famous of the Ghibelline cities. No town or city in medieval Italy could avoid becoming involved in the dispute between Guelphs and Ghibellines, and Siena lay at the heart of the

conflict for control of Tuscany. Having once decided for the Ghibellines, she never voluntarily wavered in her allegiance and, if not from
Charlemagne and Otto, at least from later emperors derived substantial benefits. It was, for instance, the great Frederick Barbarossa
who in 1186 conceded to the city, the right of self-government, which
included the election by the Sienese of their own consuls, the right
to coin money, and jurisdiction over both the city and the *contado*.

The Ghibelline allegiance of Siena was to give birth to further and
more elaborate historical legends, but the essential fact about such
manifestations of pseudo-history is not that they in any way embody
an accurate account of the city's past, but that the past they seem to
describe was one that was believed by the Sienese. Furthermore,
because the legends were accepted as true, a series of memorials based
upon them were created and displayed to the people in the city, so
reinforcing the original myth. Similarly, throughout Siena's history,
great and stirring moments came to be enshrined in tangible monuments, which served both as aids to memory and as the starting-point
for new legends. For some hundred years, for instance, the white
standard reputedly flown by the Sienese at the battle of Montaperti in
1260 was preserved in the sacristy of the hospital of Santa Maria della
Scala, together with the box used for balloting Sienese elected officials.
Before proceeding to the ballot the banner was unfurled so that, in the
words of the chronicler, 'the memory of that glorious event could
be recalled.'[1]

Legends were of particular importance in Siena because they were
a most important binding-force for a people whose social life appeared
to be characterized more by division, factionalism and violence than
by unity and civic virtue. Yet despite the perennial turbulence of Siena's
medieval history, unity and civic virtue also existed outside of the
world of myth, legend and propaganda, and exercised a powerful
civilizing force within the community. Given that the whole tendency
of the medieval world was to prefer the corporate to the individual,
and to subordinate the particular to the general, once the commune
could convey the idea of itself as the most perfect of corporate bodies,
without which salvation was impossible, it was bound to attract the
allegiance of the Sienese community as a whole.

By the twelfth century the commune had found powerful allies in
the developing legal bodies of Siena where, by 1176, a college of
judges and notaries was already in existence and public instruction
in the law was offered. Lawyers and notaries were largely responsible

for the formation of the central civic ideology. Forming as they did both a literate and a responsible secular group, with strong professional instincts, it was they who helped to formulate the important concept that only the commune embodied the absolute values of Justice and Good Government, without which civic government was impossible. Probably another consequence of this large legal presence in the city is the fact that, by 1179, Siena already had a written constitution.

Yet the ultimate victory of legalism and constitutionalism, of city and commune, over other bodies or individuals who challenged their authority, was no easier in Siena than in other Italian cities, and in some ways was never fully achieved. From the beginning, the church naturally presented a strong alternative claim to overriding authority. As in other Italian cities, after the end of the Roman empire and of the rule of the Lombards and Franks, it was under the leadership and governance of her bishop that Siena's inhabitants struggled to impose some kind of order onto a frequently chaotic world. The bishopric of Siena was rich and powerful and the bishop was therefore the most important force in civic life. It was, in fact, over their own bishop's quarrel with the bishop of Arezzo about the limits of his diocese, that the Sienese first showed any recorded sense of corporate identity or civic purpose. During these struggles, however, they were of so much assistance to the bishop that he was forced to give them an increased say in the management of Siena, although it was not until 1167 that the commune first declared its independence from episcopal control. For centuries thereafter, whenever they felt in a position of strength, the bishops still tried to reassert their power.

Like others founded elsewhere in Italy in the twelfth century, the commune of Siena was a fruit of the revival of town-life in the tenth and eleventh centuries. It was in essence an association of the city's leading citizens—*the boni homines*—by which they bound themselves together by a horizontal oath to pursue common ends, and to preserve internal order, stability and justice. The chief organ of the commune was the *parlamento*, or general assembly, first heard of in 1137, which met in the open, either in front of the cathedral or in Piazza Tolomei in front of the church of San Cristoforo (San Cristofano). Here the commune began in 1125 to choose elected representatives, the consuls, to act as an executive. Selected from among the commune's most powerful members, the consuls served for a year and were always either three or six in number.

Thus, at the very beginning of Siena's recorded independent urban existence, three entered into the civic consciousness as a significant number. Three and multiples of three were, thereafter, to play a vital role in Siena's life. The number of governors in her chief magistracy—three, twenty-four, thirty-six, nine, twelve or fifteen—and in her other administrative offices, was always divisible by three, reflecting, one suspects, the rooting of the city's government in its very structure, in the fact that Siena came into existence by an alliance of groups or tribes, each occupying a different hill or fortress. To the south-west was the oldest settlement, the Castelvecchio or Castel Senio; to the north the Camollia; and to the east the Castello di Montone, all, by the end of the thirteenth century, included within the circuit of the city-walls. This tripartite division survived to become incorporated into the subsequent division of the city into the three Terzi: Terzo di Città, Terzo di Camollia and Terzo di San Martino. Throughout the middle ages, Terzo di Città, the most ancient and where the majority of private palaces was situated, was the wealthiest and the most important.

The topography of Siena with its three hill ridges helped to perpetuate this tripartite division. So also did her most important roads, for Siena's arterial communications lead in three directions: to Florence, to Rome and to the Maremma. As a result, throughout the life of Siena as an independent city and state, the Terzi survived as small communes in their own right, corporate bodies within a corporate body. Each had its own separate civil authority, its own military and economic organization, and each levied its own taxation. On the battlefield each wore its own colours; red for San Martino, green for Città and black and white for Camollia. And thus, from the time of the consuls onwards, the Supreme Magistracy of the Republic was normally composed of a number of men drawn equally from each Terzo.

The surviving strength of this territorial division within the city suggests that the formation of the commune of Siena represented but a tentative gesture towards a corporate civic life on the part of a number of warring clans. Siena, which, rather than Verona, was the home of the first Romeo and Juliet story, was, like other Italian cities, divided into a number of systems of family alliance and patronage, each system headed by one of the noble families who initially dominated the commune. These families were of diverse origins. Some, like the Salimbeni and the Buonsignori, were descendants of foreign invaders, counts and barons of the Frankish and Germanic emperors. Others—as the Piccolomini were always to claim of themselves—may have been descendants of old Roman families. But by the mid-twelfth century, there was nothing to distinguish the five leading noble families who had come to dominate Siena's fortunes: the Piccolomini, the Tolomei, who claimed descent from the Ptolomies, the Malavolti, the Salimbeni and the Saracini, and the names of these families were, for centuries, to be interwoven with the civic history of Siena. Even today the Gothic palace of the Salimbeni, home of the Monte dei Paschi, and the nearby Palazzo Tolomei (first built in 1208), also now a bank, give clear expression to the kind of social and political predominance once enjoyed by their owners.

That predominance affected the whole life of the city, for it was based on an elaborate system of relationships and clientage which ultimately embraced the entire population of Siena. These patronage systems were centred upon the noble *consorterie* or family power-groups, a typical example of which in ninth and tenth century Siena, was that of the Ugurgieri who held a fortified quarter within the city, still known as the Castellare degli Ugurgieri, an aggregation of houses and fortresses, inhabited by their family and their clients. From here they would issue forth into the streets to do battle, occasionally with the enemies of the city, but most frequently with their noble rivals. Whole areas of the city were thus alienated from public control of any kind. In 1262, for instance, the commune interested itself in improving the street system of Terzo di Camollia:

> because there is only one road and one street there . . . and also because the men from the other *Terzi* who have to go to Camollia, neither can nor want to pass in front of the houses of certain nobles.[2]

From the commune's point of view, the situation was particularly difficult, in that the *consorterie* tended to be clustered along the principal thoroughfares which ran along the ridges of the hills on which Siena was built. The houses of the non-noble and the poor were to be found in the valleys and they could be easily dominated by the noble fortress which was at the heart of each *consorteria*. This fortress took the form of a tower, which served as a place of refuge, defence and prestige. The earliest example of a Sienese family being permitted to build such a tower by the commune is that of the Gallerani in 1186, but there is little doubt that, for at least a generation before then, other families had already been erecting their own, with or without communal sanction. By the beginning of the fourteenth century, when there were upwards of fifty in the city, the sky-line of Siena was dominated by these lofty symbols of noble power, and around them the palaces of the *consorterie* tended to be grouped. Of all these towers the most remarkable was that of the Sansedoni, which was so high that it rivalled even the Torre di Mangia.

The military effectiveness of such a tower as that built by the Sansedoni may be seriously questioned and this suggests that the real importance of any noble tower was its symbolic value, its capacity to indicate the particular area of territorial control enjoyed by a family within the city. Thus the destruction of a tower was a direct attack upon the power of a *consorteria* and it became the custom for the commune to punish unruly or rebellious nobles by destroying their towers or houses; in 1270, for instance, all the houses of the Incontri were burned or pulled down. Popular disturbances and riots often had the same result; the rioters would attempt to destroy a focus of power within the city by removing its physical manifestation. The symbolic importance of such actions is emphasized by the fact that it became the custom to use the materials from such demolished buildings in the construction of communal projects. Thus, as late as 1408, the portion of the new city-wall between Santo Spirito and San Giovanni was built with materials from former palaces of the Malavolti.

One manifestation of the territorial control exercised by the *consorterie* was their domination of local parish churches, each of which came to acquire something of the status of a family chapel. In this way, for instance, the Ugurgieri controlled the church of San Vigilio, and the Tolomei that of San Cristoforo, and even in the eighteenth century, the church of San Gregorio was still regarded as a family chapel of the Malavolti. Given this concentration of power on a territorial basis, it is scarcely surprising that, by the thirteenth century, many of the *contrade* or *popoli*—the small administrative districts into which Siena was divided—took their names from one single dominant family living within them. Nor is it surprising that the pattern of urban settlement in Siena should have been determined more by family than by occupation or employment.

Territorial control by powerful families over the city was, nevertheless, as has been implied, disliked by the commune, which spent much energy in trying to weaken it. Yet, well into the modern period, the assertion of such control by powerful families remained a reality; as late as the first half of the sixteenth century, the noble palace was still partially conceived as an offensive fortress. Hence, as a result of its domination of Siena's corporate life—economic, social, political, religious or cultural—the ethos of a noble class came to affect the whole of Siena, and many values which came to be embodied in the commune originated in the courtly world of the nobility. An aristocratic sense of honour, for example, expressed in violent terms through the blood-feud or *vendetta*, was to find its way into the official life of the city. Thus the commune never rejected the *vendetta* completely, choosing rather to try to limit its effects. Indeed in a curious document known as the *Memoriale delle Offese*, in which were recorded any wrongs done to Siena by her citizens, it tried to utilize the code of honour in the service of the city, enjoining the citizens never to forget:

> through eternity, those who deny you, who withdraw themselves from the homage they owe to you, that plot against you and bring shame to you. . . .

Such an example suggests how a noble or knightly view of the world came to permeate the whole of society, and it was nourished by the fact that Siena was a city often at war. Her major antagonist was Florence, with whom Siena was brought into direct confrontation as her rule expanded out from the city-walls into the countryside around.

Throughout most of the twelfth and thirteenth centuries, then, Siena was engaged in a series of wars with Florence, struggles so bitter that they have coloured the relations of the two cities until the present day. Some bitterness was injected into the conflict by the fact that it involved the antagonistic ideals of Guelph and Ghibelline, more by commercial rivalry between the two republics, each anxious to capture for its own merchants a monopoly of papal finances, but most by the fact that each was striving to expand its territory at the expense of the other. A unique twist was given to this conflict because Siena was unusual among capital cities in being also a frontier town, so that in any war with Florence, Siena itself was immediately and directly threatened.

From the Sienese viewpoint the culmination of the struggle was the defeat of the Florentines and the Guelph allies at the battle of Montaperti in 1260 on the day the 'Arbia river flowed red with blood.'[3] Sienese pride in the victory is reflected in the fact that today during football matches between Siena and Florence, the Sienese will bid their opponents to 'Remember Montaperti!' For all of its mythological status for the Sienese, Montaperti was, however, a short-lived victory. The pope declared a ban on Siena and withdrew his protection from her merchants; King Manfred fell at the hands of papal forces in the battle of Benevento in 1266; and in 1269 at Colle Val d'Elsa, the Florentines reversed their defeat by annihilating the Sienese forces and capturing and executing their great leader at Montaperti, Provenzano Salvani.

Such constant warfare had two important consequences for the urban development of Siena. The first was that the sheer cost of war necessitated the development of communal institutions and in particular of communal fiscal instruments. For warfare would more than double the normal annual expenditure of the commune. The two years of fighting in 1230 and 1231 were years in which the commune's expenditure ran at between £50,000 and £55,000 per annum, as opposed to a normal peacetime expenditure of between £10,000 and £20,000. The renewal of serious warfare between 1257 and 1268 raised annual expenditure to a level of about £60,000 a year and this pattern was to remain fairly constant. The need to collect revenue on such a scale meant that the commune had, very swiftly, to develop new institutions to cope with the problem.

A second major consequence of continued warfare was that it helped to sustain a view of the world in which knightly and chivalric views seemed of abiding importance. It was inevitable that the attitudes and values of those who supplied Siena with her military captains and the bulk of her cavalry, and who continued to play an important part in the government of the city-state, should continue to exercise a powerful influence on the life of the city. None the less, other powerful forces were working against the continuing predominance of the old nobility over the political and cultural life of the city. In the early twelfth century a movement began which can be closely paralleled in other Italian towns, the rise of the *popolo*. There was a time when English-speaking historians were happy to translate the word 'popolo' as people, and, by so doing, to give birth to a whole series of misconceptions about the democratic character of Italian civic government in the Middle Ages. We now recognize that those governments were in no sense 'democratic' as we understand the meaning of the word. Rather they were oligarchies, and the *popolo* a highly selected citizen-élite, whose leaders differed scarcely at all in wealth, economic interest or power from the nobility they professed to despise and with whom, in fact, they customarily inter-married and conducted their business.

Elsewhere in Italy, the organization of the *popolo* was normally based on the guild structure, but since Siena was a commercial and banking rather than an industrial city the guilds were never strong. As a result the *popolo*, like so many Sienese institutions, seems to have been topographically rooted. Its organization was related to the militia companies of foot-soldiers which were raised locally within the city.

Broadly speaking, the leaders of the *popolo* were traders, merchants, manufacturers and bankers who had risen to wealth and consequence within the city. They presided over what was, effectively, a state within a state, a corporate body, structured much like the commune itself, existing parallel to it, and sometimes, but by no means normally, in opposition to it. At times, indeed, it seems almost a parody of the commune; in 1255, for instance, the *popolo* set up its own bell, saying that the one belonging to the commune was barely audible. Like the commune, the *popolo* had its own *podestà*, or chief executive authority, its own judge, its own treasurer, notaries, heralds and messengers, General and Secret Council.

By 1147 the *popolo* was powerful enough to challenge the exclusive nature of noble control over Siena and successfully demanded a third share in the communal offices, with their own elected official, the Captain of the People, established alongside the city's *podestà*. By the end of the twelfth century the *popolo* had further increased in power and was clearly dissatisfied with its share in the city's government, for, from 1213 onwards, it emerged as a violent force in politics. This was a year of many civic disturbances which culminated in attacks on a number of noble towers. Change came eventually in 1233 with a further advance for the *popolo* when, in one of the few peaceful revolutions recorded in Sienese history, a magistracy of twenty-four was created to govern the city, a half-share of whose offices was reserved to the *popolo*. In 1270 this magistracy was further enlarged to thirty-six, although it remained equally divided between nobles and *popolani*. Finally, in 1280, the nobles were completely excluded from the supreme magistracy of the city, power being vested in 'Fifteen Governors and Defenders of the Commune and People of Siena' all members of the *popolo*.

The most significant aspect of the rise of the *popolo* within Siena is that it was an exclusively urban phenomenon, the product of a specific and unique environment. The *popolo*, in other words, was the most urban of institutions and its values were entirely civic ones. It was natural, therefore, that, in time, the *popolo* should come to be seen as the embodiment of civic virtue. Some of the suspicion felt and expressed towards the old Sienese nobility derived not only from concern over its pride and ambition, but also from a sense that the values of a feudal aristocracy, no matter how urbanized that aristocracy might be, were essentially inappropriate in civic life.

The leaders of the *popolo*, as we have seen, were businessmen—

merchants or bankers—and Siena, by the early thirteenth century, was already one of the most prosperous cities in Europe. As a city, she had always enjoyed certain natural advantages as the centre of an agricultural region which produced a variety of crops, and, in normal years, a surplus of those most vital to the economy. It included some of the best pasture in Europe and the hill-slopes of the region were planted with an abundance of olive-groves and vines. Mineral wealth was also important; in 1137 the bishop of Volterra ceded to the bishop of Siena half of Montieri with its valuable silver mines. Until the silver was exhausted towards the end of the middle ages, these were a very important source of communal income.

Siena became a major commercial centre partly because it was situated on two of the most important trunk-routes in Italy. The first of these was the old Via Francigena, the main communication route between France and Rome, down which pilgrims, in particular, passed in large numbers; by the eleventh century a number of hospices existed in Siena along the Francigena, founded by pious individuals to house and care for these pilgrims. The Francigena was sufficiently vital to the economy for the Sienese statutes of 1262 to devote considerable attention to its upkeep and maintenance, and a glance at a plan of the city explains its importance. Effectively both the Terzo di San Martino and that of Camollia existed because of and for the Francigena, which entered Siena at Porta Camollia, followed the Via di Montanini and the Via di Banchi di Sopra to the Croce del Travaglio, the meeting-point of Siena's three main streets. From the Croce del Travaglio the Francigena begins its course through the Terzo di San Martino, leaving the city at last at Porta Romana. The second important trunk road, with which Siena was linked, was that which ran from Germany and Austria to Rome and which passed through Bologna and Pistoia by way of the Futa pass. Several sea-ports also provided easy access to Siena: Follonica, Talamone, Santo Stefano and Portercole.

As a result of its favoured position in terms of medieval travel, almost anyone of any importance in the middle ages seems at some point to have turned up in Siena. Henry IV visited it on his journey back from Rome after his coronation; Frederick Barbarossa and Frederick II also stayed there; the ill-starred Conradin passed through on his way to his combat with Charles of Anjou; Giovanna of Naples and the Emperor Sigismund were both received in Siena; and, in 1469, in a series of spectacular celebrations, presided over by Aeneas Sylvius Piccolomini (later Pope Pius II) Frederick III celebrated his marriage with Eleanor of Portugal in the city. This occasion is commemorated by a pillar outside Porta Camollia as well as by the fresco by Pinturicchio in the Piccolomini library. Charles VIII passed through the city in 1494, and Charles V visited it amid universal rejoicings. Popes, as well as secular rulers, were frequent visitors, finding Siena a convenient refuge close to the turbulent Church State. During the Avignonese papacy, papal legates and administrators inevitably passed through the city on their way to Rome or Naples. For Gregory XII, Siena was a second Rome; Eugenius IV, and naturally, Pius II, were equally enthusiastic. Such visitors, with their courts and retinues, provided Siena with an important source of income which it was determined to retain; by 1345 the Innkeepers' Guild of Siena had 100 members, including ten women, carefully supervised by the communal authorities to ensure that they did not cheat their guests.

Given their city's geographical and economic advantages, it is perhaps not surprising that Siena's leading citizens, both noble and non-noble, should have emerged as brilliant bankers and merchants. By 1192 these men had their own Merchants' Guild, and, from the beginning of the thirteenth century, companies of Sienese are to be found trading at the fairs of Champagne where they soon began to retain permanent representatives. On this basis the Sienese built up their banking operations, soon offering a whole range of facilities: deposit, credit and foreign exchange. By the middle of the century the *milites et mercatores Senenses*—the Knights and Merchants of Siena—as they were known to their contemporaries, were great commercial companies with massive capital assets, dealing in the spices of the East and the cloth of Flanders, trading between Rome, Paris and London, and constantly developing their parallel banking interests.

For such men their city had a particular importance. Italian business life was structured around the family, largely because it depended upon the kind of trust which only the bonds of kinship could provide. A natural extension of the family was the *consorteria*; a natural extension of the *consorteria* was the city; to his city, then, the Sienese merchant was deeply bound. While his business might require him to travel throughout the known world, it was within Siena that he built his family residence, and to Siena that he returned to be buried in the family tomb. Whatever their differences might be within the city walls, once outside of Siena the dominant feeling of her citizens was that of being Sienese. It is no accident, therefore, that the oldest document in Italian is an account-book, written by a Sienese merchant in 1211.

A passionate patriotism affected the way of life of these merchants, a patriotism which found expression in a multitude of ways, from the assertion of the value of the Tuscan vernacular, as opposed to clerical Latin, to the eternal flame which burned always before the *carroccio*— the communal war-cart. The Sienese merchants loved their city above all things and gloried in its precious autonomy, that *Libertas* which facilitated their business affairs. As a group, therefore, they may be fairly represented by Salimbene Salimbeni who, in 1260, as the Florentine troops advanced on Siena and the commune found itself without the money to pay its mercenaries, sent to the communal meeting-place in front of San Cristoforo, a cart covered with branches of olive, to signify the joy he felt at being able to come to the city's aid in its hour of need. Inside the cart was found a sum of money sufficient to pay the wages of 800 mercenaries for the ensuing battle.

The events of 1260 seem to suggest a new sense of civic unity, which in the latter part of the thirteenth century also found expression in the first communal buildings: the Palace of the Captain of Justice, the Dogana on the site of the future Palazzo Pubblico, and the first projects for the building of that palace itself. This new sense of civic unity had developed out of the growing complexity of city life which forced the commune to shoulder more and more responsibilities, in an increasingly prosperous community, and so to impinge upon the consciousness of most of those within it.

The new prosperity itself was based on and reflected in a growth in the size of the city, which, by the mid-twelfth century, had a population of some 15,000, increasing to 20,000 by 1260. By the mid-thirteenth century Siena was thus one of the largest cities in western Europe. The increase in population came, of course, from immigration, for the death-rate in all pre-industrial cities was so high, that the urban population never reproduced itself. The immigrants themselves can be divided into two somewhat arbitrary groups. The more important, from the point of view of the commune, were men of substance from the Sienese *contado* attracted, particularly in the prosperous twelfth and thirteenth centuries, by the legal and economic advantages offered by life in the city. More problematical for the commune were the serfs or ex-serfs who came to swell the numbers of the city's proletariat; they helped to foster a kind of civic feudalism which was to be a marked feature of late medieval Siena where the most characteristic labourer was not the free man offering his labour for hire on a daily basis, but the man or woman who gave his or her labour to one of the great corporations, like the hospital of Santa Maria della Scala, or to one of the great family clans, under conditions of dependence which were not far removed from traditional feudal bonds.

Siena's population growth was also related to its continuing success as a commercial centre. Its reputation in the craft and luxury trades was particularly high—Sienese jewellers and goldsmiths already enjoyed a European-wide fame by the twelfth century—but these specialized trades were not major employers of labour. Many Sienese, however, worked in the construction industry and many more were agricultural labourers, helping to farm the estates which lay around the city and which were even enclosed by its walls. Virtually all of these estates were owned either by city-dwellers or by city corporations. And although the textile industry was never to acquire anything like the importance it held for Florence, it was by no means unimportant to the city. Certainly the woollen industry was a heavy employer of labour and was sufficiently powerful to develop its own formidable, corporate institutions; the constitution of 1262 gives clear evidence both of the existence of the Wool Guild—the *Arte della Lana*—and of the involvement in the industry of many important and powerful Sienese families.

As the population increased a number of suburbs grew up around the city-walls and forced the commune to take account of the demographic expansion of Siena. These suburbs, which were effectively demanding incorporation into the city's structures whether defensive or administrative, could not be ignored. Based on the local church, which, in turn, was dependent on the cathedral, each suburb soon had developed its own organization, both religious and secular. The local church served not only as a centre for corporate religious life, but as a place where the inhabitants could meet to discuss problems of common interest: the maintenance of streets and *piazze*; police and the prevention of crime; the allocation of taxation. Out of such meetings came the demand and pressure, above all, for inclusion within the city walls, an inclusion which would bring not only protection but also civic rights.

The demographic expansion of the city meant an inevitable extension of communal power and its administrative tasks. It meant first the constant expansion and renewal of the city-walls; in fact they were extended six times in the course of the middles ages. These walls had to be supplemented by other major defensive works; outside the city the various *antiporti*, which served as defensive outposts, and of which the most imposing survivor is that of Camollia, the last defensive barrier on the road from Florence; numerous barbicans in the most vulnerable places, like those of San Maurizio and Pescaia; and little turrets connected by service walls to the main circuit. Within the walls of the city, all around the circuit, deep ditches were dug as further defence works; these, during times of peace, were rented out and cultivated as garden plots. The existence of these ditches had a fundamental impact on the urban evolution of Siena, for they were sufficiently deep and inconvenient to form a natural barrier within the city, even after their original function was superseded by the extension of the circuit of the walls. In consequence many of the streets of the city follow the old line of these ditches.

The second major impact of the demographic expansion of Siena was that attempts had to be made to solve the problems involved in housing, clothing, creating work and, above all, for feeding an expanding urban population. For five or six centuries every government in Siena was haunted by the fear of famine: as early as 1227 the chroniclers were recording the price of 10s the *staio* as the cost of grain;* in 1258 and 1271 famine forced the commune to import grain from Sicily, while by the end of the century, when Tuscany as a whole was grossly over-populated, famine and its grim attendant, disease, had become endemic. Famine is recorded in 1302; famine and excessive mortality in 1328–9; famine and disease in 1339; and partial famine in 1346. Famine threatened the commune because it brought instability; hunger and starvation frequently led to civic disorders, such as the riot in April 1329, when the populace who were without bread armed themselves with poles and stones and attacked the Palazzo Pubblico. Such bread-riots could, and on occasion did, lead to the overthrow of regimes.

The first concern of every Sienese government, therefore, was the supply of food to the city. Various measures were taken in an attempt to solve the problem; Sienese outlaws, for instance, were granted a safe-conduct of five days, provided they brought grain with them

---

* It is fruitless to suggest modern equivalents for medieval Sienese money. The Sienese reckoned by the *lira*, which was a money of account, not a coin. There were 20 *soldi* or 240 *denarii* to each lira; i.e. £. s. d. The gold florin, also used in reckoning, was a real coin, and the long-term tendency was for the *lira* to be devalued in relation to the florin. In 1287 one gold florin was worth about 36s and in 1355 70s. The *staio* was the principal unit of dry measure in Siena, its nearest English equivalent being the bushel. Twenty-four *staia* were equal to one *moggio* (584,709 litres).

into the city to sell. The commune also maintained its own grain-
stores and placed strict controls on the sale and transport of grain out
of the city. During a famine it commandeered all private grain supplies
and fixed the price at which bread could be sold, at very considerable
cost. The famine of 1339, alone, was popularly reputed to have cost
the commune 40,000 gold florins. A more long-term solution to the
problem of food-supply lay in the expansion of Sienese authority
over the surrounding countryside, so as to gain direct control over the
city's main source of grain and the routes by which food was brought
into Siena.

There was no sudden shift to an expansionist policy. Individual
Sienese had long-established relationships with the Tuscan countryside
where they had vast land-holdings. As we have seen, many of the
immigrants into Siena were not those escaping serfs, so beloved of
popular history, but wealthier property-owners; such men, even after
they moved to the city, continued to maintain close links with the
country, and usually retained their property there as well. Throughout
the middle ages, even the moderately prosperous Sienese citizen
continued to invest in properties and farms in the *contado*, and such
informal property links were often the basis on which the Sienese
commune subsequently established a more formal jurisdiction.
Gradually, but relentlessly, the commune took over neighbouring
castles and villages, forcing the feudal lords who remained there to
become citizens of Siena, to reside in the city for a fixed period in each
year, and to fight for the commune when required. And, as the city's
economy developed, so did the drive towards expansion, especially to
the south and west, which culminated in the capture of Grosseto in
1224. This development gave Siena control over the important ore-
bearing region of Massa Marittima and opened the possibility of
building up Talamone as a commercial port to rival Pisa, then at the
peak of its commercial and cultural supremacy in Tuscany.

At its greatest extent, the Sienese state included all the river basin
of the Ombrone, the valleys of the Albegna, Chiarone, Astrone and
Bruna and the upper courses of the rivers Tasone, Fiora, Paglia,
Foenna, Ambra, Staggia, Cecina, Cornia and Pecora. It was in no
sense a state in the modern meaning of the word, with an internal,
cohesive jurisdictional uniformity, but was divided into cities and
masse, the *contado*, and at her jurisdictions. It included direct subjects,
vassals, allies and *raccomandati*. The latter were individuals or communities who were promised the right of protection by Siena, in

exchange for the acknowledgement of the ultimate supremacy of the city, but in every real sense, they were autonomous powers. They paid neither taxes, nor loans, nor tribute to the commune, and preserved their own laws, magistrates and administration. The allied towns or individuals had also accepted Sienese overlordship voluntarily, and their relationship with Siena was governed by treaty articles which varied from individual case to individual case, but, normally, they accepted a Sienese garrison force and *podestà* and paid an annual tribute to Siena on the feast of the Assumption.

Despite the variation in status of these dependencies, Siena was, nevertheless, from the early thirteenth century, no longer a city but a city-state, controlling the destinies not only of her own citizens, but also those of the many inhabitants of her *contado* and state. Without that *contado* and state, Siena could never have flourished as she did. They were vital to the city. They were a source of food supplies, of raw materials, and of manpower. They brought in tax-revenue, and were a market for Sienese goods, produce and services. They allowed Siena to control her own trade-routes through Tuscany; they were a source of profit for the Sienese ruling-classes, and a source of soldiers for Siena's armies. In 1292, for instance, 3,000 infantry from the *contado* served with the communal armies, and in 1318, 7,000.

II

The development and rule of a territorial state, the expansion of the city's population, constant warfare, family and factional feuds, and urban violence, were all problems which increasingly put pressure on the existing forms of government within Siena. The result was development, elaboration and change. Already, in 1199, the Sienese had abandoned consular rule, and, in common with many other Italian cities, had substituted rule by one man—the *podestà*—for rule by the consuls.

Several reasons have been suggested for the almost universal adoption of the system of rule by *podestà* by the communes of central and northern Italy at this date. A model was certainly provided by Frederick Barbarossa who appointed several such officials in a number of north Italian towns in the years after 1160, and experience then showed that, in dealings with an outside authority, it was usually better to have one official who could speak for the whole commune. A more powerful and compelling motive, however, probably lay in

2

the factional rivalry between the dominant families in the communes. Since, as we have seen, these families controlled and influenced whole urban areas, open conflict between them led to violent upheavals and street battles which were destructive of life, property and prosperity. The *podestà*, after 1211 in Siena normally a foreign noble, could be supposed to be above factional rivalry, and thus could be accepted as a genuinely impartial source of justice and order within the city. That this was a primary motive in impelling the Sienese towards rule by *podestà* is suggested by the fact that Siena was, proverbially, more faction-ridden than any other Italian town, and by the provision made that each Sienese *podestà* in turn must reside in a different Terzo of the city in order to preserve his neutrality.

The creation of the *podestà* was part of a pattern of rapid change in Siena's governmental institutions. These institutions were first fully described in the written constitution of 1262, drawn up at the height of Sienese power. By this constitution, all power and privilege within the city-state were reserved to an oligarchy of citizens, a situation which scarcely changed during the succeeding 500 years. Only a man who was a citizen could participate fully in the functions of government or in the formulation of public policy. Only citizens were entitled to join one of the city's guilds or to own property in Siena. To the citizens were reserved all influential or financially rewarding offices. Their business affairs were carefully protected by the commune's courts, which were particularly adept at shielding a citizen from his debtors, and would protect any citizen against external temporal jurisdictions. In time of war a citizen might have to fight for his city, but he was guaranteed free medical treatment for any war wounds, and the payment of ransom by the commune if his own resources were inadequate. He could even expect free maintenance for life in the hospital of S. Maria della Scala if he were so disabled by war injuries as to be incapable of earning his own living.

The life of the Sienese citizen was, then, a privileged one; but, at least in the middle ages, Sienese citizens did not form a closed caste. Although the normal route to citizenship was through birth, it was simple enough for a man to purchase admission if he wanted it, by paying 20s, promising to enter his properties on the tax register, building a house in Siena, residing there with his family, and performing all services required of him by the commune. He then automatically became a Sienese citizen if he received the approval of at least two-thirds of the General Council.

This Council was the principal legislative body of the city by 1262. It was composed of at least 300 citizens, equally divided among the Terzi, chosen and presided over by the *podestà*. The Consuls of the Merchant and the Wool Guilds sat by right on the Council, as did the Rector of the hospital of S. Maria della Scala.

At this period, as we have seen, the permanent executive body of the city was composed of twenty-four councillors, equally divided among the Terzi, half of whom were nobles and half *popolani*. They were chosen by election from the General Council. From this twenty-four, one man was chosen from each Terzo every fortnight to hold supreme executive power. The resulting triumvirate were known as the Priors of the Commune.

Administrative authorities were also chosen from and by the General Council. Of all the offices, the most important in the communal period was the Biccherna, Siena's main department of finance, where all business was concentrated. Throughout the twelfth and thirteenth centuries this office lacked a permanent home; located first in premises attached to the church of San Vigilio, it then moved to San Pellegrino alla Sapienza and then to San Cristoforo, until finally, at the end of the thirteenth century, it was transferred to the new Palazzo Pubblico. This lack of premises must have been a constant handicap and irritant, for the Biccherna was an immensely busy office. First mentioned in 1167, it was not only a treasury department, controlling the revenue and expenditures of the state, it also supervised many minor administrative offices. It was thus, for example, ultimately responsible for the building and maintenance of roads and streets, for the supply of regular building materials to the cathedral and other public works, and for the weapons of the commune.

The Chamberlain or Treasurer of the Biccherna was, normally, a monk from the great Benedictine house of San Galgano, near Siena, a religious being chosen for this vital office because of his presumed incorruptibility. His staff consisted of four *provveditori*—officials appointed by the General Council for periods of office of six months' duration, which began in January and July of each year. The holders of these posts were always among the most distinguished citizens of Siena, for the simple reason that a *provveditore* had to be extremely wealthy. Since Siena was no exception to the general rule that all medieval governments were always short of ready money, the *provveditori* had to have enough liquid capital to be able to advance money to the Biccherna, either to pay off their predecessors' debts, or to tide over the Biccherna until cash from its major sources of income came in.

Today the Biccherna is most widely known for its records and, in particular, for the *Tavolette di Biccherna*, that series of paintings which began life as the wooden covers of the great parchment volumes in which the Biccherna officials entered their accounts. The first of this series of *tavolette* to have survived is that for 1258 when the retiring Treasurer, Don Ugo, had his portrait painted on the cover. The Sienese love of decoration and beauty in all areas of life guaranteed that this would become a regular practice; the portrayal of one individual was followed by the portrayal of the Treasurer with his notary, seated working at his bench, or by the portrayal of allegorical figures or important episodes in the life of Siena.

By the second half of the fifteenth century, the Biccherna covers had become pure works of art, with no functional purpose. The covers of the registers were now made of leather, rather than of wood, but the officials continued to have *tavolette* painted. These increased in size, being no longer limited by the form of the register, and became more and more like normal paintings, so that the last two Biccherna covers of all, those of 1619 and of 1677–82, are not even painted on wood but on canvas.

It is significant that this practice of the Biccherna was soon copied by the office of the General Gabella, for this, Siena's second major financial office, was, by the end of the thirteenth century, almost coming to challenge the Biccherna in importance. The General Gabella had probably evolved out of the Biccherna in the mid-thirteenth century and its main function was to receive the income derived from the gabelles of Siena, i.e. taxes on a whole range of commodities and business transactions. The General Gabella had, like the Biccherna, a chamberlain, who was normally a religious, either from San Galgano or from the Umiliati, and three executors.

The Biccherna and the General Gabella were both highly efficient administrative organs, as indeed they needed to be. Constant warfare was proving to be very expensive to the commune. In peacetime too, in the later thirteenth and early fourteenth centuries, expenditure was growing as the commune was forced to intervene in more and more areas of urban life.

Among the earliest matters to force themselves on the attention of the city communal authorities were the streets of Siena. In the past, influenced by a somewhat romantic attitude towards the middle ages, writers have tended to describe the street system of Siena as a 'natural' one, as if the streets had been thrown up by some elemental forces. In fact, it can only be described as natural in that it was highly successful in fulfilling the obvious needs of the city; the two main and symmetrical streets, the Via Banchi di Sopra and the Via Banchi di Sotto, for instance, form a beautiful parabolic curve, which accords precisely to the needs of those riding on horseback at high speed, and thus was a vital part of the city's defensive system. The same curve was of equally vital functional utility during civic processions, since it permitted the processors to be both participants and observers at the same time. But the suitability of these streets to Sienese urban life does not mean that they were unplanned. On the contrary, like all the existing street-systems of Siena, they were the fruit of careful control by the commune, a form of town-planning dating back to the early middle ages. As early as 1218, the Podestà, Ugolino da Salamone, had made an attempt to systematize all the streets and squares of Siena and, by 1226, an office of three existed, charged with the care of all the streets. This office could arrange for paving, choose the workmen to be employed, and provide for the upkeep of areas which had already been paved at communal expense. This office was still in existence in the mid-thirteenth century, but by then it had acquired new powers. The commissioners were now also responsible for keeping the streets clean and unblocked by refuse; they had power to order the removal of overhanging gables, which were both a fire-hazard and an obstruction to light and fresh air, and, most important of all, they had the power to create new urban thoroughfares.

How far the commissioners were actually able to exercise these powers must remain questionable. One glance at any fourteenth-century narrative painting by a Sienese artist, including *Good and Bad Government*, will suggest that in the matter of balconies, projections and outside staircases such statutes remained for the most part pious hopes rather than enforceable regulations. In all areas of medieval administration, the theoretical and the practicable coincided only rarely. Thus, as we have seen, communal officials in Siena were attempting to control a people whose sole concept of space was that it was not public but private property, and to interfere with powerful families who exercised considerable territorial control within the city. The communal statutes seem to recognize this problem when they make those whose houses lined a street responsible for paying for any improvements made to it.

Whatever the economic advantages such improvements might bring, from the commune's point of view they had the added advantage of reducing the power of territorial control which a *consorteria* might exercise. For this control was based on a system, common to most medieval cities, that each quarter was totally self-contained and virtually forbidden territory to outsiders. The streets were so narrow, twisting, and illogical as to form what amounted to an arcane maze, only penetrable by initiates. Communal authorities, therefore, controlling this situation and trying to maintain or to create an urban network of streets within Siena, came into conflict with private interest and were themselves subject to private influences which prejudiced the impartial exercise of their office. Consequently, in 1292, authority over the streets and roads of Siena and its *contado* was vested in a new official—the Judge of Streets—who was to be a foreigner born outside of Tuscany. To him complete control was given over all matters concerning roads, bridges and fountains in both city and *contado*.

The addition of the supervision of fountains to this list of duties is significant, for this was another area in which circumstances forced the commune to take an active role and so helped the development of overall city planning. The provision of water in adequate quantities was an essential prerequisite for a flourishing urban community in medieval Italy; not only was it vital for drinking and washing, it was essential to all of the major textile industries and to leather-working. By 1262 the government of Siena was already concerned that the woollen industry might suffer through a lack of water and therefore decided to provide basins and fountains that would be reserved exclusively to that industry's use.

The difficulties involved in such an enterprise were manifold, for the problem of providing Siena with a good water-supply had already engaged the commune for more than a century. The difficulty was created by the very nature of the Sienese water-supply which was drawn from vast underground aqueducts, called *bottini*, which fed the public fountains. Over the centuries an underground acquatic world was created beneath the streets of Siena, which was to provoke wonder in even so eminent a visitor as Charles V who declared that Siena was more remarkable below than above ground. No private interests could have created or maintained this complicated system and the only alternative source of water-supply consisted of private cisterns. In addition, water was so precious that the fountains were made an integral part of Siena's defensive system. Each, as the architecture of those which survive suggests, was a fortified strong-point, a mini-fortress. Those which lay beyond the city walls like Fonte dei Pescaia, were, like the antiports, defensive points outside the city, while those which lay within the walls were small communal fortresses inside the urban complex.

So much care and concern was lavished upon the fountains of the Sienese, whose attitude to water frequently bordered on the idolatrous, that they became, even in the middle ages, one of the city's most famed features. Each was carefully designed to include a series of basins to serve different functions. In the first, the water was collected, and this clean water was restricted to domestic use. The second basin was for the watering of animals; the third for washing clothes or for industrial purposes. In the more sophisticated fountains, the surplus water was then collected and channelled off, 'so that it is not lost but returns to the use of the community.'[4]

By the early fourteenth century the provision of an adequate water-supply for the growing city had clearly become a matter of most urgent concern. In 1295 the *Operaio del Duomo*, or Master of Works of the Cathedral, was commissioned to institute a search for the mythical river—the Diana—which was reputed to run under the city, a search which was to earn for the Sienese the characteristically uncharitable derision of Dante.[5] In the same year a commission composed of the painter, Duccio, and four stonemasons, was instructed to sink wells, on behalf of the commune, wherever they deemed it appropriate.

More and more frequently the General Council debated the question of the shortage of water: 'which is one of the four elements, without which life is impossible.'[6] The commune both encouraged the construction of private wells and cisterns and provided new public fountains itself; in 1302 land was purchased in Vallerozzi to build the Fonte Nuova, which was finally completed in 1323; the Fonte Pino was constructed in 1338, and the Fonte Gaia was also first projected in these years.

The result of all these measures to improve the street-system and the water-supply was that, by the end of the thirteenth century, the commune had effectively taken to itself much of the responsibility for the appearance of the city. The constitution of 1309 even forbade the erection of any new buildings in the city unless previous planning permission had been received, in order to 'prevent those who build from trespassing on public streets or any of the rights of the commune'.[7]

By 1300 some 300 decrees on the statute book were directly or indirectly concerned with civic development and a committee was being appointed annually to survey the town and advise on any projected building plans for that year. The office of the Judge of the Streets was not only in existence but reasonably effective; he was already establishing a norm for the width of the streets of six *braccia* and insisting on a uniform brick paving for the streets.

A related area in which communal control was (by the end of the thirteenth century) fairly extensive, was public health. A provision of some kind of medical service had always been a concern of the commune, and, from 1250 onwards, one of the most sacrosanct of fixed charges on the communal revenues was that which went to pay the master who taught medicine in the University. But the avoidance of disease was a matter of even greater concern to the civic authorities. For this reason the most stringent controls were exercised over the sale of all fresh foodstuffs. The problem of keeping the city clean was attended to equally carefully. Indeed the constitution of 1262 shows a positive obsession with the subject, extending its concern not only to the streets but also to such areas as the squares and the streets around the churches, particularly those of the friars, to the Campo, and to the other open spaces of the city which were to be kept free of all refuse. In an attempt to see that, at least in this area, its decrees were observed, the commune ordained the appointment of one man in each *contrada* who was to be responsible for supervising the cleaning of streets and other public spaces. These decrees were further strengthened in the 1309–10 constitution which places a universal ban on the emptying of refuse, slops or latrines into the street, and forbids the keeping of pigs or sheep within the city. A further decree of 1334 appointed a non-Sienese official who was to prevent the keeping of swine within the city-walls.

Fire was another danger of city-life which in Siena fostered government intervention. The majority of houses were either built of wood or had a wooden infrastructure, and Siena, like all medieval cities, was full of stables, stalls, grain and hay-stores. Even the smallest fire might therefore spread with alarming rapidity. In 1153 the church of San Vigilio was completely destroyed by fire; in 1260, virtually the whole of Terzo di Città; and in 1302 the palaces of the Saracini and the Scotti, along with many other buildings in their immediate vicinity. The commune responded to the hazard in various ways: by issuing building regulations designed to minimize the fire-risk, by disciplining certain hazardous occupations, and by punishing severely anyone found guilty of causing a fire. Except for the house in which a fire had started, the commune paid compensation to the owners of houses destroyed in this way and to those whose houses might be destroyed in order to prevent a fire spreading. It also made itself responsible for fire-fighting, delegating the task to eight master-carpenters who were paid an annual salary for their services.

As a consequence, therefore, of a series of empirical responses to a number of external threats and internal problems, by the end of the thirteenth century, the Sienese commune enjoyed a very elaborate structure of government. This can be illustrated by a study of the Sienese archive, which, even for richly-endowed Italy, is unusually comprehensive for the thirteenth century. Statutes of the commune exist from the middle of the century, records of income and expenditure date back to 1226, and the reports of the General Council begin in 1249.

A study of these records reveals, as we have seen, a city with a high concentration of population, expanding through constant immigration, largely from the *contado* and region around Siena. It reveals a city with a mixed economy of commerce, industry, services and agriculture, but one in which commerce was the pacemaker of economic change. It uncovers an embryonic, if not very powerful, guild system and a far more powerful and very sophisticated political organization, designed to protect the interests of the city and its citizens. It reveals a highly complex administrative structure in which the vast majority of citizens participated, presumably at the expense of their other obligations and commitments. It has been estimated that, by 1257, when the adult male population cannot have exceeded 5,000 there were some 860 offices held by Sienese in the city, involving every aspect of city life. Among these officials were 171 night watchmen, 114 supervisors of tolls and customs, and 90 officials concerned with tax assessment. In addition, there were coiners, supervisors of weights and measures and of grain and salt sales, custodians of the fountains, gaolers, executioners, the officials of the streets and houses, trumpeters, six 'good men' charged with supervising the inns and preventing swearing, and another six who were responsible for keeping out wild donkeys, pigs and lepers, and for preventing people from spinning wool in the street. Even those men who did not participate in the government of the city by holding one of these offices, or by sitting in the city councils, might yet participate in decision-making at a local level, in Terzo or *contrada*, or they might be members of any

2*

one of the numerous *ad hoc* or permanent committees created to supervise the daily administration of the city. Such widespread participation in the tasks and responsibilities of government, fostered a pride in the city and an enthusiasm for its well-being, which in turn shaped the cultural life of the city, expressed through its religious and secular ceremonies, through its urban architecture and city-planning, and through its educational services.

By the second half of the thirteenth century, men had a clear idea of the difference between city and country life, and of the advantages offered by the former. Social mobility was undoubtedly easier in the city, and Siena offered a particular attraction as a place in which to obtain specific kinds of training. Its *Studio* or university, carefully fostered by the commune, which paid the salaries of its masters, offered instruction in Law, Medicine, Grammar and Dialectic. It was within Siena also that a man might be trained professionally, as a notary, for instance, or as a goldsmith, a painter, a mason, as a merchant or a banker. In the thirteenth century this was as true as it was to be in 1360 when Maestro Naddo di Corbo, a carpenter from Montesevoli, declared that his original reason for moving to Siena had been to provide his sons with an education and that they were now, 'satisfactorily trained in the art of manufacturing wool' and 'unable to work the land'.[8] We hear also of the sons of Bandino di Salvuccio who, according to their father, were of 'good habits, suited to the civil and urban life, rather than to that of rustics,'[9] and of Tolomeo del fu Meuccio di Compagno who left the village of Percenna for Siena because he was avid for knowledge 'and he knew that he would acquire no learning if he stayed in the country'.[10]

What we glean from these examples is that, by the beginning of the fourteenth century, a clear sense existed of the distinct superiority of city life, not just among men like Ambrogio Lorenzetti and his patrons, but among many of Siena's ordinary citizens, such as, once again, the four brothers who emigrated from the hamlet of Pietralata and declared that they did so because they knew they were born to enjoy the delights of the refined life of the city. They would, they maintained, infinitely prefer to live as only humble artisans in Siena, than till the land like the peasants of the *contado*. It was this emergent bourgeois mentality, this sense of the immense value of city life and of its unique qualities and opportunities, that, in Siena, helped to create the great cultural achievements of the fourteenth century.

3

The Rule of the Nine

'Or fu giammai
Gente si vana come la Sanese.'
Dante

THE BATTLE of Colle Val d'Elsa in 1269 effectively closed a chapter in Sienese and in Tuscan history, bringing to an end the period of Ghibelline ascendancy. Whatever the traditional sympathies and emotional attachments of the Sienese, and there is some evidence in the proverb coined by the Florentines at this time to describe their neighbours—*La Lupa puttaneggia*, i.e. The She-wolf plays the whore—that they remained Ghibelline orientated, there was now no question of the city choosing any foreign policy other than alliance with Florence and membership of the Tuscan league.

In the cultural history of Siena this was a development of profound significance, for it gave a completely new direction to Sienese art with remarkably beneficial results. The new Guelph alliance placed Siena, for the first time, in regular and close contact with both Naples and France, and so brought to the city new artistic influences. In 1310, Robert of Anjou was actually in Siena, concluding an alliance between the Angevins and the Tuscan Guelphs; his arrival was to be of immense significance in the career of Simone Martini who worked for Robert in Naples. The Guelph alliance thus opened for the Sienese the world of French Gothic and Martini's *Maestà* provides the first evidence of their direct contact with French painting. French influences were also being transmitted to the Sienese at the same time through the building of the new Cistercian abbey of San Galgano, close to the city, which, although it had been begun in 1244, was not completed until 1288. Here for the first time, the Sienese came directly into contact with the verticality and elegance of northern Gothic architecture, which during the next hundred years they were to adapt, transform, and absorb into characteristic Sienese architectural forms.

Since Siena now formed an important link in the Tuscan Guelph alliance, it was essential that power within the city should be vested in a magistracy of Guelph sympathies and so, in 1287, the ruling magistracy of Fifteen was reduced to Nine members of the *popolo*, the famous, 'Lords Nine, the Defenders of the Commune and *Popolo* of the city and district of Siena, and of the jurisdiction of the same.' This magistracy was to give to Siena two generations of stable, prosperous, and peaceful government in which the city reached its highest peak of civic development; when, in the words of one chronicler, Agnolo di Tura:

> The Sienese and their city lived in great peace and tranquillity, everyone attended to his own business affairs both in the city and in the *contado*, and all loved each other as if they had been brothers.

It was a period subsequently looked back on almost as if it had been a golden age. Filippo Agazzari was to recall it in his *Assempri* as a period in which:

> Siena was in such great peace, and in such great abundance of all earthly goods, that almost every feast day, innumerable weddings of young women were celebrated in the city.

The magistracy which presided over this wonderful period in Siena's history was drawn from what was, unquestionably, a restricted oligarchy, from which the nobility, the judges and the notaries were specifically excluded. All candidates for the ruling magistracy of the Nine, which appointed its own successors, had to be over thirty, members of the *popolo* and of the Guelph party. The majority of those successful in obtaining the highest office also turn out to have been closely related to each other. Nor was oligarchical control restricted to the ruling magistracy. It was extended into all areas of civic life. Members of the Nine or their kin were preponderant in the Biccherna, and usually served as ambassadors, castellans, war captains and directors of public works. The Nine and their relatives tended to be in the majority on civic committees and in public councils. The necessity of placing their supporters in all the really key positions of government also led the Nine to make some changes in traditional communal practices. The possibility that having the General Council select the members of the Biccherna might lead to the election of opponents of the Nine was too great a risk to be ignored, and the Nine chose the Biccherna members themselves, in consultation with the Four Consuls of the Merchant Guild. The Nine were also careful to appoint their own supporters to the leading police offices, and it is an indication of the importance they attached to urban planning that the Supervisors of the Streets were also appointed directly by them. The Sienese militia companies were headed by men who were amongst those most trusted by the regime, and, from these companies, a further élite corps was created, composed of eight men from each company, 'lovers of the pacific state of the city of Siena', who, at the least sign of disturbance, were to hasten to defend the Palazzo Pubblico.

A distinct concern for law and order was also a marked feature of a regime which invested heavily in building new communal prisons. A large police-force was created, with about one law-enforcement officer for every 145 inhabitants, and this force was supplemented by the night-watch, composed of small groups of citizens. Siena was subject to strict curfew, with only authorized persons—the night-watch, visiting doctors and priests, rubbish collectors—moving around the city after dark. Among many who paid the 20s fine for infringing the curfew was the Sienese poet, Cecco Angiolieri.

Yet although an oligarchic and a frequently repressive regime, the Nine must be seen as representative of a very large body of Sienese citizens. Although they were described as being drawn from the *gente di mezzo*—the middling sort of people—and as 'good and loyal merchants, devoted to the Guelph party', such a description disguises the fact that among the Nine there were wide disparities of wealth and status, as well as a diversity of occupation. While bankers and international merchants undoubtedly predominated, among the Nine there were also wool manufacturers, spice-dealers, a goldsmith and even an innkeeper. Many of the Nine were also large-scale property owners in the *contado*.

Again, a high proportion of the moderately wealthy Sienese must have sat on the ruling magistracy or Consistory* at the time of the Nine, for this was rotated on a bi-monthly basis. Therefore, between 1287 and 1355, some thousand men must have sat on the Consistory. Even those who did not so serve probably enjoyed considerable experience of government in the many other posts which were still available in the Sienese administration, and whose number continued to proliferate under the rule of the Nine.

* Before the development of the Bal*i*a in the fifteenth century, this was the name always given to the ruling magistracy, whatever its composition. It is also known, somewhat confusingly, as the *Signoria* and the Senate.

It is also abundantly clear that the Nine did not wish to be associated with any particular clan, class or faction, that their rule was, in no sense, partisan. Among all medieval regimes, not only in Siena, but in the whole of western Europe, the rule of the Nine is remarkable for its flexibility and for its refusal to be tied to any one set of attitudes; in 1355 the General Council enunciated the view ultimately derived from Justinian that: 'it is fitting that human statutes be changed according to changing times.'[1]

There is no doubt, in fact, that the Nine tried to govern in an equitable fashion and in the interests of the whole community or the Common Good. Many works of art commissioned by them essentially proclaim the determination of the Nine to oppose any privileged group in society, and in the administration of the law, to give Siena, in reality, justice and good government. Members of the great noble clans, like the Piccolomini, and even relatives of the Nine, were unable to escape punishment with all the rigours of the law when their conduct merited it. As a result of major offences, the houses of even such powerful families as the Tolomei were destroyed. The Nine, for the same reason, fearlessly asserted the rights of the commune over the clergy of Siena, even when such a policy brought them into direct conflict with the bishop armed with his threat of excommunication. Within four years of their seizure of power, they felt strong enough to support their *podestà* against Rome, when he was excommunicated for beheading a priest, 'an act of justice . . . which was approved by everyone.'[2] For similar reasons, the Nine asserted the right of the secular authorities to control the hospital of Santa Maria della Scala.

All citizens were to be equal before the law, and to have free access to justice. The city's statutes were translated into the vernacular, 'to avoid all ambiguity' and 'to the end that poor folk and other persons who know not Latin may be able to see and copy the same at their will.' Those too poor to have any civic rights were still protected by three Judges, one from each Terzo, who were known as the Advocates of the Poor. They were employed and paid by the commune to serve as lawyers for paupers in both civil and criminal cases, and, for these services, they were not allowed to charge their clients a fee. So, in theory at least, no man in Siena might claim that he was denied justice because of his poverty.

Taxation was also spread broadly and fairly and matters were arranged in such a way that, when direct taxation became inevitable, the wealthier members of the commune bore the brunt of payment.

As was made clear in 1307 when the annual *contado* liability for taxation was reduced, 'because equity and justice must be served in every city and every community,'[3] the principle on which the system was based was closely associated with the important role assigned to Justice in the state. Taxation must be fairly spread because, 'whatever is unequal is intolerable.'[4]

Normally, the major part of civic income came from the *gabelle*, particularly from sales and excise taxes, farmed out to companies of Sienese businessmen, and from the rent of communal properties in the city and *contado*. Voluntary loans at a high interest provided additional income as did court fines, profits from the communal salt-monopoly, and various fees. If the sum of these did not meet current needs then the Nine either had recourse to the *Lira*, a graduated property tax, or to forced loans, levied on the wealthier inhabitants of the city and *contado*. In such circumstances, it was always from those best able to pay that the greatest sacrifices were demanded.

The Nine's concern for the community as a whole is also shown in strenuous and, normally, successful efforts to ensure an abundant and inexpensive food supply for the mass of the urban population. The purchase of Talamone in 1303 was a part of this strategy, for it was intended to develop it into a flourishing port to rival Pisa and Genoa. The Nine also carefully fostered industry and the nascent guild structure. The wool industry, in particular, enjoyed a brief period of great prosperity, producing cloth for an expanding local market. From 1338 onwards there was a considerable investment by the Wool Guild—*Arte della Lana*—in new premises and properties, but even so a petition of 1341 records that:

> there is a great shortage of cloth in the city. For the wool manufacturers do not . . . respond to the opportunities available in Siena.[5]

The difficulty as far as the woollen industry was concerned lay in keeping pace with an expanding population, for the increased prosperity of Siena was reflected, as we have seen, in a continued growth of population. The years between 1287 and 1330, saw a great influx of immigrants into Siena from the *contado* and the neighbouring states with the result that by 1330 Siena's population had reached its highest peak. Much of this expansion may be explained by the increased availability of employment in Siena during these years, in which the cathedral was being enlarged, the streets reorganized, fountains rebuilt and the Palazzo Pubblico erected. And immigration, particularly when it involved prosperous, skilled or professional men, all of whom were, of course, potential taxpayers, was overtly encouraged. The Nine shared the conviction, general among contemporary Italians, that a city's strength was to be measured largely by the size of its population.

By 1318–20, therefore, it has been estimated that the population of Siena was already 52,000. This made it very large indeed in medieval terms when even a population of 800 could give a settlement urban pretensions. In 1323 it became necessary to build new walls and gates in the region of Valdimontone in order to reduce urban congestion. In the following year the commune purchased land from the Church of San Martino which lay between the old and the new gates of Valdimontone. This area became the new district of Borgo Santa Maria. It is typical of the attitude of the Nine that they should have used this opportunity to improve Siena's amenities; after 1306 any new citizen was required to build a house in Borgo Santa Maria which was to be valued at, at least, £100.

Such urban programmes were but one aspect of the most remarkable feature of the rule of the Nine: the great programme of public works which the regime financed. Since, in addition, they consistently favoured any projects which celebrated their city or enhanced its prestige, Siena, as it is today, is in large part their creation. It was the Nine who gave to the city the Campo, the Palazzo Pubblico, the Torre del Mangia, the project for the new cathedral, and the new buildings of the hospital of Santa Maria della Scala. They were responsible for the paving, widening and straightening of many city-streets, for the rebuilding of Porta Romana, the most majestic of Siena's city-gates, for the creation of public parks, and for many other communal projects.

The motives for such public works were always a combination of the idealistic and the intensely practical. The Nine did want to embellish the city for beauty's own sake, but they also wanted to impress foreigners with the splendour and the power of their community. Thus they normally explained their activities by the traditional formula: 'for the honour of the commune of Siena, and for the beauty of the city.'[6] The Nine wanted to suggest that their city was powerful, by displaying its wealth, but they also wanted to enrich Siena. They wanted to give pleasure to the citizens, but also to control the activities of those citizens. Such a mixture of motives was involved in the decision of 1309 'to make a park between the gates of Camollia', which was to be both, 'for the beauty of the city and . . . for the delight and joy of citizens and foreigners',[7] but which was also to help foster trade by providing a site where fairs could be held. Similarly, a grant to the Wool Guild in 1346 to build the fountain of Vetrice may certainly be seen as a way of improving the city's appearance, but it was also intended to assist the development of the textile industry. Equally, there is no doubt that although the ruling élite were alive to the aesthetic qualities of space and light in the urban framework, their overriding concern in improving the street-system of Siena was a desire to control the populace more effectively, by eradicating those decayed areas of the city which fostered crime, violence, murder and rape.

A similar mixture of motives explains the careful fostering of learning which is so marked a feature of the rule of the Nine. The University was encouraged because the pursuit of knowledge was recognized as valuable for its own sake, but also because an internationally famous University attracted foreigners and, with them, trade and business to the city. The international reputation of Siena was also enhanced. One indication of the seriousness of purpose of the Nine, in relation to the University, is their instruction to their representatives in 1348 to spend whatever sums they found necessary in order to persuade the Pope to bestow on Siena the coveted title of *Studium Generale*. Although, in this ambition, the Nine were thwarted, they were more successful in expanding the scope and improving the quality of the Sienese University. A solid financial basis was provided, for the first time, by the conversion of the Casa della Misericordia, a hospital, originally founded by the Blessed Andrea Gallerani, into the Sapienza or residential college of the University. Privileges, particularly tax-exemptions, were accorded to any scholars or teachers who came to Siena, and an especially warm welcome was extended to those who moved from Bologna in 1321. They were given an official reception in the Palazzo Pubblico where they were addressed by Messer Biagio di Montanini. The schools of Medicine and of Theology seem particularly to have profited from the careful nurture of the Nine, the esteem in which Theology was held by the ruling regime being demonstrated in 1340 in the public funeral given to the Augustinian, Fra Gherardo da Siena, the author of several major theological works. Secular learning also flourished and one member of the old nobility, Gianpaolo di Meo Ugurgieri, translated the *Aeneid* into Sienese prose during the regime of the Nine.

Under the rule of the Nine, Sienese civilization achieved a new maturity. Two poets of international repute and remarkable sophistication, Cecco Angiolieri and Bindo Bonichi, himself a member of the ruling élite, helped to win for the city a reputation as a place of wit, grace, elegance and humanity, celebrated in verse by Fazio degli Uberti:

> By that road that takes the easiest route
> We made our way to the city of Siena,
> Which is situated on a strong and healthy site,
> Full of gaiety, and good customs
> Of attractive women and courteous men,
> A city with a sweet, mild and serene air . . .

A contemporary at this time described Siena in admiring terms as a city which had, 'an abundance of men of letters, of experts in civil and canon law and practitioners of other professions and occupations'.[8] Among such professions and occupations it seems natural to count the visual arts in a period when Giovanni Pisano, Duccio, the Lorenzetti and Simone Martini were all active, along with a host of minor artists. In 1311 an incomplete taxation record of Terzo di Città shows that in this area of the city alone, there were ten painters, twenty-one goldsmiths, two miniaturists and twenty-one stonecarvers.

The most remarkable characteristic of the large number of artists and craftsmen supported by the commune at this date, is the very high quality of their work. The painting, the architecture, the sculpture, and, indeed, the literature produced during the rule of the Nine is all both innovatory and of the highest quality. The *Dolce Stil Nuovo* in the arts found no happier a home than in Siena, and for this the Nine must take much credit, for they created an ambience in which all of the arts could develop.

In the free and reasonably peaceful Siena of the late thirteenth and early fourteenth century, learning, as we have seen, both flourished and was encouraged to flourish. The existence of a tradition of civic learning, exemplified by the University and by courses of public lectures, was reflected in the works of painters like Ambrogio and Pietro Lorenzetti with their philosophical and mathematical bent. It also contributed to the work of the Sienese sculptors and architects, and, in particular, to Giovanni Pisano.

The free and dynamic society of Siena also facilitated the process, so marked in all the arts, by which the different artistic disciplines learnt from each other, and were inspired to experiment. The advances in sculpture at the end of the thirteenth century were, for instance, a prerequisite for the development of a new, naturalistic style in painting, and themes, first explored in sculpture, such as the *Madonna Lactans*, were then taken up by painters. Literature, also, had a marked effect on the visual arts. In this context, it is important to remember that literature whether religious or secular was not in fourteenth-century Siena a private but a public experience. Arthurian romance, for instance, was a part of the stock-in-trade of the *cantastoristi*—ballad-singers—who performed in the Campo, as well as being a cult of the Sienese nobility, whose world is explored in the poetry of Folgore da San Gimignano. He compared the young nobles of Siena to Priam's sons:

> Valiant and courteous more than Lancelot
> Each one, if need should be, with lance in hand,
> To fight in tournament at Camelot.

Such feudal romances became a major source of inspiration in the work of Simone Martini.

Other themes in painting also originated in the literary world. Martini's own portrayal of the Virgin in the *Maestà* as the Queen of Heaven, derives not from any visual model, but from the Italian religious lyrics which became so popular in the later thirteenth century, and, most probably, from a poem of Giacomino da Verona, the *De Jerusalem Celesti*, which pursues the theme of Saints and Angels pressed around the Virgin to render her a courtly homage. An equally important influence on painters were the popular *Laudi* or sacred songs which were sung by bands of pious men and women throughout Tuscany and Umbria, and which were especially popular in a city which, in Bianco da Siena, produced one of the best and most-loved authors of *Laudi*. These songs were the source for the beautiful motive of intercession which is expressed in Duccio's *Maestà* by the four kneeling saints—the advocates of Siena—and by the invocation of Duccio himself:

> Give to Siena peace. Give to Duccio eternal life because he has painted you so.

Nor can music-making, which is so important and attractive an element in Sienese painting, from the time of Martini to that of Rutilio Manetti in the early seventeenth century, be seen apart from the other arts at this time, for music was also designed for public rather than for private entertainment, and was a necessarily shared dimension of the communal experience. Among the most important servants of the commune were the musicians of the Palazzo Pubblico. These, in 1314, included five trumpeters, one drummer, a bag-piper and a man who played the *maccara*—a pair of copper Saracen drums. These musicians participated in all public functions and festivals and accompanied the Nine on all ceremonial occasions.

One reason for the high quality of all the arts at the time of the Nine, then, was their public nature. The only important patrons were public, and the most important of all was of course the government. For it was not only the Nine, as the supreme civic magistracy, who provided artists with the opportunity of employment on public works. Other government offices also acted as important patrons: Ambrogio Lorenzetti's *Annunciation*, for instance, one of the finest and most original works produced in fourteenth-century Tuscany, was painted in 1344 for the Gabella officials whose names can still be read on its base. In 1322 the Biccherna commissioned Simone Martini to paint a St. Christopher to symbolize the protection they offered to the poor and the weak.

The ruling authorities realized the importance of extensive patronage in controlling society. In this context, expenditure on such ephemera as public festivals was perfectly acceptable. Even in the fourteenth century, Sienese festivals were already famed throughout Europe, for the art of their management was perfected at the time of the Nine. Their value, of course, was the opportunity they provided to restate and to emphasize in public the order of society and its essential hierarchies. They also provided an opportunity for the Nine to harness potentially unruly forces and passions in the service of their regime. To this, for instance, the Sienese owed the introduction of a Palio or horse-race in 1306 which was to be run in honour of the Blessed Ambrogio Sansedoni. Sansedoni had died in 1288, and, immediately, a highly popular and undisciplined cult had sprung up around his name. The Nine, in a sense, were now diffusing that cult by making it official and diverting the violent emotions and passions of the crowd into the running of the Palio.

Public displays and festivities had a further effect on the city in that they encouraged a similar public display by private individuals. All possible occasions for festivity and ostentation were taken advantage of. Betrothals were celebrated in public on the Campo before a notary. Marriages were occasions for riotous extravagance. Even funerals became elaborate and expensive festivals, ending with a splendid feast. The funeral of a citizen, described as 'poor' in 1294, ended in a meal at which were consumed one hundred loaves of bread, a barrel of wine and one hundred fish. Charities were founded to pay the expenses of burial for those too poor to leave money for the purpose.

The nobility, in particular, outdid each other in lavishing money on public display which indicated their power within the city. The bestowing of knighthoods on their sons was celebrated with public banquets and balls. It is this aspect of life in Siena which is reflected in the poetry of Folgore da San Gimignano, whose *corona* of fourteen sonnets was addressed to a group of twelve young Sienese noblemen, who spent their days in a round of diversions: feasting, hunting, jousting and making love to beautiful young women. There is little evidence here of that sobriety which is normally held to be a mark of bourgeois society.

We should, however, see such expenditure as much more than simple examples of conspicuous consumption. Ultimately they derive from the same impulse as led the Nine to make heavy investment, not just in ephemeral festivities, but also in the visual arts and in town planning; the recognition that the effective use of visual symbols could help to mould society in desired directions. The Nine thus had both the motive and ability to patronize an enlightened programme of civic artistic development.

The Nine were not, therefore, financing projects for their own personal and private enjoyment, but projects to be seen, enjoyed, experienced and learnt from by the Sienese public as a whole. To a certain extent, such a programme of patronage of the arts had long been built into the commune's statutes. The *podestà*, on assuming office, swore 'to maintain and conserve the cathedral of Siena and the hospital of Santa Maria, and all the venerable places of the city and *contado* of Siena', and successive communal governments had made frequent contributions to the building and decoration of churches within Siena. This policy the Nine maintained; in 1309 they provided 100,000 tiles and a quantity of mortar for the rebuilding of San Domenico. In 1329, in response to a plea by the Carmelites, they contributed £50 towards the important painting they had commissioned from Pietro Lorenzetti, and in 1339 they made a grant towards the rebuilding of San Francesco.

What was common to all these projects was their corporate and public nature. As we have seen, the Nine were prepared to patronize the arts because they saw that, in this way, they might influence the commune as a whole. In consequence, participation in the artistic event was expected of every citizen in Siena. Thus an anonymous chronicler records of the installation in the cathedral of Duccio's *Maestà* which had taken three years to complete and had cost the commune 3,000 gold florins, more even than Nicola Pisano's deservedly famous pulpit:

> On the day when the new picture was brought to the cathedral all the shops were closed, the bishop having ordered a great procession to accompany the painting to its destination. Priests and monks, therefore, together with the Council of the Nine, the city officials, and all the inhabitants marched in solemn procession. One behind the other, the city dignitaries marched beside the great picture, each carrying a burning taper, with women and children bringing up the rear with great devotion. After this manner was the altar-piece brought to its resting-place in the cathedral. Right round the Campo the procession paced, as is customary; meanwhile the bells pealed the 'Gloria' in honour of the beautiful painting for the high altar.

Such descriptions vividly reveal the integration of art into the whole life of the community, so that it was natural for Simone Martini to sign his *Maestà* by the simple statement:
Siena had me painted by the hand of Simone.

As an expression of the corporate life of the people, and totally relevant to its experience, art played a highly functional role in Sienese society. Under the Nine, the Campo was carved out of the city in order to create a neutral ground in which impartial government and justice might flourish; buildings like the new cathedral or the Palazzo Pubblico were designed to fulfil specific religious and civic functions. Paintings and sculpture were commissioned for celebratory, didactic or minatory purposes. Thus a new secular emphasis was brought to both architecture and to painting. For artists this was often a great liberation, providing them with unprecedented opportunities to explore the new realism which was at the time such an exciting force in Italian painting.

An example of secular minatory painting was the commission to Simone Martini in 1330 to paint a portrait of the rebel, Marco Regoli, in the Sala del Concistoro in the Palazzo Pubblico, and a combination of the celebratory and the minatory are to be found in the famous and entirely secular fresco which Martini painted of Siena's war-captain, Guidoriccio da Fogliano, to record his victory over the *contado* nobles of Montemassi and Sassoferrato. This work was originally commissioned in 1328, despite the fact that that year was one of great famine, urban rioting and attacks on the city's grain-stores by the starving populace. As originally conceived, the fresco did not show what we see today, the isolated and noble figure of Guidoriccio, but the power and majesty of the Sienese commune and the penalties of rebellion. It was, in fact, part of a much larger fresco which illustrated all the castles conquered by Siena since 1314, running continuously round three-quarters of the Sala del Mappamondo.

The art which the Nine patronized could also teach a less distinctly political lesson. Let us consider the anonymous chronicler on Duccio's *Maestà* again:

> . . . the altar-piece was completed, brought to the cathedral and placed above the high altar after the previous picture had been removed; this one now hangs above the altar in the church of San Bonifazio and is called 'The Madonna with the Great Eyes' or 'The Holy Mother of Mercy'. This latter picture was the one which heard the prayers of the people at the battle of Montaperti when they vanquished the Florentines. The two pictures therefore exchanged places, the new picture being much more beautiful, larger and more devotional. The back of the picture also shows scenes from the Old and the New Testament. . . . During the whole day of the procession, prayers were offered unceasingly and to the poor alms were distributed. To our advocates, Our Lord and His Mother, prayers went up entreating Her in Her infinite mercy to preserve us from all evil and disaster and to protect Siena from the hands of traitors and enemies. . . .

The chronicler is aware of the aesthetic value of the *Maestà* but does not perceive this as its chief value. It is also an aid to devotion and a means of instruction. The scenes from the *Life of Christ and of the Virgin* on the reverse of the painting fall within the tradition of narrative painting, encouraged by the friars as providing a bible for the illiterate. Most interesting of all, however, is the chronicler's attribution of virtually magical powers to a painting which he sees as a charm against all the enemies and evils which constantly threaten a city. What is in question is a typical emphasis by Siena's ruling élite on that aspect of religion which acted as the strongest binding-force in the pre-industrial city, its protective, restorative and predictive magic, which assisted the individual in adjusting to the natural divine order and protected the community from all the insecurities which were inherent in the social and physical world.

It was, in fact, in such magical-mystical qualities that the Nine themselves probably saw the greatest value of any work of art, for those qualities could also be used to develop civic consciousness at the expense of family and factional differences. As we have seen, in the Italian city-state, law, order and the common good fought a constant and often losing battle against the forces of individualism, faction and lawlessness, and only the gradual evolution of a corporate, civil consciousness, over a very long period, eventually put an end to this struggle. At the time of the Nine the conflict in Siena had reached its zenith, when the simplest incident might threaten the whole fabric of state and society. In 1325, a simple game of *Pugna* on the Campo escalated into a full-scale battle:

From apparently nowhere, banners and shields appeared, helmets were donned and lances, swords and even spears were used, the noise increasing to such a roar that it seemed the world was being turned upside-down, so great was the crowd of struggling men. Troops of armed soldiery were ordered to the scene.... The Nine sent a herald to proclaim order: the noise was so great that his voice could not be heard and the fighting continued ... Many of the soldiers' horses were killed and even a few of the soldiers themselves. Meanwhile, more and more men, armed with crossbows, axes and knives entered the Campo so that the battle waged even more furiously. Neither the Nine nor any other authority seemed able to bring a stop to the destruction. At last the Bishop ordered the priests and the brotherhoods of monks to accompany him to the Campo. They appeared carrying a Crucifix before them and paced slowly in and out of the combatants; whereupon a slight cessation of the struggle was felt. Finally, succumbing to the persuasion of the priests, Bishop and monks, the crowd gradually dispersed and all fighting ceased....

As this incident demonstrates, the Sienese crowd was highly excitable and quick-tempered, likely to break out into violence on the slightest provocation. Despite all the appearances of legalism and constitutionalism with which the Nine surrounded their regime, they lived in an age of very considerable violence when bloodshed and street-fighting were every-day matters. It was therefore the concern of the Nine to try to channel some of the volatility of the Sienese mob into acceptable and peaceable manifestations, and so help to impose upon the community a sense of civic, communal purpose, finding expression in an ordered and lawful existence. In achieving this laudable end, the work of art had an essential part to play through the utilization of its magical qualities and symbolic values. Thus, in 1315, Simone Martini's *Maestà*, a painting concerned with the twin themes of Justice and the subordination of the will of the individual to the Common Good, was commissioned for the General Council chamber in the new Palazzo Pubblico, so that the Virgin might actually be present at the council-meetings and inspire the councillors in their decision-making. The desires of the Nine and their purposes for civic government were placed in the mouth of the Virgin who, surrounded by the city's patron saints —Savino, Ansano, Victor and Crescenzio—appears as Siena's ruler, and admonishes the communal officials to govern fairly and wisely. Her meaning is defined by the inscriptions on the steps which lead up to her throne. 'The roses and lilies which spangle the fields of heaven delight me not more than wise decision' she advises the Sienese, and warns that: 'The prayers of the saints will bring no profit to those who spread discord in my city.'

In such great works of art we can discern the aim of the Nine to bring peace and prosperity to their city of Siena. Such an aim, however difficult it was to achieve, gained widespread support for the Nine. Opposition did, of course, exist, and occasionally issued—as in 1311, 1318 and 1328, and successfully in 1355—in major plots against the regime. Fully aware of the danger of such plots, the Nine relied heavily on an elaborate spy-system to warn them of possible areas of unrest and to uncover any serious conspiracies.

Three main groups in society may be identified as persistent opponents of the Nine: some disaffected nobility in the city and *contado*, the city's butchers, and the notaries. Although the rule of the Nine was broadly-based, it resembled regimes in other Tuscan communes in that it was founded on exclusion and proscription. In particular, the victory of Guelphism throughout Tuscany led to the exclusion of the nobility from government which, in theory, rested solely in the hands of the *popolo*. So, in Siena, as elsewhere, the nobility were expressly forbidden by statute from serving on the supreme magistracy of the Nine. Yet it is unlikely that this was a major cause of disaffection for the nobility were not prevented from holding office in every other important position in Siena. They continued to serve regularly in the Biccherna, as commanders of communal forts, as governors, *podestà* or vicars in the smaller communes of the Sienese state, and as ambassadors. Socially, they mixed freely with the Nine whose daughters they often married. Economically they also benefited from the rule of the Nine; the Tolomei, for instance, had virtually all of their wealth invested in

France, and were, therefore, bound to a maintenance of the Guelph alliance.

There were no real occupational differences between the Nine and the nobility. Like the nobility many of the Nine were great *contado* landholders. Like the Nine, the nobility were involved in a diversity of other occupations and businesses. Thus the Salimbeni, although they held more lordships in the *contado* than any other family, were also important merchants and bankers, and the Buonsignori, among the oldest and most aristocratic of all the noble families, were also the largest and most important Sienese banking firm in the thirteenth century. The only major difference between the Nine and the nobility was a tendency for the nobility to invest more heavily in urban property. Since the economic and social interests of the Nine and the nobility were so close, it is unlikely that any differences between them resulted from the opposition of the nobility to the policies of the Nine.

The real cause of conflict between the Nine and the Sienese nobility lay rather in the *mores* of the noble class, for the continued lawlessness and blatant individualism of some families brought them into constant conflict with the Nine's attempts to subject all citizens to the rule of communal law. This was particularly true of families like the Forteguerra and the Tolomei, who automatically opposed a regime which enjoyed the support of the Salimbeni, with whom they continued to wage a *vendetta* which had already lasted for centuries. A factional struggle between the Salimbeni and the Tolomei kept the whole city in uproar between 1320 and 1326, and the following decades were disturbed by similar squabbles between the Saracini and the Scotti, and the Malavolti and Piccolomini, which were only brought to an end in 1347 by a reconciliation forced on the parties by the papal legate and the Nine.

Clan rivalry of this nature underlay the first major conspiracy against the Nine in 1311. Encouraged by the approach of the imperial candidate, Henry VII, whose entourage included at least one important exiled Sienese nobleman, Niccolò di Bonifazio di Buonsignori, a large group of Sienese nobility threatened to overthrow the government. Clan rivalry was certainly at work in 1314 when on 17 April the Salimbeni and Tolomei resorted to arms and engaged in a pitched battle through the streets of Siena over a period of some forty-eight hours. In order to bring these hostilities to an end, the Nine had a lighted candle placed in a window of the Palazzo Pubblico and let the combatants know that if they did not lay down their arms before the candle burned out, they would all be exiled from Siena and deprived of their property. When a temporary lull in the hostilities occurred, the Nine:

... sought to cut off the two families from any friends living outside in the *contado*, fearing that adherents might gradually gather together to help one side or the other. An order was therefore formulated forbidding the presence in the city of any stranger from the *contado* under whatsoever pretext he might try to enter the city gates; and whoever disregarded this order would have his foot cut off. Many there were who regarded this order as quite unjustifiable; there were others who had some good reason of their own for entering the city, while many were simply dare-devils. No one could really believe that so great a penalty would be exacted and they took it for granted that three days in prison would suffice.... But agents of the Podestà searched the city and seized seven peasants from the *contado* in one day. The following morning there stood before the palace of the Podestà the block and axe ready to cut off the foot of each of the delinquents. While this rough court of justice was being prepared, the Campo gradually filled with a seething crowd of citizens protesting against the crippling of so many men for so small an offence. Hardly had the Podestà brought out his seven prisoners than stones began to fly in all directions, thrown by the crowd and the shopkeepers on the Campo. The blinding hail of stones wounded many of the Podestà's servants and covered the escape of six of the prisoners. The Podestà was a man of ungovernable temper, and now, blind with fury against the populace, he led his one remaining prisoner to the upper floor of his palace, had the block and axe brought to him and there and then beheaded the peasant, throwing the body out of the window upon the crowd as a warning ... the crowd rushed to arms ... and the regime was within an inch of being overthrown.[9]

Similar disturbances were provoked by a conflict between the Tolomei and the Salimbeni in 1322 and such incidents serve to explain why the Nine could never afford to treat the possibility of noble rebellion lightly.

Like the opposition of the nobility, the opposition of the butchers, who revolted against the Nine both in 1318 and 1324, also stemmed directly from the attempts at 'good government' on which the Nine so prided themselves. For butchers in fourteenth-century Siena were also, normally, animal dealers; thus they resented statutes passed by the commune which were designed to keep down the price of meat and which forced them to sell their animals only in Siena at a much lower price than they could have obtained elsewhere. They also seem to have resented communal supervision, dating from the earlier thirteenth century but rigorously enforced by the Nine, to prevent the sale of bad meat, the passing off of one kind of meat as another, and the use of false weights.

Like the nobility, the judges and notaries of Siena were specifically excluded from the Nine. This, however, does not seem to have been a major cause of their opposition to the regime. Rather, they, like the butchers were professional victims of 'good government'. Throughout the period they enjoyed power, the Nine, in accordance with their commitment to the ideal of equal and cheap justice for all, made strenuous efforts to keep down lawyers' fees and, in 1318, these efforts culminated in a direct attempt to deprive lawyers of all independence of action.

It was this move against the lawyers that led to one of the more serious risings against the Nine, for it produced an alliance between the butchers, led by the wealthy Cione del fu Vitaluccio, who, according to the chronicler, Agnolo di Tura, was designated the commune's future *Bargello* or Chief of Police; the lawyers; and the disaffected noble clans of the Tolomei and the Forteguerra, who attempted to overthrow the government during the night of 26 October 1318. Yet even the united efforts of these three groups were insufficient to remove the Nine and what the revolt really showed was the general acquiescence of the population in the regime and a broad approval of its policies.

Such widespread acceptance and approval make it legitimate to ask how it was that in the end the Nine did fall from power. The proper answer to this question may be found in the deep structural changes which affected Europe in general and Tuscany in particular in the midfourteenth century. Famine became more common and more widespread. In Siena there were food shortages in 1302, 1319, 1328, 1329, 1340 and 1346. Both in 1340 and 1346 and, again, in 1347, the commune was forced to raise large loans and to pawn communal property in order to raise money for the purchase of grain to be distributed freely or sold at less than cost price to the needy.

In the same period trade declined and was often disrupted by warfare. In Siena, as in Florence, Lucca and Pistoia, this decline was associated with a series of spectacular bank-failures. The worst of all was the failure between 1298 and 1306 of the bank of the Buonsignori, known throughout Europe as the *Gran Tavola*, but in the second decade of the fourteenth century mercantile and banking firms headed by the Tolomei and the Malavolti also collapsed. The Nine found the communal finances severely strained by these bank-failures and by papal pressure for repayment of the debts of the Buonsignori company. A measure of this strain is the increased use of novel taxes after 1348 as the Nine strove to tap additional sources of revenue; thus, for instance, in April 1350, a special forced loan was imposed on innkeepers and others who did business on the pilgrimage route, on the assumption that they would be making large profits in Jubilee Year; and, in the winter of 1351, another forced loan was imposed on the clergy.

Meanwhile the communal finances were facing new demands. Marauding companies of mercenary soldiers began to harass Tuscany in the 1340s, Siena suffering particularly in 1342 from the attentions of the 'Great Company' of Werner von Urslingen who called himself the 'Enemy of God, Piety and Mercy'. Money had to be found either to drive these companies away by force, or to pay them to remove their unwanted attentions elsewhere.

There was, in addition, a revival of interest in Italy on the part of the ultramontane powers. The invasion of Italy by Henry VII led to an expensive and exhausting campaign in the Sienese *contado* which sparked off a series of local rebellions among the subject communes, and, in 1342-3, the Duke of Athens, who had been made Lord of Florence, was actively trying to induce the nobility of Siena to rebel against the Nine. Although he was not successful in producing the outright rebellion he sought, the Duke certainly succeeded in nourishing and encouraging a deepening mood of dissatisfaction among the nobles of Siena. Of this the Nine were aware and, in consequence, they became increasingly afraid of alienating the nobility. They were now less ready to subject members of the ruling clans to the full rigours of communal justice, so that, in the words of the chronicler:

> The people of low estate were taken and destroyed, and the nobles were merely exiled, even though they might have been captured, like the little men.[10]

Gradually the feeling began to grow that the regime was no longer administering the city fairly or justly, and that, on occasion, the justice it offered was frankly partisan and politically motivated.

In 1348 a further blow struck the city in the terrible shape of the

Black Death. In this epidemic Siena suffered as much, if not more than, any other city of a comparable size in Europe. Its devastating nature and psychological impact were graphically recorded by Agnolo di Tura:

> It was all so dreadful and so cruel that I hardly know where to begin to describe the terror which then reigned; one felt that the very sight of so much suffering would drive a man mad. No words can do justice to the horror, and he is fortunate who has never faced such sights. . . . Father fled from son, wife from husband and brother from brother. . . . Loneliness encompassed the dying, for there was no one who would bury the dead either for money or for friend-ship's sake. If they could do so, blood relations would carry their own dead to the grave without a priest, without any ceremony and without even a funeral bell. I . . . buried all my five sons with my own hands. There were some who were buried too close to the surface, so that the dogs came and scratched them up, devouring the bodies on the open streets. . . . The city of Siena appeared to be deserted; one met no one in the streets . . .[11]

The death-toll was indeed tremendous. It has been estimated that between one-half and one-third of the population died, the poor and the clergy suffering the highest proportionate losses. By the spring of 1349 the militia companies had been reduced from forty-three to twenty-one and the number of *contrade* fom sixty to forty-two. In the city all industry ceased. In the *contado* the fields were neglected and animals left untended. Mills closed down, in some cases for a year or more. On 2 June 1348 the General Council ordered the suspension of the civil courts until September and did not itself meet again regularly until 15 August.

Although, despite all the difficulties, some parts of the administration did manage to limp on throughout the epidemic, the pestilence was a disaster from which the Nine never fully recovered. Public confidence in the regime had been undermined and was not to be regained, for in those areas of public life on which the Nine most prided themselves the Black Death had the greatest impact. A reduced population must bear a heavier tax burden, but the principle of equality in taxation had to some extent to be abandoned. The regime began to rely more heavily on gabelles, which burdened the masses more than the upper classes, rather than on direct taxation, and there was more frequent recourse to voluntary loans which profited the already wealthy.

The administration of justice also suffered. The Nine found that one unfortunate consequence of the epidemic was that it was difficult to find judges, notaries or foreigners to serve in posts such as that of the *podestà* or Captain of the People. The shortage of notaries was particularly acute and in 1350 complaints were made to the General Council that:

> the notaries who survived the mortality are so swollen up with pride that they could not care less about anything. . . .[12]

Profiting from their scarcity the notaries refused to accept posts with the commune:

> for these days they have no need to earn anything and . . . they hate the idea of putting themselves out or working, also they do not care to take work in the offices of the banks in this city . . . And so, between refusals and excuses, the months pass. . . .[13]

In consequence, a host of illegal entrepreneurs, false notaries and unscrupulous clerks came to act in the city. Inevitably the administration of justice suffered. The epidemic, in any case, seems to have sparked off a long outbreak of licence and a consequent increase in the number of crimes of violence. In 1350 the General Council was still lamenting the ease with which criminals could evade justice by leaving the city; in 1352 the commune appointed a new 'official for the custody of the city',[14] to share the Podestà's police powers, but the experiment was not a success and had to be abandoned after a two-months' trial. It is scarcely surprising, therefore, that these years saw an increasing number of charges of dishonesty and favouritism against the Nine. Such criticisms were most frequent and most bitter when they came from members of the old noble *consorterie* or from the new men who had grown rich as a consequence of the economic changes wrought by the Black Death, and who neither belonged to the old oligarchy nor appreciated its management of the city. As a result of such mounting hostility, by 1352 the instability of the Nine was already so apparent that in order to keep order during the Festival of the Assumption, they had to call out the militia companies of Terzo di San Martino and summon extra troops from the *contado*.

Even so, the regime endured for another three years until in 1355 the Emperor-Elect Charles IV visited Siena on his way to coronation in Rome. Hardly had he entered the city-gates, on 25 March, when the cry went up: 'Long live the Emperor and Death to the Nine!' This outcry seems to have been inspired by the Piccolomini and other noble families who, on the following day, succeeded in rousing the whole city. On 27 March, to the general acclamation of the crowds, the Emperor rode from his lodging in Palazzo Salimbeni to the Palazzo Pubblico in order to receive the abdication of the Nine, while the young nobility of Siena led the crowd in a riotous sack of the palaces of the Biccherna, the Merchants' Guild and the Wool Guild, releasing prisoners and hunting down the *podestà* and the War Captain. Although the Emperor saved the persons of the Nine from the fury of the mob, he did nothing to prevent the destruction of their houses and the ransacking of their property. A regime which had preserved peace and prosperity in Siena for some sixty years was thus brought to an end in an orgy of violence and disorder, presided over by the man who was, theoretically, God's secular representative on earth.

4

The Cathedral

'Truly, this is the most beautiful building in the city.'
                    Agnolo Niccolini, Governor of Siena, 1559

ONE OF the most evocative memorials of the rule of the Nine is the skeleton of the new cathedral which stands so hauntingly on the summit of the Castelvecchio. It is a lasting reminder of how often the aims and ambitions of the Nine bore little real relationship to the actual condition of the Siena over which they ruled. Seen from afar, however, this skeleton tends to melt into the surrounding fabric of the city, and the sky-line of Siena is dominated instead by the city's few remaining medieval towers and by the magnificent, hexagonal cupola of the old cathedral or *Duomo*, glistening in its dress of dark-green, pink and white marble.

In the Tuscany of the twelfth and thirteenth centuries, such marble was reserved as a building material for ecclesiastical buildings, and in consequence, the cathedral is distinguished from all other buildings in Siena, which are predominantly pinkish-brown in colour. In Sienese paintings, too, the cathedral always stands out as the dominant element in the townscape; it is by depicting the cathedral that a painter normally identifies the city he is illustrating as Siena. Yet, once within the actual walls of Siena, this sense of dominance vanishes. The cathedral is not even easy to find. No street runs directly to it. It is glimpsed, almost accidentally, between other buildings, and, until one climbs into the cathedral square, there is no sense of its towering vigilance over the city. In fact, the cathedral seems to stand aloof from the centre of civic life—the Campo—which lies below it.

One might, therefore, be forgiven for assuming that this semi-isolation of the cathedral, particularly from the Campo, reflects a profound opposition between church and state, between the sacred and the secular. Yet nothing could be farther from the reality of the experience of Siena; a city in which all the buildings and all the space express

3

the combination in careful equipoise of the religious and the civic spirit. This, as we shall see, is particularly true of both the Palazzo Pubblico and the hospital of Santa Maria della Scala, which is opposite the cathedral. But the cathedral also can only be understood if it is seen, not as the expression of some aloof, heaven-orientated, ecclesiastical authority, but of the people of Siena as a whole.

It was, after all, to the cathedral and not to the Palazzo Pubblico that the people of Siena and her dependencies owed their allegiance, and it was to the cathedral that they all processed—excepting only the very poor, the sick, and those whose personal enmities were so great that they dared not risk leaving home—on the fourteenth of August every year during the celebrations of the feast of the Assumption. Here, in sign of homage, they offered to the Board of Works of the Cathedral a wax candle, which, with a typical Sienese love of decoration, had been carefully carved with scenes from the Old Testament alluding to the Virgin or with other devout images. Each candle, therefore, like the cathedral itself, was simultaneously a sacred object, a symbol of temporal authority, and a work of art. A similar ceremony occurred on the following day when the subject communes, territories and lords, made their offerings in the cathedral.

This annual ceremony was the most important in the Sienese year. Before the loss of independence in 1555 it was a ceremony which represented both the submission of the rights of the individual to the Common Good, and the uniting of disparate corporate groups into the context of the city. For, although each person made the presentation of his candle as an individual, he was required by statute to do so as part of a group. The constitution of 1310 specifically required him to go:

> in company with those of the *contrada* wherein he dwells; and although he may be registered for purposes of taxation in another district, yet every man shall go with those of the *contrada* wherein he dwells.

So the dedication of the fourteenth of August was, therefore, a territorially-based one; the submission of the *contrade* of Siena to the authority of the commune, found its symbolic expression in the cathedral. It was the moment each year when the commune asserted its rights over all other bodies, corporations or systems within the city; the Nine, for this reason, ordering in 1309 that all shops should be closed and all commercial dealings prohibited during the Assumption celebrations. In 1346 they made the point even more emphatically, interfering even with the solemn obligations of the blood tie and the *vendetta*, and decreeing that on 14, 15, 16 August there should be a solemn and universal truce between all citizens and subjects of Siena, so that they might safely perform their devotions. So important and out of the ordinary were the Assumption Day celebrations that they even required different clothes. It was for these festivities that the communal servants were annually issued with new liveries, and in the fifteenth century it was only on these three days that women were allowed to wear silks and velvets in public.

This expression of the city-state ethos within the cathedral was, however, but one among a myriad of civic occasions which had their focal point in the cathedral. Both within the civic and the religious calendars there were many ritual moments which directed the attention of the citizens upon their cathedral. Thus, for instance, on the second Sunday in June, for centuries after the Black Death, that urban disaster was annually commemorated in a solemn mass offered in the cathedral at the expense of the commune. And, as an example of a religiously-inspired festival, we may take the annual Corpus Christi Day celebrations of the later Middle Ages in which the whole city participated, processing to the cathedral in an order carefully arranged on the basis of the city-guilds.

The cathedral also housed a vital source of spiritual protection for the city of Siena and its inhabitants, a protection which was and is perceived as emanating literally from within the cathedral walls. For, above everything else in the middle ages the cathedral was a shrine for many important relics which provided remedy and relief in every crisis of life. In the early eighteenth century, Gigli reckoned the number of these relics as thirty-one, including the veil of the Virgin, the remains of Siena's patron saints, Saints Ansano, Savino, Crescenzio and Victor, which were exposed on the High Altar during the Feast of the Assumption, a tooth of San Bernardino, some remains of San Galgano, relics of the Blessed Sorore, the mythical founder of the hospital of Santa Maria della Scala, of the Blessed Andrea Gallerani, the Blessed Ambrogio Sansedoni, the Blessed Giovacchino Piccolomini Pelacani, the Blessed Francesco Patrizi, the Blessed Giovanni Colombini, founder of the Gesuati, and of the Blessed Agostino Novello. Most prized of all was the arm of St. John the Baptist, presented to the city by Pope Pius II in 1464 and housed in the chapel of the Baptist in the left transept of the cathedral. With a true eighteenth-century rationalizing instinct, Gigli suggested gathering all these relics together from the altars where they were dispersed and forming one central Sancta Santorum or Holy Despository:

> To which one might have recourse with greater confidence, than anywhere else, on the occasion of any disaster.[1]

This role of the cathedral as a source of protection for the city endured, of course, after the loss of independence, and indeed is still important today.

The cathedral was, then, an expression of the spiritual dimension first of the commune and later of the city. In consequence, its construction was a matter of considerable urban significance, far too important to be left to ecclesiastics. The building operations were rather directed by bodies of Sienese citizens, responsible to the communal government, the ecclesiastical authorities playing only an advisory role. The resultant relationship between commune and cathedral is well set out in a decree of 1310 which states that:

> It is evident to all that the office of the Lords Nine should have care and solicitude and love for the building of the Blessed Mary the Virgin and should concern itself with the conservation of its affairs, curtailing useless expenditure and accepting and preserving those things which may promote it.[2]

In effect, the building works of the cathedral were a government department and the responsibility of the commune. The financing of the works came directly from communal income, for the most part, and any Master of Works who found the building-fund in difficulty would turn automatically to the communal authorities for financial aid. In 1343, as a result of one such request, the commune decreed what was in effect a direct tax whose proceeds were to go to the cathedral. Any person making a will in Siena was required to leave at least ten florins to the cathedral building fund:

> which the Master of Works may demand, even if the sum is not written into the will, for the good of the Board of Works and for the salvation of the soul of the testator.[3]

Many individual Sienese citizens were, of course, to donate far more than they were required by law to the building-fund; Bartolo di Fredi was typical of many in leaving twenty-five gold ducats, and in later centuries substantial gifts by wealthy Sienese citizens were to pay for particular decorative projects.

The income of the cathedral and the power of spending it were delegated by the commune to the *Operaio* or Master of Works, who was a communal appointee, paid an annual salary. The fact that, in the thirteenth century, between 1258 and 1285 the Master of Works was a religious, a monk from San Galgano, has less to do with the ecclesiastical nature of the work than it has to do with the reputed honesty and proven competence of the Cistercians in communal work. Since the office of the Master of Works was seen as a full-time and exclusive post, the salary, particularly once the post began to be filled by secular appointees, was high. When Jacopo della Quercia was appointed in 1453, for instance, he was paid one hundred gold florins a year for his life, and, in addition, the commune also contracted to provide his widow with the annual interest from one hundred gold florins. Such a salary reflects the fact that the Master of Works of the Cathedral held one of the most important posts in the Sienese administration. He was responsible for hiring the architects who designed, and the contractors and masters who actually built, the cathedral. He also organized the majority of feasts and receptions offered by the commune to distinguished visitors. In addition, he was often in charge of other important public works in Siena; the Palazzo Pubblico, the Fonte Gaia and the Loggia della Mercanzia, were all, for instance, ultimately the responsibility of the Master of Works of the Cathedral.

This Master was appointed or reappointed by the commune every six months. Although, in the thirteenth century he was a religious, subsequently, he might sometimes be a practising artist in his own right, like Jacopo della Quercia, or, occasionally, he might be a high-ranking artisan. But more normally he was a merchant, familiar with the organization required for the running of the large-scale business which is what the building works of the cathedral were.

It is clear, from the history of the building of the cathedral, that a strong-minded Master of Works, with determination and vision, could have a very important impact on the way in which the cathedral was built. One of the most critical decisions taken in the whole history of Sienese cultural development was that by Fra Melano in 1265 when he summoned Nicola Pisano to Siena to build the cathedral pulpit, one of his finest works, because Melano believed that contemporary Sienese stonecarving and sculpture were simply inadequate. An even better example is to be found in the fifteenth century in the great period of office of Alberto Aringhieri, who was twice portrayed by Pinturicchio, once in youth and once in old age, in the chapel of

St. John the Baptist. Between 1481 and 1498, it was Aringhieri's energy and drive which led to the building of that chapel and to the completion of the Baptistery, and some of the best sections of the cathedral floor. In the two side naves Aringhieri was responsible for the Hermes Trismegistus, and the Sibyls, who prophesied the mysteries of the Incarnation and Redemption, designed by such distinguished artists as Matteo di Giovanni, Antonio Federighi, Guidoccio Cozzarelli and Neroccio di Bartolomeo, and also for the completion of the floor of the right transept with Benvenuto di Giovanni's *Expulsion of Herod* and Matteo di Giovanni's *Massacre of the Innocents*, and, in the left transept, *Jepthah's Daughter* by Bastiano di Francesco.

Despite the fact that a strong-minded Master of Works could impose his individual impress upon the cathedral, characteristically he did not operate on his own. A marked feature of the patronage exercised throughout the whole chequered history of the building of the cathedral, is its corporate nature, the Master of Works consulting with and being controlled by groups of Sienese citizens at all stages of construction and decoration. Thus the Master of Works always worked with a board of appointed members, which had its own house and workshops by the cathedral where artists could work. This board consisted of between four and six men of whom one was normally a canon of the cathedral. For obvious reasons, membership of this board was frequently given to practising artists, as in the case of Taddeo di Bartolo, whose first recorded office was when he was elected a member in 1388, or that of Cristofano da Chosana, who had himself worked on the cathedral before he was elected to the board in 1379. The inclusion of such artists among the board members was immensely valuable for although, as we shall see, it did not prevent either bad workmanship or bad decisions it did contribute to a situation in which the Board of Works could exercise its patronage with a considerable degree of aesthetic self-confidence.

Of the board's members, one man would normally act as Treasurer and one as Notary or Clerk of Works. Together, all members were responsible for keeping the accounts, collecting revenues from property which had been bequeathed to the cathedral, and for fixing contracts and wage levels. They reported back to the commune regularly, and it was on their recommendation that the city government appointed the Master Mason or *Capomaestro*, who was responsible for the day-to-day administration of the building.

Essentially the Master Mason was the cathedral's architect. This post was thus of the first importance and it was frequently filled by one of Siena's most distinguished artists. Holders of the position include Giovanni Pisano between 1287 and 1296; Pisano's most distinguished follower, Tino di Camaino; sculptor of the beautiful monument to Cardinal Petroni, Francesco di Giorgio Martini who was appointed in 1499; and Baldassare Peruzzi who held the position from 1532.

Despite the fact that the Board of Works was frequently manned by such distinguished artists, it still did not normally take major artistic decisions on its own, but only in association with a larger committee, composed of a number of citizens. Usually these were selected on the basis of their presumed expertise. Thus, for instance, the committee created in 1388 to decide on the design for the *testiere* of the choir-stalls was composed of fifteen artisans. Of those who can be identified, six were painters and included Luca di Tommè and Paolo di Giovanni Fei, four others were woodcarvers, one was a stonemason, and one a goldsmith.

Nor were such committees the only check on the activities of the Board of Works. In the dispensing of money in particular, the communal authorities maintained a direct and careful watch on the Board, the General Council being kept 'fully informed of its income and expenditure'.[4] The detailed control which the commune exercised may be illustrated by the problems that arose in December 1308, when the Master of Works complained that the work on the cathedral was suffering because at mealtimes the workmen went off either to their homes or to the local taverns. The solution he proposed was simple enough. Drink should be served to the masters and the builders actually on the site of the cathedral because: 'they cannot be expected to work all day without drinking'.[5] But even this small expenditure could not be authorized by the Master of Works before he had obtained the prior consent of the city government. Again, in 1369, the General Council authorized the expenditure of 100 florins by the Board of Works, but only on condition that the financial officers of the commune supervised what was done with the money; and, in the following year, it was the General Council that determined the salary to be paid to Francesco di Tonghio during his work on the choir-stalls of the cathedral.

In no area of civic government, therefore, did the Sienese mania for corporate decision-making manifest itself so consistently and so regularly over so long a period as it did in the building of the cathedral. And such corporate decision-making was bound to have artistic and cultural consequences. Perhaps the most significant of these resulted from the determined preference shown by the communal authorities for Sienese artists, artisans, and architects when it came to the hiring of men. Other considerations being equal, Sienese citizens were chosen before other artists. There were, of course, good practical reasons for the exercise of this preference. It helped to avoid local unemployment and, in any case, as Jacopo della Quercia pointed out in 1438, the employment of foreign artists and craftsmen invariably involved 'greater delays and greater expense'.[6] Yet one also suspects the intrusion of aesthetic considerations. A case in point is the door for the marble tabernacle of the font in the Baptistery; the Sienese simply did not like the Florentine Donatello's original version and, although he was paid for his labours, the door was finally made by the famous Sienese goldsmith, Giovanni Turini. At this critical period in the development of the early renaissance, such a decision represents a positive attitude on the part of the Sienese towards their own native traditions and a typical suspicion of Florentine innovation. It was part and parcel of that natural good sense and taste which ensured that the cathedral of Siena, despite the incorporation within it of many different styles, and the length of time over which it was built, should none the less exhibit a very homogenous appearance. It seems more than probable that the continuing dominance of this good taste owed a great deal to the corporate and probably conservative nature of the patronage which created the cathedral.

The fact that the cathedral is so perfect an expression of Sienese civic idealism also stems from the patronage which created it. The particular role that the cathedral played in the life of the city is reflected, for instance, in the iconographical and decorative schemes of the Duomo all of which are civic in their inspiration. Chief among these is the exposition of the Virgin's role as protector and advocate of Siena. This is expressed in a whole range of projects which stretch from Pisano's original elaborate exposition of the Virgin's part in the history of the Redemption on the façade, to the portrayal of the Virgin and her glorification by God and Man on the central bronze doors, first projected in 1457 but not executed until 1558 when Enrico Manfrini's realization was paid for by the Monte dei Paschi. We should also note the specific emphasis, both within and without the cathedral, on saints with a specifically Sienese connexion. The medallions on the spandrels of the façade, for instance, contain seventeenth-century busts of three Sienese saints: Giovanni Colombini, Ambrogio Sansedoni and Andrea

Gallerani. And, within the cathedral, in the left transept, there is a corner chapel, dedicated to Saint Ansano, which contains a fine canvas, painted in 1596 by Francesco Vanni, and showing *Saint Ansano Baptising the Sienese.*

Such quintessentially Sienese concerns reflect, in their turn, the fact that behind the communal committees and councils, responsible for the building of the cathedral, lay the whole body of the Sienese citizenry who were deeply committed to this building. Their concern may be illustrated by the fact that, in fulfilling the needs of the cathedral, the communal authorities felt free to abrogate all normal communal laws and obligations. Thus, artists and workmen were permitted to work on official holidays, and even criminals might be pardoned, if it were for the benefit of the building; in 1281, a certain Ramo Paganelli, banished for the crime of fornication, was pardoned and recalled to work on the cathedral because he was, '. . . one of the finest . . . stonecarvers . . . in the world'.[7] It is equally significant that the officials of the Board of Works were not normally allowed to leave the city, and that artists and workmen, employed by the Board, were specifically contracted to work for it solely and continuously.

This total commitment to the project on the part of the whole community both created and reflected the deep civic pride of which the cathedral was an expression. Every Sienese citizen was positively encouraged to concern himself with the appearance of a building which, it was said in 1430, 'both is and ought to be the mirror of all the citizens'.[8] The cathedral's construction was constantly watched, discussed and, on occasion, vigorously criticized. Thus, a directive from the commune, written with some urgency to Jacopo della Quercia in Bologna in 1435, instructed him to return home immediately to resume his position as Master of the Works since:

> God alone knows the fuss that is being made and the number of complaints there are from our citizens.[9]

Again, in 1440, the decision to cancel a project for a stained-glass window, which had already been commissioned, was made because a large number of citizens complained bitterly about it on the grounds that it would obstruct the light.[10]

One consequence of such citizen involvement was a reiterated insistence that the cathedral must be splendid, magnificent and beautiful. Thus the contract given to Francesco del Tonghio and his son, Jacomo, specified that their work be done:

3*

according to the design drawn up by the said Master Jacomo or that
it should be made even more beautiful if they can manage it.[11]

Similar attitudes are still apparent a generation later when the Master of
Works petitioned the government for permission to build a new
sacristy:

> because the present one would not do even for a small castle, and is
> a matter of shame for the whole city; for this church ought to have
> a beautiful sacristy as befits so praiseworthy and honourable a
> building.[12]

Such high-minded aesthetic considerations could and did co-exist with
more mundane economic reasons to explain the degree of public
involvement in the cathedral. For several centuries her cathedral was
Siena's major investment. It was also the major employer of artists
and workmen; every Sienese artist of any significance worked at one
time or another on the building. And it was the chief purchaser of
luxury building-materials and so had a peculiar significance for Sienese
contractors and merchants.

For centuries, therefore, the cathedral was a vital element in the
city's economic life. Few cathedrals have such a long building history;
the mosaics of the façade were added only in the last century, and the
doors, as we have seen, in this. In fact the Sienese were constantly
tinkering with, rebuilding, or redecorating a building which, for all its
splendours in which they took such justified pride, never seems really
to have satisfied them. It is, in consequence, a most curious blend of
styles, both externally with a lower part of the façade and a *campanile*
which are Romanesque, and a general appearance which is pure Gothic,
and, internally, with a range of decorative forms which date from the
earliest period to the present day. Nothing in the eighteenth century
was to cause the Sienese more embarrassment than the eclectic nature
of their cathedral which defied every attempt to systematize it in
accordance with the dictates of neo-classical taste. And nothing in the
nineteenth century was to cause more heart-searching than the Baroque
elements in the cathedral interior which no amount of enthusiasm for
the Gothic revival could persuade the Sienese to remove.

It is not known when the first building was erected on the present
site, although tradition maintains that a temple of Minerva once stood
there, and that the first church of Our Lady of the Assumption was
built on the ruins of this pagan shrine. Certainly, although the present

cathedral dates only from the twelfth century, some kind of Christian building has existed there since at least the tenth century. The bulk of construction work on the present building was completed in the twelfth century for, by the beginning of the thirteenth, the nave, aisles and the lower part of the front and side walls of the present cathedral were already completed. The choir, however, was still under construction in 1259 when a commission of nine citizens, drawn three from each Terzo, was appointed to consult with the Master of Works: 'and whatsoever those Nine or a majority of them think should be done about the choir, that shall be done'.[13] In the following year the General Council reiterated its concern with the progress of the building and urged its expedition. Four years later the cupola was completed and in 1265 Nicola Pisano began work on the pulpit.

The influence which this elegant, octagonal pulpit, with its seven narrative reliefs, classically-inspired yet clearly influenced by the new French Gothic style, was to have over the subsequent development of the arts in Siena was immeasurable, and it illustrates how, by the second half of the thirteenth century, the cathedral was an important artistic training-ground, as well as a major source of artistic employment. Since the cathedral attracted the best talent, not only from Tuscany but from all over Italy—Pisano, himself, came from the South—master-craftsmen and artists in Siena were bound to be influenced by and learn from the building project with which they were constantly involved. In the course of time the educative quality of the building was even to have some kind of official recognition; in 1505 Ventura di Ser Giuliano Turi was given a post in the Office of the Works, but only on condition that he agreed to train eight apprentices in metal casting.

Within the context of this teaching and training dimension of the cathedral's creation, a very important cultural landmark for Siena was the appointment in 1284 of Pisano's son, Giovanni, as Master Mason. For more than twenty years thereafter Giovanni Pisano was a figure of central importance both in the history of the cathedral and in the cultural history of Siena. He was mainly employed in building the complicated façade, the most richly decorated of any Italian façade at that date; as a result of this important work, Giovanni's influence spread rapidly through the city, as it was subsequently to spread throughout Italy.

Since the cathedral was an integral part of Siena's civic life, it was inevitable that any political change in the city would have an impact on the building. It was, for instance, not unknown for the Master of

Works to be removed from his office after a change in regime. Thus, given their grandiose assumptions about Siena's role and their own self-confidence, the Nine were bound to become dissatisfied with the first cathedral which Pisano's work had virtually completed.

Although the cathedral building-fund was in serious difficulties by 1299, largely because the Nine were currently engaged in so many other prestige building-projects, in 1316 it was decided to expand the existing building to double its previous size, at least partly to take account of the increased size of the population, since the theoretical ideal remained that the entire population of the city should be able to worship together in the cathedral on the major festivals of the year. In the new rebuilding scheme, neither Pisano's remarkable façade nor the already famous cupola were to be touched, but the chancel was to be lengthened out over the steep slope of Valle Piatta by the addition of several more arches. These were to be supported by the Baptistery of San Giovanni, which was to be built at a lower level so that it might serve as a foundation for the new chancel. At the same time, it was planned to extend the cathedral transept.

In 1322 when this new building had already made considerable progress, it was discovered that, following subsidence in the foundations, the old and new masonry had begun to gape and the Master of Works commissioned a report from a number of consulting master-workmen as to what should be done with the building. Their unanimous advice was that the project should be abandoned; instead the old cathedral should be demolished and replaced by a new, much larger building:

> vast and most beautiful, with over-all measurements of length, height and breadth in the perfect harmony of proportion which a fine church demands.[14]

It was not, however, until 1339 that the decision was taken by the General Council to begin building a completely new cathedral which, by its size and magnificence, was intended to surpass all other cathedrals in Italy and, most particularly, its neighbouring rivals under construction at Florence and Orvieto. The architect, Lando di Pietro, was summoned home from Naples, where he had been working for King Robert, to superintend the works as Master Mason. The task of architectural design faced by Lando di Pietro was not an enviable one. The existing cathedral, with its now lengthened chancel, was not after all to be demolished but was to remain standing and serve as the transept of the new building. Two major difficulties, therefore, confronted the architects. The first lay in adapting the new nave, designed in the formal Gothic style so that it coincided with the existing pillars of the transept and aisles, and which with its high vaulting would have to cut through the old one. This created the second major problem faced by the architects: the very difficult task of reconstructing the cupola to fit in with the new building.

Despite such daunting problems, a beginning was made with the extension of the choir and the erection of the new nave and façade whose delicate and frail skeleton still rises above the Campo. However, it was inevitable that, with so ambitious a project, the building fund would soon run into difficulties, and it is scarcely surprising, therefore, that in 1343, alarmed by mounting costs, the General Council should have decreed that no new work be undertaken until the choir was finished.

The project for building a new cathedral was thus already in very serious difficulties even before Siena was overwhelmed by the tragedy of the Black Death, which immediately halted all construction work. Building does not seem to have been resumed again until 1356. Then new problems immediately became apparent; the Master of the Works, Benci di Cione, reported that not only were the finished parts of the new cathedral in a weakened state after so long a delay, they were actually of defective construction and unsafe. A report made in the same year by Domenico di Agostino and Master Niccolò di Cecco advised that to continue with the original building scheme would mean an expenditure of at least a further 150,000 florins:

> and it is our opinion that if you go ahead with this new church . . . according to plan, and without an increase in the normal income of the Board of Works, it will not be completed in a hundred years.[15]

Since it was now clear that to continue with the building would be both dangerous and, in the weakened economy of post-plague Siena, financially out of the question, the Master of Works proposed abandoning the enlargement of the cathedral and his plans were, albeit reluctantly, accepted by the commune.

These new plans involved bringing the work to completion on a considerably more modest but also more realistic scale. The chancel of the original cathedral was, therefore, extended out over the present Baptistery, and, within two years, the extension of the vaulting had been finished and Duccio's great chancel window transferred to its present position. The Baptistery itself, with its façade, designed by Mino di Pelliciaio, was completed in 1370. Simultaneously, what had been the main aisle of the cathedral was raised to correspond to the new extension of the choir and, in 1377, the west façade was finished by Giovanni di Cecco. The cathedral was thus virtually complete as we know it today, although some building work was to continue until well into the fifteenth century.

The completion of the fabric of the cathedral is not, of course, the end of the story. Equally important in the cultural development of Siena, largely because of the stimulus it provided to continued artistic activity, was the decoration and internal embellishment of the building. Always a continuous process, this has continued to the present day, but the greatest period of activity occurred in the fifteenth and six-teenth centuries and thus coincided with the emergence of renaissance ideas within Siena.

That the interior of the cathedral should have been lavishly decorated is itself significant. By and large, the churches of Siena are not pro-fusely decorated or ornamented. San Martino, Santa Maria dei Servi, San Francesco, San Domenico and the church of Santa Maria della Scala are in fact largely remarkable for their austerity, and even the Baroque church of Santa Maria Provenzano is very simple. It was, therefore, only in the cathedral that the Sienese mania for decoration could be given full rein with the series of terracotta busts of popes and emperors, the carved and inlaid wooden choir-stalls, and the high altar designed by Peruzzi. This altar can indeed be seen as the Pantheon of the decorative arts in Siena at the time of the renaissance, for all the leading artists of the day contributed to it. The bronze tabernacle is Vecchietta's, and is surrounded on either side by light-bearing angels, designed by Giovanni di Stefano. Below are the enchanting angels by Francesco di Giorgio who was also responsible for the lateral half-figures. Other contributors to the altar were Cozzarelli and Beccafumi, who also designed the beautiful angels on the columns leading towards the nave.

Such decorative schemes within the cathedral are of major impor-tance since, for certain periods, they represent the only large-scale artistic effort being made in Siena. Such a period, for example, occurred in the late fourteenth and early fifteenth century when the decoration of the choir, certain chapels and the sacristy were completed, the Baptistery was being decorated, and the creation of the uniquely elaborate marble pavement in Siena's cathedral was under way. The most important stages of the pavement were those of 1372 exhibiting the figure of the symbol of Siena, the she-wolf suckling her twins, surrounded by the symbols of Siena's allied towns; of 1434 when Domenico di Bartolo executed his portrait of the Emperor Sigismund; of Antonio Federighi's *Allegory of the Seven Ages of Man* in front of the Chapel del Voto; and the period of Alberto Aringhieri's office as Master of Works, to which we have already alluded. The pavement was only finally completed* in the early sixteenth century with Pinturicchio's *Allegory of Fortune* and Beccafumi's Old Testament scenes which are distributed between the high altar and the space under the cupola.

Nothing could have been better suited to the ingenuity and the decorative genius of the Sienese than this pavement with its two-dimensional quality and its dependence on line and design. Nothing, further, could be more typical of a society in which close relationships existed between artists and craftsmen. The pavement was actually created by the artist first making his design on paper. This was then sent to specialised craftsmen who were able to translate the artists' designs into marble. Only in a traditional society in which the relationships between creative artists and craftsmen remained very close could this have been done so effectively.

Such conservatism is clearly reflected in the contracts entered into by artists involved in the decoration of the cathedral. They show a consistent pattern of employment through several centuries. Like Sienese society itself, and certainly like the majority of Sienese governmental departments, the Board of Works was remarkably resistant to change. By and large, therefore, whatever alterations in the status of the artist were occurring in Europe as a whole, particularly in the fifteenth, sixteenth and seventeenth centuries, these are not reflected in any difference in the treatment of artists by the Board of Works of the cathedral of Siena. All workmen, artisans, craftsmen, and those whom today, we would probably think of as creative artists, tended to get the same treatment. At all stages of their work they were subject to the strictest control, both in the design and in the execution of their work. 'In order to avoid subsequent disagreement',[16] and to prevent fraud, they were first requested to submit a design or an example of their work to the supervisory committee. If this was accepted, it was then normally registered with a notary. The progress of the work was then regularly monitored by the Board of Works. When it was completed,

---

* Subsequently, of course, it has been constantly changed, altered, repaved, repaired and restored.

payment was normally by valuation; a completed piece would have its value assessed by two men, one a nominee of the artist and one of the Master of Works. If these two could not agree, the deadlock would be resolved by a third mutually acceptable arbiter, or, after 1559, by a nominee of the Grand Duke of Tuscany. The ability of these arbiters to decide upon a sum was, to some extent, facilitated by the fact that contracts often included clauses which stated the upper limit of the possible price to be paid, and sometimes the lower limit as well. Contracts also contained clauses relating specifically to conditions of work; customarily the materials and scaffolding were provided by the Board of Works, and on most occasions the Board also provided food, wine and living accommodation as well.

The fall of the republic and the loss of independence seems to have produced no great break in the continuity of these traditions. The Board of Works continued to be organized in the traditional manner; contracts continued to be couched in familiar terms; and artists were rewarded for their work in the way in which they had always been rewarded. Even as late as the seventeenth century the Board of Works still treated artists as if they were merely craftsmen and there is little recognition of the claims due to genius. As late as 1608 the Board included in a contract made with Ventura Salimbeni for 'certain Sienese saints'[17] the somewhat surprising clause that the artist promised:

> with divine help, to put into that work, all the skill and diligence of which he is capable.[18]

Similarly, the amount of latitude left to an artist in his designs by the Board of Works remained severely limited. The contract given to Francesco Vanni for his painting of Saint Ansano in 1593 warned the artist to stick to the design he had provided; he might improve it or enlarge it but only: 'according to the good rules of his art.'[19]

Such conservative customs may have had a restraining, though not necessarily a constraining, influence on the artists who worked for the Board of Works. They should be considered, however, in the context of the fact that they were balanced by a more liberal and open-minded private patronage. And in relation to the decoration of the cathedral, individuals and powerful families had in the end as great an impact as the Board of Works. Sassetta's lovely and artistically advanced *Madonna of the Snows* of 1430, for instance, although it has long since been removed, was originally commissioned for the cathedral by Madonna Ludovica, whose husband, Turino di Matteo, had once been

Simone Martini, *Maestà*

Simone Martini, *Guidoriccio da Fogliano at the Siege of Montemassi*

Palazzo Sansedoni and the Campo

The Palazzo Pubblico

Ambrogio Lorenzetti, *Allegory of Good and Bad Government*

Ambrogio Lorenzetti, *Allegory of Good and Bad Government*

Facade of the Cathedral

a Master of the Works. Many of the major Sienese families, like the Piccolomini and the Chigi, had their own family altars in the cathedral, and they vied with each other to make these the most outstanding, the most valuable or the most up-to-date. Thus, the Piccolomini altar, commissioned by Cardinal Nani Todeschini, the nephew of Pius II, as his intended sepulchre, and begun in 1485 to a design of Andrea Fusina of Milan was among the loveliest and most innovatory works of the renaissance. So, too, was the Pinturicchio library which the Cardinal had built to house the books bequeathed to him by his uncle. It is among the greatest decorative triumphs of renaissance Europe. Of the same nature is the Capella del Voto, a riot of gold and lapus lazuli in the right transept of the cathedral, built in 1661, by Benedetto Giovannelli for the Sienese pope, Alexander VII, to enshrine the precious Madonna del Voto.

Equally significant, if slightly less obvious is the impact which the Petrucci family had upon the interior of the cathedral, for Pandolfo Petrucci used his important position within the government of Siena to impose his personal taste upon it. During Petrucci's ascendancy every artistic decision concerning the cathedral was taken in his presence. He was a member of every important artistic committee, contracts were drawn up in his palace, and payment for works completed was made 'as it shall appear suitable to the Magnificent Pandolfo Petrucci'.[20] It was Pandolfo who, in 1506, moved the high altar from under the cupola to its present position. It was Pandolfo's decision— one showing a remarkable disregard for Sienese tradition and sentiment—to remove the Duccio *Maestà* to a side-aisle and to replace it with Vecchietta's Tabernacle which was moved from its original position in the church of Santa Maria della Scala. Thus the whole atmosphere of the present cathedral derives to a large extent from the artistic tastes of the Petrucci family.

The impact of the cathedral of Siena, like that of all great cathedrals, derives from a fusion of an intense spirituality and a magnificent and imaginative artistry. In the case of Siena both elements in turn represent a combination of the corporate and the individual, of the public and the semi-private. The sense in which this is particularly true of the cathedral's aesthetic beauty should already be clear. Whereas its basic formal structure is the inspired result of a corporate and communal patronage and thus expresses a corporate ideal, the furnishing and the embellishing of the cathedral often reflect private and personal tastes. If we except the important work done on the interior of the cathedral in the seventeenth and eighteenth centuries—when the side-altars were modified and systematized, the valuable old Sienese paintings were removed and replaced by paintings by the best contemporary artists, and the two panels of the *Maestà* were separated and placed, one in the chapel of the Sacrament and one in the chapel of San Ansano— what we are left with is a building in its essence Gothic, combined with an interior decor whose style and taste are largely of the renaissance. Uniting in this way magnificent monuments of the major and most distinguished periods in the city's cultural history, the cathedral of Siena is a splendid treasury of the city's artistic and creative life. As such it remains an object of intense and continuing fascination for all visitors to Siena. Even in the eighteenth century, when it seemed so clearly to offend against the established canons of taste of the day, all travellers made the cathedral at least one obligatory visit:

> under the impression that, enclosed within it, is everything which this city has which is either beautiful or noteworthy.[21]

5

The Campo

Un giorno ancho a me toccherà
Lascia' il fagotto e anda' di là. . .
Un ci venì a trovammi
Cercami in Piazza
Mi ci troverai.

Ferdinando Giannelli

WHERE THE three hills of Siena converge, at the very heart of the city, there opens out that famous, semi-circular space which is known as the Campo. Eventually any Sienese street will bring you to this natural meeting-place, where, in front of restaurants, bars and souvenir shops, the brick pavement slopes down to the Palazzo Pubblico. The open space is crossed and recrossed by children on bicycles, by wandering tourists, or by purposeful Sienese. The Fonte Gaia, one of the most-photographed works of art in Italy, is a natural rendezvous, and one has the impression that, if one were to wait here long enough, all the world would eventually pass by. Nor would such a wait be tedious, for meanwhile the eye could rest on one of the most rewarding complexes of buildings and space ever created, whose humane dimension makes them instantly comprehensible and enjoyable. There is a familiarity about this place and, entering suddenly from one of the dark passage-ways which feed into it, one's breath is taken away, not by a sudden sense of sublime beauty, nor by wonder at a display of wealth and power, but because entering the Campo of Siena is like coming home.

What Gigli wrote remains as true today as in 1722:

> our *piazza* has been created with so magnificent and so beautiful a symmetry, that anyone, at the first glance can tell whether the person he seeks is there.[1]

The Campo is one of the most successful uses of space in any city, with an articulation which is unique. Both an autonomous and a total work of art, every element is essential to the whole, and no one part has any artistic value without the rest. It is a perfect example of urbanisation, created at a time when shape and proportion were determined neither by a surviving classical model—it was created too late for that—nor by the rationalizing, linear demands of renaissance architecture which it was early enough to escape. It was rather an intuitive, intentional adaptation to the needs of the medieval town. Reflecting the corporate organization of Siena, the Campo was the deliberately designed centre of the secular and administrative life of the city, distinct from, but always related to, its religious heart which lay in the area around the cathedral.

The Campo has always inspired admiration, and frequent attempts to explain its significance have been made by means of metaphor, symbol or simile. Montaigne, for instance, described it, quite erroneously, as a circle, because the circle was a symbol of perfection. For much the same reason, romantic writers have always emphasized the Campo's irregularity, at the expense of its symmetry, and concentrated upon its shell-like qualities. Others have likened it not to a shell but to a fan. Commonly it has been compared to a theatre, 'especially constructed for great festivals and popular feasts'.[2] It was Siena's sixteenth-century historian, Orlando Malavolti, who first described the Campo in these terms, and, after the introduction of the *palio alla tonda* in 1627, it became even easier to see it as a 'theatre of life' with the surrounding windows and their balconies serving as seats for spectators. Certainly, seen from the windows of the Archivio di Stato in Palazzo Piccolomini d'Aragona, it does look like a vast amphitheatre, with the houses above it climbing the slopes to the cathedral, playing the role of spectators; from this perspective too, one has the sense of mass and volume, characteristic of a Roman theatre, but normally completely lacking in Sienese architecture.

Perhaps the best metaphor for the Campo, however, is the popular Sienese one, which sees it as the cloak of the *Madonna della Misericordia*, a favoured subject of Sienese painting and a common theme in Sienese writing. In this image as Sermini explains, the Virgin appears in a protective role: 'And covers all your city with her holy mantle.'[3]

Paintings often show Siena's citizens huddled together for protection under this mantle; an early example is seen in the *Madonna* of Niccolò da Siena in the Pinacoteca. Later good examples are those by Bartolo di Fredi at Pienza, in which the Virgin's cloak is held up by angels, that of Giovanni di Paolo on the cover of the Liber Vitale of the hospital of Santa Maria della Scala of 1458, and the same artist's delicate altarpiece in Santa Maria dei Servi. Among the finest of Vecchietta's works is his *Madonna della Misericordia* for the Palazzo Pubblico and in 1481 the subject was enchantingly treated by Benvenuto di Giovanni for Palazzo Salimbeni. Other examples of this same subject are to be found among the *tavolette*; in one of 1451, the Virgin hovers to the left of the picture, her mantle spread over Siena, in another of 1467, attributed to Francesco di Giorgio, the Virgin protects Siena from an earthquake, and a third was painted by Neroccio di Landi in 1480. The *Madonna della Misericordia* refers, of course, to the battle of Montaperti, when on the night before the battle the Florentine sentries:

> beheld as it were a mantle most white, which covered all the camp and city of the Sienese . . . and there were those who said it seemed to be the mantle of Our Mother, the Virgin Mary, the guardian and defender of the people of Siena.[4]

Again, at the battle of Camollia in 1526, as it is commemorated in the painting in San Martino by Giovanni di Lorenzo Cini, a similar cloud spread over the city and its defenders and was taken to represent the cloak of the Madonna. If the form of the Campo does derive from such myths and images and does indeed represent the Virgin's cloak, then all that occurs there can be seen as, in a most literal sense, taking place beneath her protection. The Campo then becomes an essentially sacred place.

Circle, shell, fan, cloak or mantel—such varied metaphors illuminate the perspectives of those who use them more than they define the reality of the Campo. But their very variety suggests the difficulty of achieving an accurate definition. Perhaps history alone provides a solution. The Campo is, after all, an historical creation, consciously shaped in a process by which the communal authorities responded to the needs of the Sienese people. Hence, fully to understand its meaning, we must look to the historical circumstances which engendered it and which, over the centuries, continued to shape it.

A study of these circumstances immediately reveals that the Campo, although preconceived, was not in a strict sense designed, and suggests that in this fact lies its dynamic secret. It was, in fact, created by a variety of forces; by, for instance, the topography of the city, by the problem of its water-supply, and by its traffic flow. The Campo is situated just outside the most ancient area of settlement in the Castelvecchio; in the early middle ages, it was clearly a central point where the three main streets leading from the three *nuclei* of the commune converged. This already gave the area a certain importance, underlined when the commune itself began both to build new roads, also converging on this point, and, towards the end of the twelfth century, to purchase land and property in the same area.

Another powerful force in the shaping of the Campo was the fact that it began to fulfil certain social functions which were very important to the city. From the beginning, for instance, it was a fortunately neutral territory where the contentious city might meet, a public area to which all might belong. It was large enough to accommodate the whole body of citizens, but remained an area where no one individual family or faction could predominate. It lay at the confluence of all three *terzi* but belonged to none of them, just as today it belongs to none of the Sienese *contrade*. For this reason, in normal times, it was an area in which arms and weapons were not used except in play and where all violence was ritualized. To enforce this point, draconian measures were sometimes resorted to. So in 1554, during the siege of the city, a certain Antonio Rieti, who had drawn his sword on a shopkeeper in the Campo, was hanged from a window of the Palazzo Pubblico by order of the French commander, Piero Strozzi.

The Campo was thus a physical expression of the ideal of good government, of that substitution, sought by the commune, of love for the city, in place of loyalty to faction, clan, family, *terzo* or *contrada*. It was here that ordinances were proclaimed, here that government could be seen to reside, here that the public gallows was erected, and here that civic celebrations and festivities took place. Such a celebration occurred, for instance, in 1451 during the visit of Frederick III and Eleanor of Portugal, when a vast wooden stage was erected in front of the Palazzo Pubblico and a great ball was staged for the delight of the Emperor and his new bride:

> and the virtuous and beautiful lady, Battista Berti, wife of Achille Petrucci, gave a Latin oration, with rare elegance and wit, for which she was embraced by the Emperor and created a countess, and, when asked what further grace would most please her, asked to be exempted from the laws which forbade the wearing of brocade and jewels.[5]

Similar celebrations were held in 1465 for the visit of the Duchess of Calabria when a ball was held in the Campo and:

> a great golden wolf was built from which there issued a band of twelve persons who were well and richly arrayed, and one was

dressed as a nun, and they danced to a song whose words were: *I don't want to be a nun any more....* A great feast was set out of marzipan and a quantity of other sweetmeats, and every kind of fruit that was in season . . . and the said celebrations cost the commune of Siena twenty-four thousand florins. . . .[6]

More than two centuries later the Campo was to see another, remarkably similar celebration, when the Sienese welcomed their new governess, Princess Violante of Bavaria, on the evening of 12 April 1717. The Campo was illuminated with a host of blazing torches and decorated by fifty coats-of-arms of the house of Bavaria:

> each surrounded by six great illuminated globes, to represent the arms of the ruling house of Tuscany: all of which but made a crown for another coat-of-arms, placed upon two columns and supported by two figures of Fame, placed in front of the Palazzo Pubblico, on which were combined the arms of the royal family of Tuscany and that of the Electoral family of Bavaria. The decorations were continued with countless torches and lamps, placed in all the windows which look onto the Campo, and the façade of the Palazzo Pubblico was most majestically illuminated, so that the great theatre had the most wonderful appearance.[7]

The Campo was also a natural theatre for such events as the sermons in 1427 of San Bernardino, who was forced to preach in the open because no church in Siena was large enough to hold all those who wanted to hear. A faithful visual record of these dawn sermons is to be found in the paintings of Neroccio di Lando and Sano di Pietro. They show much of the appearance of the Campo and of the Palazzo Pubblico at the beginning of the fifteenth century; they also show how, for the occasion, an altar was set up between the two windows of the Palazzo, with, in front of it, a pulpit. To the left of the pulpit, a platform was erected for the communal officials, while in the Campo below were gathered the women to the right, the men to the left, divided by a curtain so that their attention should not be diverted by members of the opposite sex. Naturally, therefore, the Campo was also the centre for the celebrations relating to the canonization of San Bernardino in 1450 when:

> celebrations occurred throughout Siena, each man giving food and drink to anyone who wanted it, and the Bishop of Siena sang mass in the Campo.[8]

It was in the Campo, likewise, that the Sienese were to be found at play as a community, in that series of ritual games which then served and still serve as a binding-force uniting the city against the outsider. The recreational value of the Campo was recognized by the commune as early as the first years of the fourteenth century, when a decree ordered the shopkeepers to clear away the mountains of rubbish which were so fetid and unpleasant that they prevented the citizens from taking their ease in the Campo after dinner in the cool of the evening.

By a natural process, therefore, every major event in the life of Siena came to centre on the Campo. Despite its ideal existence as a centre of civic unity and harmony, it was no doubt inevitable that the open space it provided should also make it the frequent scene of riots, civil strife and factional battles. Often it also witnessed more pathetic and distressing events in Siena's history, such as those which followed the earthquake of 1320, when the inhabitants of the city fled to the Campo where they believed they would surely find a safe refuge.

More mundanely, for centuries the Campo was also the major market-place of Siena and, as such, the fulcrum of its economic life. In earlier centuries, the centre of the Campo was filled each morning by stalls, selling such goods as grain, fruit, vegetables, fish, which were kept in basins at the foot of the Fonte Gaia, wood and, until 1346, when the animal market was moved to Fontebranda, all kinds of livestock. As, over the centuries, more specialized markets developed in other parts of Siena the Campo gradually lost its primary importance as an economic centre; but it was still busy in the late nineteenth and early twentieth centuries and, even today, some traces of the old market remain in a few morning fruit and vegetable stalls.

Until the nineteenth century, the Campo also played another important role, as the place where the commune literally nourished its people, for it was here, in time of famine, that the commune distributed grain to the poor and starving. So common was the mental association between the Campo and grain distribution that we have the story of the Marquess Zondadori in 1799 during the terrible famine:

> riding from Salicotto, and being told by certain women that rather than diverting himself, he would do better to send grain into the Campo.[9]

The Campo, therefore, fulfilled many important roles in city life. We have seen how in the earlier middle ages it already served as a central meeting-place, at the natural confluence of the major thoroughfares of Siena, and acted as an urban market. Thus, by around 1200, it was already a clearly-defined area, but one still unrefined or polished, a steep and open slope at the end of a valley down which water ran from the heights of the old city above it, yet already crossed by important thoroughfares and divided by a wall, built at communal expense in 1194 to prevent soil erosion on the site subsequently occupied by the Palazzo Pubblico. The Campo's importance in public life by this date is suggested by the existence of special officials appointed to look after it and to supervise the many activities which already occurred there.

By the end of the thirteenth century the Campo's importance as a public centre had been considerably enhanced in that it was virtually the only remaining open space of any size left in Siena. There was, therefore, a natural pressure towards the preservation and systematization of the Campo and, as with so much else in Siena, it was the Nine who took up the challenge to turn this space into a veritable work of art. It was they who developed it into the definitive form it retains today. From 1293 onwards they were buying up property in the vicinity, and in 1297 they issued the famous decree which said that, in order to create an harmonious whole which might reflect the harmony of civic society, the windows of all buildings facing onto the Campo should be adorned with small columns and devoid of all balconies. The Nine also emphasized the significance of the Campo by further encouraging the process by which all the streets of the city tended to converge on it. In this area the most spectacular intervention of the Nine was that of 1299 when they constructed a new road which gave direct access to the Campo from the Terzo di Camollia. The completion of this part of their work came between 1297 and 1349 with the actual paving of the Campo in the nine compartments which still recall Siena's great city-makers. For this the commune contributed two-thirds of the cost; the remainder was paid by the owners of property adjoining the Campo.

Despite their insistence on the principle of uniformity in decoration in palaces facing on to the Campo, the Nine never tried to impose a total uniformity of appearance on these buildings and they therefore displayed a natural irregularity and rhythm, fully consonant with the traditions of Sienese culture. During the renaissance, however, when new ideas about the importance of symmetry in urban design began to make their way to Siena from Florence and Rome, various leading Sienese citizens, including Pandolfo Petrucci, canvassed the idea of adding a series of porticoes to the fronts of the palaces, in order to give

the Campo a greater unity, a project defeated only by a lack of available funds. The idea was revived again in the eighteenth century but,
fortunately, again proved too expensive. All that was achieved was the
imposition of a degree of symmetry on the palaces, consonant with
contemporary principles of order. What such innovators failed to
realize, the medieval Sienese knew full well, which is that the uniformity of Siena, whether in its parts, as in the Campo, or as a whole,
is created by colour and by material; by the brownish-red—the famous
Burnt Siena—of its bricks and not by any formal stylistic unity.

This colour and its dominance in the Sienese townscape were also
determined, in so far as it is possible for such things to be determined,
by the decision of the Nine to erect their important buildings and to
pave the Campo in brick and not in stone. Before the time of the Nine,
stone had been extensively used throughout Siena, but the Nine, as we
might suspect from the Lorenzetti frescoes, which show only brick
houses, consciously rejected stone as a building material. Brick production in the fourteenth century was clearly a communal concern, for
bricks in vast quantities were needed for rebuilding the city-walls.
Bricks were also cheaper, for the materials used in their production
were to be found near at hand in the *contado*. The Nine, therefore, not
only made extensive use of brick in communal buildings, but also in
1309 ordered that brick should be used in all new houses to be built in
Siena. Thus, in the end, the colour of Siena would become determined
by the colour of the Campo.

The aim of the Nine throughout had been to make the Campo the
centre of civic life, and few aims have ever been so triumphantly
realised. It immediately became a great source of civic pride, vividly
expressed by a contemporary chronicler who recorded that in 1347:

> ... the Campo of Siena was finally completed. It is held to be one of
> the most beautiful of all squares which can be seen not only in Italy
> but in the whole of Christendom, both for the loveliness of the
> fountain and for the beauty of the buildings which surround it.

A similar sense of the beauty and the special quality of the Campo was
expressed in a petition to the Council of the Popolo of 9 April 1398
which recorded that:

> ... in every well-governed city, provision is made for the embel-
> lishment and the improvement of that city, and you have in this
> Campo of yours ... the most beautiful square that can anywhere
> be found. ... [10]

From the beginning the Campo clearly belonged to the people. Yet its true meaning lies in the fact that, within it, this popular element is balanced by the other important forces which have gone to shape Sienese urban life. The arc of the Campo is defined by a series of palaces which illustrate the importance of noble and mercantile families in Siena,* the religious element is represented by the chapel where mass was said daily—the shopkeepers on the Campo participating from their doorways—while the natural completion of the whole complex is the Palazzo Pubblico, representing the official forces of Justice and Good Government.

The Palazzo Pubblico, as the nine merlons, or battlements, of its central tower remind us, was also the work of the Nine. Originally the commune of Siena, like other Italian communes, lacked a permanent location where its authority could be seen to reside. Meetings of the city's ruling bodies had to take place in a church, or, from the late twelfth century, in rented private residences. For obvious reasons, such a situation was unsatisfactory and one of the first decisions taken by the Nine, after their seizure of power, was to provide a new and independent seat of government in the Campo where the Dogana del Sale—the communal salt-store—and the mint already stood.

In 1282 a commission of twelve men, equally divided among the *Terzi*, was nominated to plan the whole enterprise, and two years later, according to Agnolo di Tura, the Podestà Guido da Romagna took up residence in the Dogana del Sale; 'on the Campo of the commune, and he was the first Podestà to reside there'.[11] In 1288 the commune purchased some adjoining houses, in order to provide a site for the communal palace, but a long and costly process lay ahead, so costly, indeed, that in May 1297 the General Council agreed to spend £2,000 every six months on the project. The slopes which fall so sharply below the Campo had first to be built up with enormous earthworks and foundation walls. Some idea of the scale of the undertaking can still be gathered by climbing up to the Loggia of the Palazzo Pubblico, which was completed in 1304, and looking down at where the building slopes down to the valley below it. There were continual difficulties over the

---

* Reading around the Campo from the right-hand side of the palace, these are: Palazzo Petroni, Palazzo Piccolomini Salamoneschi, Palazzo Piccolomini d'Aragona, Palazzo Ragnoni, Palazzo Mexolombardi-Rinaldini, Palazzo Tornaipuglia Sansedoni, Palazzo Vincenti, Palazzo Piccolomini, Palazzo Rimbotti, the Mercanzia, Palazzo Saracini, Palazzo Scotti, Palazzo Accarigi, Palazzo Alessi, Palazzo Mattasala Lambertini.

supply of materials for such a massive enterprise. The chroniclers record in 1307 that:

> in order to build the palace . . . the Sienese purchased the tower of the Visdomini. . . . And the said tower cost the commune £700 to destroy it and to recover the stones and the bricks.[12]

Not surprisingly, therefore, costs continued to mount; between 1307 and 1310, payments of at least £10,000 were made out of the Biccherna towards the project, and, in addition, in the years of maximum effort, 1308–9, there were further extraordinary payments of £6,400. But, despite such difficulties, by 1310 the original nucleus of the palace was already complete.

At the ground level, a stone façade was pierced by four arches which gave access to the interior. This was surmounted by a brick building, decorated with four three-mullioned windows—the characteristic Sienese *trifore*—which corresponded to the arches on the floor below. The ground floor was occupied by the Biccherna, the upper floor by the General Council. The whole edifice was crowned with a row of merlons. But, almost immediately, the building was found to be inadequate and a third floor with five *trifore* was added, subsequently reduced to four in order to impose stylistic symmetry on the building. By 1310 the sidewings had been completed, but even so construction work continued until 1342. At this date the building had taken its first definitive shape with a central body at that time two floors higher than the wings. This form was a symbolic embodiment of the nature of the commune, for the palace represented the balance and relationship between Justice and Good Government; Justice in the shape of the *podestà* occupied one wing of the palace, Good Government in the shape of the Nine, the other; while, in the centre, the balance between them was kept by the city's financial office, the Biccherna, and the commune's most representative institution, the General Council.

The story of the Palazzo Pubblico does not, of course, end here, for through succeeding centuries it was to grow and develop, to be decorated and redecorated both within and without, in response to changing situations within Siena. This we can perceive by examining the façade, a task which can be performed perfectly adequately from a bar on the opposite side of the Campo. The communal era is recalled by the *balzana* in a repetitive motif above every door and window. But, equally prominent now, are the arrogantly placed arms of the Medici and their grand-ducal crown erected in 1560 which recall the extinction of Siena as an independent republic. More obvious than even this aggressive secular symbol, and replacing the arms of the Visconti, which were once placed there, is the mystical monogram of Jesus, which appears so prominently in late medieval illustrations of the Campo and which has, reputedly, saved Siena from disaster on many occasions. Commissioned in 1425 from Master Battista di Niccolò of Padua, at a price of £440, and bronzed by Turino di Sano and his son, Giovanni, for 40 florins, it recalls Siena's civic piety, as well as the dramatic impact which San Bernardino had on the city.

These themes are all reflected and elaborated upon inside the building, which is a treasure-house of Sienese art. For, from the beginning, the Palazzo was conceived of as an aesthetic object, as a work of art, expressing the aspirations of the Sienese people. Monumental wall-paintings were an integral part of its design, beginning with Simone Martini's *Maestà*, painted in 1315 for the great council hall, in which Sienese government and the rule of law are celebrated, and the Virgin is made an active participant in civic life. Elsewhere in the Palazzo Pubblico the same themes are alluded to; in the Lorenzetti *Allegory*, in the allegories of Taddeo di Bartolo in the antechapel, and in those of Beccafumi on the ceiling of the Sala del Concistoro.

Frescoes also celebrate Siena's saints and her civic religious life; apart from the patron saints of the city in the *Maestà*, the Sala del Mappamondo has portrayals of San Bernardino by Sano di Pietro, of St. Catherine by Vecchietta, of Saints Ansano and Victor by Sodoma, and of the Blessed Bernardo Tolomei. Another group of frescoes celebrates military victories: again in the Sala del Mappamondo, Martini's breathtaking *Guidoriccio da Fogliano at the Siege of Montemassi* and the two very inferior monochrome frescoes, representing the *Victory of the Sienese over the Company of the Capello at Torrita* in 1363, and the *Battle of Poggio Imperiale* between the Florentines and the Duke of Calabria in 1479.

Another overall theme of the frescoes of the Sala del Mappamondo is that of the obligations of the governed to the governing. The *Maestà* certainly expounds the ideals upon which good government should be based, but we should remember that it was also commissioned in the context of a struggle between the Nine and the noble clans of the city. Thus the *Maestà* carries an implied warning about the dangers of faction and the determination of the commune to assert the rule of law in the face of noble lawlessness. And this, of course, was also a theme of the *Guidoriccio* and the original frieze of which it once formed a part, showing other noble castles conquered by the commune, beginning with Giancaro in 1314 and continued with Martini's now-obliterated Arcidosso and Castel del Piano. To contemporaries, Guidoriccio therefore appeared as the symbol of law and authority and the upholder of communal rights against lawlessness.

The most important work of art in the whole Palazzo, however, lies in the room adjoining the Sala del Mappamondo and this is Ambrogio Lorenzetti's famous *Allegory of Good and Bad Government*. In these frescoes we find a distillation of Augustinian and Thomist thought and an indication of the achievements of medieval science, combined with a statement about the value of human experience in this world, expressed through popular images and a vigorous vernacular art. For Ambrogio Lorenzetti's greatest achievement as an artist was his ability to realize universal themes neither through the medium of a somewhat tired Byzantine style, such as had been employed by his immediate predecessors, nor through that of a somewhat derivative International Gothic, such as Simone Martini, who was his contemporary, used. Lorenzetti employed instead a robust and genuinely Sienese vocabulary. This means, for example, that his work is distinguished by its use of telling naturalistic detail. In the *Presentation* at Assisi, for instance, his Christ-child is the first illustration of its subject in which the baby is portrayed as clearly under a year old. Similarly, in his famous *Madonna Lactans* in the Seminary of San Francesco in Siena, it is a real baby we see, sucking its finger and curling up its toes. And, at the very centre of *Good and Bad Government* the traditional image of the she-wolf and the twins is saved from being a dull stereotype by the robustness of the twins and the original touch of the mother-wolf turning to caress her foundlings with her tongue.

Such vigorous naturalism means that the Lorenzetti frescoes are immediately readable at the literal level. If we look at that section of the frescoes which represents the effects of Good Government, we see that beneath the hovering image of Security—incidentally one of the first, if not one of the more successful, attempts in Christian art to portray a nude female—city-life goes on within the protective circuit of Siena's walls. We understand the picture as it was understood and described by San Bernardino in the fifteenth century:

I see merchants buying and selling, I see dancing, the houses being repaired, the workers busy in the vineyards or sowing the fields, whilst on horseback others ride down to swim in the rivers; maidens

I see going to a wedding, and great flocks of sheep and many another
peaceful sight. Besides which I see a man hanging from the gallows,
hung there in the cause of justice. And for the sake of all these things
men live in peace and harmony with one another. . . .[13]

Much of the attraction of these frescoes has always lain in their recognizably human qualities and we should certainly enjoy them at this
popular and literal level. Nor is there any reason why we should not
also enjoy them as outstanding examples of Sienese *Trecento* painting.
But to understand their significance in the urban life of Siena we must
go further and look at the allegorical meanings which underlie them.

To understand the *Allegory of Good and Bad Government* as allegory
we also need to know something of the context out of which the
frescoes emerged. They were probably painted between 1338 and 1340,
to a commission of the Nine. They were designed to decorate the very
heart of that regime, the council chamber of the Nine, a room in the
Palazzo Pubblico which, since at least the fifteenth century, has taken
its name from the supposed subject-matter of the paintings and is
called the Sala della Pace.

The primary function of the frescoes at the time they were painted
was a decorative and a celebratory one. They were to add to the glories
of Siena which were being created by the beneficent rule of the Nine.
They fell, in fact, within the terms of a document of 1316 which refers
to murals to be executed within the Palazzo Pubblico and explains
that the interior:

> should please the eye, bring joy to the heart and satisfy every one's
> senses; (it is) to the glory of the whole community that the leaders
> and rulers of the commune should enjoy surroundings which are
> fine, beautiful and honourable.[14]

The frescoes were also intended to be didactic for this was the primary
object of all medieval painting and, indeed, its major justification as the
Sienese painters themselves explained in the preamble of their guild
statues: they are 'by the grace of God, expositors of sacred writ to the
ignorant who know not how to read'.[15]

If the Lorenzetti frescoes are didactic then we need to know to
whom their teaching was directed. The answer must be that they were
designed for the eyes of the ruling élite of the city, for few, outside of
that charmed group, ever penetrated to the innermost rooms of the
Palazzo Pubblico. And it is clearly the Nine who are addressed by the

words which appear above the head of Justice in the fresco: 'Love Justice, you who rule the earth.' Thus, these frescoes should be seen as a fourteenth-century statement about the obligations of the governor to the governed, rather than about the obligations of the governed to the governing, a subject which, as we have seen, is dealt with very effectively in the adjoining Sala del Mappamondo.

The frescoes occupy three walls of this large rectangular council chamber in which the single, and rather inadequate, source of light is a window which faces south. The short wall opposite this window is a natural point of departure for the reading of Lorenzetti's allegory. On the left, as we should expect in any Sienese statement about the relationship of governor with governed, Justice is prominently painted. This, like the other figures, was to become an important prototype in Sienese art; numerous variations were to appear in succeeding centuries. Signifying that form of justice which gives to each citizen what the public good demands, Lorenzetti's interpretation is strictly Aristotelian, within the mainstream of medieval learning, but the emphasis which is placed upon such justice is particularly and specifically Sienese. It was a theme which had already been predominant in Martini's *Maestà* and one which was to become increasingly insistent in Sienese culture. The Sienese, well aware that Augustine, in *The City of God*, had taught that no regime could survive which was not founded in Justice, saw the pursuit of such justice as the first end of all civil government. Since Justice alone could uphold the *vita civile* the fair administration of justice was a primary justification of any regime. By a natural extension, the existence of injustice came to be seen as justification of rebellion and *prima facie* evidence that a regime was tyrannical. It is, therefore, a curiously ironical footnote to these frescoes that, as we have seen, the major contributory factor leading to the overthrow of the Nine in 1355 was the fact that they could no longer guarantee a fair administration of justice in Siena.

An inscription in the *cartello* in the border below spells out the message for those who cannot read the visual image:

Wherever this holy virtue—Justice—rules, she leads many souls to unity, and these, so united, make up the Common Good.

And on the east wall this theme receives further elaboration:

Turn your eyes, you who rule, to look carefully at Justice, who, for her glory, is presented and crowned here. She always gives each man his rightful due. See how much good comes from her and how sweet life is and full of peace in the city where this virtue is to be seen, which is more resplendent than any other. She guards and defends those who honour her; and she sustains them. From her light comes the reward of those who are good and she gives to the evil their deserved punishment.

Here, then, as he says, Lorenzetti shows Justice enthroned. But, in accordance with strict Thomist thought, Divine Wisdom, on the higher level of the theological virtues, hovers above Justice, holding a balance, the scales of which are kept in equilibrium by Reason. Justice looks upwards towards Divine Wisdom, thus illustrating the relationship between divine, natural, and human law, for true justice is always inspired by reason. On the left, one angel metes out distributive justice, on the right, another commutative justice. Cords running from the scales, come together in the hands of Concord, enthroned below. This is as it should be, for, next to justice, concord was seen as the binding-force in Sienese society, and the absence of concord, expressed through factionalism, the major cause of tyranny.

Concord carries a heavy carpenter's plane which symbolizes the equality of citizens, since, in a well-regulated society, no one individual should stand above others, all citizens standing on the same level as if that society had been literally planed down. Concord passes the cord on to a group of twenty-four Sienese citizens. The presence of this twenty-four alerts us to an identification between Siena the ideal city and the City of God as portrayed in the book of *Revelation*. The numerical composition of Lorenzetti's fresco follows exactly the numerical composition of St. John the Divine's city, the twenty-four Sienese citizens represent the twenty-four elders about the throne, Justice the 'one sat on the throne';[16] the seven virtues to the right of the picture the 'seven lamps burning before the throne which are the seven Spirits of God';[17] and the four figures—Faith, Hope, Charity and Divine Wisdom—who hover at the top of the picture, the four beasts, 'in the midst of the throne and around the throne'.[18] Thus Lorenzetti clearly identifies the City of God and the city of Siena through the apocalyptic vision of the New Testament.

The twenty-four elders or Sienese citizens carry the cord they have received from Concord in procession to *Ben Commun*—the Common Good—in whose right hand the cord ends. The *Ben Commun* while a universalized portrait of the common good, is also a particular image

4

of the commune of Siena. This we know because the figure is robed in black and white, Siena's traditional colours, his shield is the official shield of Siena, and, at his feet, are nestled the wolf and the twins, which, as we have seen, is the most ancient of all Sienese symbols.

Common Good sits in the middle of a long bench and is flanked on either side by three virtues: Peace, Fortitude and Prudence are on his right; Magnanimity, Temperance and Justice on his left. Above Common Good hover the three theological virtues, Faith, Charity and Hope.

These allegorical figures are linked by a band of soldiers and two groups of lancers to the lower group of figures. As well as the twenty-four citizens, this includes a number of prisoners and two kneeling knights who are donating their castles to the city of Siena. The introduction of such *genre* material is a typical Lorenzetti touch. The secular figures do not merely illustrate an allegory, but form a link between it and the reality of Sienese life which thus becomes amalgamated with an ideal world. It is a device characteristic of Dante, who also shows a compelling capacity to proceed from reality to an allegorical or a symbolic meaning.

As for the interpretation of Lorenzetti's allegory, the key to this is again given in the *cartello* directly below the fresco. Justice, as we have seen, creates unity, and the united body of the citizens are the Common Good. The rulers of the state keep 'the glorious faces of the virtues' always about them, and 'for this reason taxes, levies and . . . estates are given . . . in triumph. Hence civic welfare follows, without war, and is useful, necessary and happy.'

Here is a world familiar enough in Thomist political thought. Nowhere had St. Thomas's doctrine of the supremacy of the common good over the good of each individual been so enthusiastically received as in the Italian city-state, where it had been rapidly propagated by the preaching of the friars. Its best-known expression was a tract, *De Bono Comuni*, written in about 1300 by a Dominican friar, Remigio de'Girolami, a work which it seems fairly safe to assume was known to Lorenzetti. The reasons for the success of the doctrine in Italy are illuminated by the example of the *Allegory of Good and Bad Government* for its acceptability lay in the fact that adherence to the community as a whole, at the expense of particularist interests, seemed to offer the security of civic peace and unity without recourse to despotism. No wonder that in Siena, which always showed a tendency to relapse into factional struggle, the idea should have been preached so enthusiastically and been embodied in both Martini's *Maestà* and in *Good and Bad Government*.

Another aspect of Thomist thought sheds further light on Lorenzetti. If we look at the *Allegory of Good Government* as a whole, four figures stand out, either because of their size, or position, or because of their pose, as in the case of the classically-draped Peace. These figures are: Justice, the Common Good, Concord and Peace. In the political philosophy of St. Thomas justice and the common good are always related to concord and peace. Thus peace and concord, as the most desirable effects of good government, are emphasized and provide a necessary thematic link with the east wall of the Sala della Pace on which is painted that section of the Lorenzetti frescoes normally referred to as *The Effects of Good Government*.

Here, in one of the first essays in landscape in the Western tradition of painting, Lorenzetti has depicted medieval Siena and its *contado*. The picture is naturally divided by the painted city-wall, so that the town and its *contado* form two compositional halves in the overall conception, linked by the thickly peopled commercial street, by the noble hunting-party which is just riding out through the city-gate, and by the peasants driving their donkeys into the city. It is a composition which boldly asserts the value of city-life, because it provides a secure, ordered and busy existence.

In the vernacular tradition which Lorenzetti was utilizing here, a city's walls were an object of pride to its citizens, because they defined the community—the *civitas*—through which men found freedom and were relieved from the dangers concomitant with life in the open country. The wall symbolised all that was good in the city, detaching it from the wild and lawless countryside and converting it into a region of order and justice. For this reason, Giotto's allegories in the Arena chapel at Padua show Justice residing within the city and Injustice lurking outside the gate. Presumably for the same reason, the beggar in Lorenzetti's frescoes is located outside the city-wall.

Lorenzetti conveys a sense of the value of urban life even more subtly, by showing the city teeming with life, a beneficent vitality which is extended into the countryside where, under the protection of the city-wall, peasants are seen tilling the land and where there are many settlements. The further one's eye wanders from Siena, however, the more empty the countryside becomes, and fortified castles take the place of villages and farms, until, at the far right edge of the fresco, Siena's newly-acquired port at Talamone is identified by an inscription.

For those who have failed to take his point from the extended visual image, Lorenzetti provides a key in the scroll, held by the presiding figure of Security:

Let every man go without fear, and let every man sow for as long as this lady rules, for she has taken power from all the guilty.

What we see depicted on the east wall of the Sala della Pace is in fact a statement that the city is the only possible complete form of human existence; that without cities there can be no civilization. The whole construction of the fresco depends on this assumption; the centre of the painting, where the dancing-girls celebrate civic life, is the point from which all the architectural diminution runs, and the point from which all the light flows both in the city and in the *contado*. Thus the fresco must be read outwards from this central point.

This visual impression is confirmed by the detailed allegory of this section of the frescoes, an allegory which is an example of medieval thought at its finest and most subtle. The figures we see engaged in various pursuits have not been randomly selected but are specifically designed to illustrate the mechanical arts, those skills and occupations, which, in the middle ages, were held to be necessary for the maintenance of life and which in many cases could only be found in the town or city. Of these arts San Bernardino was later to comment to the Sienese:

... how vital to the city are the arts and the crafts and how useful it is when they are legitimately exercised. ... This is our foundation, and we shall see that it is impossible to live well, if the arts and crafts are not properly exercised. ...[19]

Lanificium, the art of procuring and weaving material, and without which, according to Duns Scotus, no community could survive, includes also the manufacture of all clothing, sails, ropes and nets. Lorenzetti represents *Lanificium* by the tailor at his bench, by the dyers and wool-sorters under the arch and by the cobblers at work in their shop. *Armatura,* the art of metal working, is represented by the goldsmith's shop, but also by the five workers building a house, for *Armatura* in the medieval *schema* also embraced the subsidiary art of *Architectura*. *Navigatio* or trade was, according to many medieval theorists, among the more important of the mechanical arts, for it was trade which brought with it peace and well-being. San Bernardino claimed to have learnt from Duns Scotus that trade must be exercised for the Common

Good and that without it no town or city could flourish. Trade certainly enjoys pride of place in the Lorenzetti frescoes, being represented by the buying, selling and transport of goods, while the portrayal of the harbour at Talamone represents *Navigatio* in its more restricted sense of shipping.

Agricultura as well as embracing the more obvious skills—ploughing, sowing, vine-tending, stock-farming and shepherding—also included the art of gardening, an art which Lorenzetti skilfully and amusingly indicates by his numerous well-kept pot-plants, the woman at the inn who is busy gardening, and the gardens attached to the *contado* farms. *Venatio*, the hunt, included not only game-hunting, bird-catching and angling, all of which are illustrated in the fresco, but also baking and cooking, activities which Lorenzetti represents by his inn. *Medicina* is certainly represented by the spice-seller and possibly by the lecturer or teacher. The seventh of the mechanical arts was *Theatrica*, including both dance and music, activities which all medieval commentators agreed were necessary for procuring the health and happiness of each individual. Under *Theatrica*, therefore, we place the dancing-girls in their Lucchese silks, figures whom Lorenzetti's contemporaries would have recognized as allegorical, not only because they are over-large and appear in the centre of the picture, but also because they are seen participating in an activity—street-dancing—which had been explicitly forbidden by the statutes of 1309-10. It is unlikely that Lorenzetti would have represented on the walls of a room which was, by this date, the centre of civic government, an illegal activity and have expected the viewer to accept a literal interpretation of the scene. It could scarcely, in such a case, have been a picture of *good* government.

The west wall of the council chamber is, unfortunately, in a very bad condition. At the time when he saw it, San Bernardino recorded:

> only man destroying man: the houses are not repaired but demolished and gutted by fire; no fields are ploughed, no harvest sown, no riders go down to bathe in the river, nor is the fullness of life in any way enjoyed. Beyond the gates I see no men, women, only the slain and the raped; no flocks are there except those which have been plundered; man kills man in mutual betrayal. . . .[20]

The fresco, in other words, clearly illustrates Tyranny and its consequences. The Tyrant is surrounded by vices: Cruelty, Treachery, Fraud, Fury, War and Discord who wears a divided gown on the black half of which is written 'No' and on the white half 'Yes', to symbolize the incessant factional squabbles which divide the Common Good. Pride, Avarice and Vainglory hover above the Tyrant's head and, at his feet, is the bound figure of Justice, her scales now cast to the ground. The city over which the Tyrant rules is without meaning because it has no centre, no point of rest or concentration, none of the harmony to be found in *Good Government*. Both it and the *contado* are filled with scenes of violence and bloodshed, with soldiers looting, fighting and quarrelling. Armed bands wander through the desolate countryside, two soldiers abduct a struggling girl while others demolish a house. The countryside is uncultivated for here, instead of Security, Fear holds sway. His scroll reads:

> Because he seeks his own welfare in this world, he subjects justice to tyranny. Thus no one treads this road without fear, for pillage is rife both within and without the city-gates.

The inscription on this border re-emphasizes the centrality of Justice in the life of the well-regulated state:

> Where justice is bound nobody struggles for the Common Good or fights for the law, but rather permits the rise of Tyranny, which has no desire to do anything against the base nature of the vices which are here united with it, in order to give fuller rein to evil. Tyranny persecutes those who wish to do good, and attracts all those who plan evil. It always defends those who use force, or rob or hate peace. For this reason, Tyranny's land is uncultivated. . . .

A further inscription reminds the viewer:

> To avoid unhappiness, everyone must bow to justice. Banished be all those who are against her, for the sake of our peace.

Further elaborations of the allegory are to be found in the quatrefoils which are interspersed in the borders above and below the frescoes. Some are, sadly, so spoiled that their subjects can no longer be made out but enough remain to show the true extent of Lorenzetti's learning and his symbolic and allegorical vocabulary. Thus Good Government is bordered by the sun shining on its regime, by the kindly planets, Venus and Mercury, by the moon and by the papal crossed-keys to symbolize ecclesiastical authority. The medallions in the lower border depict the Liberal Arts: Grammar, Dialectic and Rhetoric—Rhetoric has subsequently been obliterated by a door set into the wall—Arithmetic, Geometry, Music, Astronomy and Philosophy. These figures impress us by their solidity and their suggestion of a classical model and it is more than probable that their immediate source was Nicola Pisano's recently completed pulpit in the cathedral of Siena, where the central pillar bears upon its base personifications of the Liberal Arts. Certainly for Lorenzetti and for Pisano the Liberal Arts bore the same significance; they represented natural wisdom, inherited from the past, and valuable because that natural wisdom prepared the way for the divine wisdom revealed in Christ.

In the medallions above *Bad Government* were depicted the un-favourable planets—Saturn, Jupiter and Mars—Autumn and Winter and the coat-of-arms of Guelphic France. Siena, we are reminded, was the most Ghibelline of all Italian cities, even in periods, like the early fourteenth century, of nominal Guelphic allegiance. In the lower frame of the fresco there were probably depicted five famous tyrants although only the name *Nero* is now decipherable.

In these magnificent frescoes, Ambrogio Lorenzetti thus ranges with consummate ease over the whole wealth of medieval learning, drawing upon it to create, if not a *Summa* of knowledge, at least a *Summa* of all contemporary knowledge about political life. But that knowledge is interpreted in a way peculiar to Lorenzetti for it is used to universalize the particular image of Siena by placing it within an overall structure of traditional medieval ideas. It is not just any city which is presented in the Lorenzetti frescoes. Siena and its life are used to define the concept of the city. Under Bad Government it is *Siena's* houses and palaces that are ruined, *Siena's* streets which become insecure, a theatre for rape and assassination, *Siena's* countryside which is devastated. Equally, under Good Government it is *Siena* which becomes the home of Concord, Justice, Peace and Good Government, an ideal City of God. There still exists in the Loggia of the Palazzo Pubblico the now-ruined traces of another work by Lorenzetti in which he made, yet again, a passionate plea for civic concord. Here the Madonna was portrayed, holding a black and white globe in her hand representing Siena. The Christ Child is in the act of blessing the globe and beneath it a scroll instructs the observers to 'love one another', quoting explicitly from *John*, xv, 34. Thus the instruction given to the apostles after the Last Supper, is particularized for the Sienese commune. Even more significant in this context is the tradition that the Nine also commissioned from Ambrogio Lorenzetti that map of the world from which the Sala del Mappamondo takes its name. In that map Siena was placed at that focal point which the medieval theorist normally reserved for

Jerusalem. Siena and Jerusalem, as prototypes for the perfect civilized life, had become conflated in the Sienese imagination, and this conflation has ever since remained a central feature of Sienese cultural life.

As a work of art, the Palazzo Pubblico was thus a celebration of the commune of Siena, and an expression of the city's intense cultural vitality, of that love of beauty and decoration which spilled over into every area of existence. Yet the palace had also to be a workable unit. Inevitably, therefore, the passage of time brought modification and change within the building. Thus, although, initially, as we have seen, the heart of the building had lain in the Sala del Mappamondo and the adjacent Sala della Pace, other rooms and areas subsequently acquired an equal or a greater importance. In the original structure, the chapel was on the ground floor, but, with the elaboration of the bureaucracy of urban government, the need for increased office-space became acute. In order to provide this, it was decided in 1406 to move the chapel to its present position next to the Sala del Mappamondo. This involved some expensive reconstruction, including the building of four great arches into the wall to provide what remains the only source of natural light. The chapel also involved costly decoration; money was lavished upon it and love and devotion poured out upon it by the artists who worked on the project. Most notable of these was Domenico di Niccolò, ever afterwards known as Domenico of the Choir, who created the twenty-two Gothic choir-stalls, which are ranged along the chapel walls and which illustrate the Nicene creed, work of so demanding a nature that it took thirteen years to complete. Here also, in 1406, Taddeo di Bartolo was commissioned to paint a series of frescoes illustrating the life of the Virgin, which were to be completed in the remarkably short space of three months, in anticipation of the arrival of Pope Gregory XII in Siena.

These frescoes of Taddeo have not always received the attention they deserve. They are important because they represent the culminating moment of the International Gothic in Tuscany, adapted as only a Sienese could adapt an international style to the tastes of his fellow-citizens, to local themes and conditions. They are the works of an artist who is both aware of the latest innovations in the world of painting and inclined to dwell upon traditional Sienese artistic concerns. Taddeo's Gothicizing impulses are best seen in the episode of the *Transport of the Virgin*. In a Sienese context, the city of Jerusalem/Siena which appears behind the figures is an innovation, for the cathedral, so prominent in earlier paintings, is here not even indicated by its cupola.

That the city is Siena we know only from the two wolves who appear
on the gate, and this Siena Taddeo has transformed into a Northern
Gothic town. But that he was not unresponsive to his Sienese heritage
is suggested by the fact that we may, for instance, discern, even at the
distance of nearly a century, the influence of Duccio in the scene representing the *Farewell of the Virgin to the Apostles*, and from the fact that
these frescoes are the work of an artist who looked at the world of
Siena round him and incorporated what he saw into his paintings. In
the illustration of the *Assumption*, the golden light of the setting sun
illuminates the broad outline of the city of Jerusalem/Siena very much
as, seen from a distance, it is illuminated by the setting of the sun
today.

These frescoes then suggest the continued vitality of Sienese traditions in the early fifteenth century. Certainly, they must have impressed contemporaries and satisfied the state, for, in the following
year, Taddeo was commissioned to paint the huge figure of Saint
Christopher, representing the care of the commune for the weak,
which dominates the antechapel, and, in 1413, to complete the decoration of the antechapel's remaining walls.

For the decoration of the antechapel, however, a new dimension was
added to the patronage of the commune. This was to be as ambitious a
project as any undertaken in Siena since the painting of Lorenzetti's
Good and Bad Government. Taddeo was, once again, to take up the
theme of those frescoes but, so important was the project to the ruling
regime, that they directed he should not be given the free hand he had
been allowed in the decoration of the chapel; rather he should paint a
programme to be devised by two leading Sienese scholars. One was
the humanist, Master Pietro de' Pecci, a doctor of law and a teacher
in the University, and the other, Ser Cristoforo di Andrea, who, with
occasional brief interruptions, had been Chancellor of Siena since 1404.

The fresco cycle again concentrates on the virtues which are needed
for the life of the good citizen; in this case they are Justice, Fortitude,
Magnanimity and Religion, all personalized by famous men, portrayed
either in medallions or in the full-length figures that cover the main
wall facing the chapel, and the walls inside the arches which lead to the
chapel and the Sala del Mappamondo. Those portrayed include Brutus,
the slayer of tyrants, and Cicero as well as two heroes who could only
appear in a Sienese context: M. Curius Dentatus, the Roman consul at
the time Siena was reputedly founded, and Furius Camillus, founder of
the colony from which the Terzo di Camollia was believed to derive

4*

its name. The purpose of these figures is explained by the figure of
Aristotle, who introduces them to the viewer:

> As exemplars of the *vita civile*, I show you these men; if you follow
> in their sacred footsteps, your fame will grow at home and abroad,
> and liberty will always preserve your honour.[21]

And, on the main wall, the message is elaborated for the benefit of the
governing élite of Siena; they should pursue the Common Good and
justice, and above all remain united since this is the only guarantee of
liberty.

It seems unlikely that these frescoes were without impact on the
political life of Siena. They were clearly well known and their widespread and early influence is suggested by the direct allusions to them
in the work of the fifteenth-century writer Gentile Sermini. Sermini,
too, reminded his readers that it was pride and factionalism that
destroyed the liberty and the glory of the ancient Roman republic, and
suggested that:

> He who rules the state should take example from this,
> He who destroys the law,
> Is certainly no lover of the Common Good.[22]

From Taddeo's antechapel, one can pass to another room of great
importance in the cultural life of Siena, the Sala della Balìa, the only
room in the palace whose decoration was carried out by an artist who
was not Sienese. It is largely the work of Spinello Aretino. Yet, although
Aretino's style is not Sienese, his subject-matter continues to reflect
traditional Sienese concerns. He has depicted the life of the great
Sienese pope, Alexander III, and, characteristically, several of Aretino's
scenes concern the struggle of the Italian communes against Frederick
Barbarossa, at the period when so many of Siena's traditional liberties
were won.

For the remaining century of Sienese independence, those traditional
liberties continued to provide the theme of the decoration of the
Palazzo Pubblico in many works by Sano di Pietro, Vecchietta and
Sodoma, and culminated in the great Beccafumi ceiling for the Sala
del Concistoro, commissioned in 1529, at one of the most difficult
periods in Siena's history. Completed in 1536, this ceiling once more
refers back, through the frescoes of Taddeo di Bartolo, to those of
Lorenzetti, expounding for the Sienese the value of the political virtues; Justice, who boldly declares, once again, *Per me regnes regnant,*

Concord and Patriotism. These virtues are then illustrated by episodes
from Roman and Greek history which could be seen to have Sienese
analogies.

One of the greatest and most exquisite of mannerist decorative
schemes to be found anywhere in Europe, Beccafumi's ceiling, was to
be the last expression of republican glory in Siena, a fit epitaph for a
great commune. Of course, the palace continued to be enriched with
decorative paintings after the fall of the republic. Until well into the
eighteenth century, many notable painters were to work there, including Francesco Vanni, Ventura Salimbeni and Rutilio Mannetti, as well
as a whole host of more minor figures: Sebastiano Folli, Pietro Sorri,
Cristofano and Francesco Rustici, Bernardino Mei, Christofano Casolani, Deifebo Burbarini, Annibale Mazzuoli, and Francesco Nasini.
But however skilled these painters were, there was little scope for
great work in the subjects they were asked to paint: celebrations of the
deeds of a series of peculiarly uninspiring Grand Dukes, or episodes of
Sienese history from a past so remote that it could have no impact on
or relationship with contemporary Sienese life.

Only with the nineteenth century in the much undervalued *Sala del
Risorgimento* did Sienese painting find an inspiring theme once more.
The Sala was created out of a part of the palace, previously occupied
by offices, as a civic shrine for the tunic worn by Victor Emmanuel II at
the battle of San Martino, and was opened in 1890. Its decorative
scheme is difficult to ignore, but while the chocolate-box ceiling, from
which Italy, between Liberty and Independence, looks down on her
miscellaneous and all equally insipid sixteen regions, may have little
to recommend it, the six history paintings on the walls are remarkably
fine. They show a mastery of technique in fresco painting which suggests
that, even in the nineteenth century, the strong traditions of Sienese
Trecento art had not been forgotten, for these are the work of the best
contemporary Sienese artists: Cesare Maccari, Amos Cassioli, Pietro
Aldi and Alessandro Franchi. They are, therefore, as much a part of
the traditional Sienese civic world as are any other of the decorations
of the palace.

Both externally and internally the Palazzo Pubblico is a remarkable
and a beautiful building. It is rendered unique by the incredible tower
—the *Torre del Mangia*—which William Dean Howells described as
leaping, 'like a rocket into the starlit air',[23] and of which he wrote:

When once you have seen the Mangia, all other towers, obelisks, and columns are tame and vulgar and earth-rooted: that seems to quit the ground, to be not a monument but a flight.[24]

It was between 1325 and 1348, at first to the design of two Perugian brothers, Minuccio and Francesco di Rinaldo, but subsequently to that of the painter, Lippo Memmi, that the Mangia was built. That this tower had a significant role to play in the development of civic life is indicated by the elaborate ritual which surrounded the laying of its foundation stone:

> It was a great occasion; the priests assembled to bless the laying of the first stone with prayers and the chanting of psalms, the Master of the Board of Works depositing a sum of money at the foot of the tower. At each corner of the foundation a stone was set carrying Hebrew and Greek lettering, to protect the tower from thunder, lightning and windstorms . . .

The tower was, of course, meant to make the Campo more beautiful; that it is successful in this is unquestionable. Its harmonious relationship with the Campo, which its shadow describes through the day as if it were some gigantic sundial, is truly remarkable, as are the elegant proportions of the tower itself. But the tower was also originally designed for specific utilitarian functions and came to be called the Torre del Mangia after the man who was appointed to sound the hours on the tower's bell in 1347; he was known as Giovanni di Balduccio, *il Mangiaguadagni* (i.e. the consumer of gain), from his reputation as a wastrel. The tower existed to house the bell of the commune, and the bell was the voice of the commune, regulating the life of Siena throughout the day. It recalled the citizens to their obligations, it summoned the councils of the commune, the Balìa, and the Consistory. In time of warfare or of civic disturbance it was the bell in the Mangia which summoned the citizens to arms, just as, on festive occasions, the ringing of the bell was a sign of public rejoicing. It was also a manifestation of Sienese religious sentiment. At dawn, the ringing of the *mattino* put an end to the curfew and signified the opening of the city-gates, the renewal of urban life. At midday it rang, along with the other bells of the city, to signify the break for lunch. In the evening it announced the sunset and, three hours later, the reimposition of the curfew.

The marking of the passage of time by the bell in the Mangia symbolized the significance of the Mangia in Sienese life, for it was an assertion of civic values as opposed to those of the nobility. The tower itself was a symbol, stolen from noble life. But the bell, and subsequently the clock which was added to the tower in 1360, spoke of an essentially urban concept of time and space and modified the function of the tower as an ancient symbol of noble power. It was an assertion, too, of communal authority, its fantastic height determined by the necessity for it to be higher than the highest private family tower in Siena, and as high as the highest point of the cathedral.

A secondary function of the Torre del Mangia was to identify the location of communal power. Easily seen from any point within the city, and for many miles outside it, the Torre del Mangia immediately fixes the idea of the location of the Campo in the mind of the viewer and helps to suggest that this is the heart of the city. So closely was the Torre del Mangia identified, therefore, with the commune that it gave rise to a significant proverbial usage; a Sienese was and is defined as: 'One born in the shadow of the Mangia.'

The Torre del Mangia was completed by the construction of a chapel at the base of the tower, actually built in the third quarter of the fourteenth century, but originating in a vow made to the Virgin in 1348, as a memorial of the deliverance of the city from the Black Death. It is easy to see in the artistic aspect of the chapel, so stylistically different from the rest of the Palazzo Pubblico, an expression of that great cultural gulf which separates the pre-plague and the post-plague world, not only in Sienna, but in the whole of Italy.

In 1352 the project was first entrusted to Domenico di Agostino in his capacity as Master of Works to the cathedral; but the building was probably only first realized in 1376 by Giovanni di Cecco, Master Mason of the cathedral, who, like a number of artists, had been involved in the completion and decoration of the Cathedral and Baptistery, and was influenced by contemporary Florentine art in a way that no pre-plague Sienese artist ever was. The Florentine quality of the chapel was subsequently accentuated when, nearly a hundred years later, the fine Sienese renaissance architect, Antonio Federighi, raised the original roof and added the upper portion of the structure, with a frieze of griffins and wreaths encircling the arms of Siena; and finally consummated by the painting of the Madonna and the patron saints of the city, 'all very beautiful figures',[25] commissioned from Sodoma in March 1537.

The last major addition to the Campo also had echoes of Florentine art. This was the Fonte Gaia, the seemingly miraculous fountain, whose name derives from the rejoicings that accompanied the first arrival of water in the Campo in 1343 by means of an elaborate system of *bottini* and aqueducts which stretched for some twenty-five kilometres. To get water to flow into their Campo was obviously a symbolic necessity for the Sienese, for whom, as we have seen, water had an almost mystical importance, but to achieve this desired end involved one of the greatest and most remarkable of all medieval engineering feats. It was an undertaking which for years absorbed a considerable quantity of communal resources and even more communal energy, for it was a much-accentuated form of the normal Sienese struggle to obtain water and to lift it up steep hillsides in sufficient quantities.

The project was initiated and completed in its first and most vital stage at the time of the Nine, probably the only medieval Sienese regime with sufficient self-confidence to embark on such a daunting project. They entrusted the work in December 1334 to the master stonemason, Jacopo di Vanno dei Ugolini, who was persuaded to attempt the difficult task by the very high salary he was offered. But, although there is no real evidence to suggest that Jacopo neglected his duties, by 1339 he had made little progress and the commune appointed two other men to assist him. By 1341 the problem had been handed over to a civic committee of three who were assigned all the income from Grosseto in order to finance the enterprise. Two years later, after nearly a decade of effort, water flowed into the first Fonte Gaia, which like its successors, was dedicated to the Virgin.

The commune was fully aware of the importance of this fountain and the significant contribution which, in the end, Jacopo di Vanno had made to the life of Siena. Their recognition of the debt they owed him came in their subsequent treatment of his descendants. It was a compliment to his father's skill that Jacopo's son, Giovanni, was made civic Provveditor of Fountains, and in November 1356, the General Council conceded to Giovanni's own orphaned children, Domenico and Giovanni, an annual pension of twelve gold florins:

> Because Master Jacopo was the occasion of so much beauty and utility in the fountain on the Campo and in the other fountains that depend on it.[26]

The Fonte Gaia which we see today is a large rectangular basin, walled on three sides. Water spouts from the mouths of six crouching wolves and from two metal pipes at each extremity. On the outside of the fountain, the enclosing wall is decorated with attractive panels of a leafy design, done in characteristic Sienese black-and-white marble, while on the inside, a series of niches contain monumental figures carved in high relief. This is, of course, but an incomplete nineteenth-century copy by Tito Sarocchi of that fountain built by Jacopo della Quercia between 1409 and 1420, which, despite its original splendours, was in such a state of decay by the early nineteenth century as to be an offence to Sienese civic pride. Through the determined efforts of a group of leading citizens money was raised to replace Jacopo's great work, and to move the site of the fountain slightly to regularize its relationship with the buildings behind it. Today one may still see the remains of Jacopo's greatest masterpiece in the Loggia of the Palazzo Pubblico, but it requires great imaginative effort to reconstruct the fountain as it once was or to guess its original impact upon the Sienese.

Much of that impact depended upon the fact that the original contract to Jacopo della Quercia was given in the first flood of republican enthusiasm and the revival of the communal spirit in Siena following the overthrow of the Visconti overlordship in the early fifteenth century. The creation of the fountain was seen as a reassertion of those communal values which had produced the earlier glories of the Campo, and which find expression in the original iconographical programme of della Quercia's great work of art, a programme much influenced by the communal committees appointed to supervise the building of the fountain.

In the centre, the perennial theme of the protection of the city by the Virgin was expressed in a portrayal of the Madonna and child, flanked by two adoring angels. This image was, of course, of great civic importance, for it is in this guise that the Virgin was portrayed on the city's shield. The same image was used by Simone Martini in his *Maestà*, where, in one of the medallions at the bottom of the fresco, there appears an image of the Virgin, Child and two angels with the legend, *Salvat Virgo Senam quam signat amenam*. And it also appears on the shield of the figure of Good Government in the painted Biccherna *tavoletta* of 1344, which has been attributed to Ambrogio Lorenzetti.

On each side of della Quercia's *Madonna* were placed portrayals of those moral and religious virtues, which Lorenzetti had also seen as necessary for the leading of a full and a good life in a civic context: allegorical figures representing Fortitude, Justice, Charity, Wisdom, Hope and Faith. Then, on the front of the fountain, della Quercia moved from the representation of divine attributes and personified virtues, to take up themes directly relevant to the human community in general and to the life of Siena in particular. The creation of Adam and the expulsion of Adam and Eve from the earthly paradise, which were depicted on the fountain's sides, represent the two moments in universal history which most directly determined the subsequent nature of human life on earth. On the front of the fountain, two great statues of Rea Silvia, the royal mother of Romulus and Remus, and Acca Laurentia, the goat-herd's wife who subsequently cared for the twins, were intended to recall to the Sienese their Roman origins and their obligations to maintain the Roman virtues, while the city's own heraldic devices called them to reflect on Siena's post-classical history.

Thus the Fonte Gaia, like the Lorenzetti frescoes in the Palazzo Pubblico opposite—to which there can be little doubt the fountain makes direct reference—was both a celebration of Siena's past and contemporary glories, and a didactic monument, designed to instruct the Sienese in the obligations of citizenship. It was, like the Lorenzetti frescoes, an imaginative, visual representation of that whole complex of interacting creative forces which the Sienese believed went into the making of a city, a blending of the material and the spiritual to produce prosperity, justice and that ever-elusive 'Good Government' of which the whole Campo is a celebration.

6

Art in Society in the Republic of Siena

Men of skill always increase the honour and the fame of republics.
Petition of 1531 to the General Council of Siena

I

IN THE Europe of the later middle ages, Siena was known for her bankers, her saints, and her artists. Of her bankers we have already spoken and with her saints we shall be concerned in the following chapter; here we shall consider her visual artists. It is perhaps through studying these artists and their surviving works that we can come closest to understanding the dynamic features of Sienese urban civilization in the centuries before its independent existence came to an end in the mid-sixteenth century. For nowhere in Europe were the visual arts so closely integrated with every aspect of social life as they were in this city. Here, the very chests in which government documents were stored were elaborately decorated, while the surviving *tavolette* of the Gabella and of the Biccherna are the happiest examples of the perfect marriage of bureaucracy and art within Siena.

The Sienese artist was ready and willing to articulate the ideals and the aspirations of his city, since almost every aspect of his individual life was intimately bound up with the collective life of the city around him. The Sienese artist was never an outsider. Although one of Sacchetti's short stories portrays a wife addressing her artist-husband in anger, demanding: 'What malediction ever married a woman to a painter? You are all fanatics and lunatics, and always drunk and not ashamed of it!', and although Duccio was fined for a breach of the peace, there is no evidence of particularly anti-social or rebellious attitudes among Sienese artists before the excesses of the eccentric and spendthrift Sodoma in the sixteenth century. On the contrary, far from being an active critic of the society in which he lived, the Sienese artist identified with it, playing a very full part in its civic, political, religious, economic and recreational life.

In the first place, every Sienese artist was a member of one of the city's guilds—the Painters, Stonemasons, Sculptors or Goldsmiths—for, without such a membership he could not practise his art in the city. Again, most artists were also members, frequently very active, of one or other of the city's numerous religious confraternities; Paolo di Giovanni Fei, for instance, joined the brothers of the Company of Mary which met in the crypt of Santa Maria della Scala in the 1380s and was to act as its treasurer in 1386, 1388, 1399, 1404 and 1408.

Artists also played a frequent and direct part in the political and administrative life of Siena. At all times they acted as officials and servants of the commune in a whole range of different capacities, and, during the second half of the fourteenth century, when the government of Siena was as open to members of the artisan classes as any Italian city-state government was ever to be, they served in all magistracies, including the most important of all—Consistory. Lippo Vanni, for instance, served on the supreme magistracy in 1360 and 1373, and Luca di Tommè in 1373 and 1379. Paolo di Neri, one of the followers of Ambrogio Lorenzetti, was elected to Consistory in 1363 and 1378, as was Niccolò di Buonaccorso in 1372 and 1377. Bartolo di Fredi was elected in 1372, 1380–81, 1382 and 1401, and served as Podestà of Massa in 1376. His contemporary, Paolo di Giovanni Fei, was equally involved in civic life; he first entered the General Council in 1369, and served again in 1370 and 1371. In the latter year he was also Standard-bearer for the militia company of his own district of San Quirico in Castelvecchio. In 1372 and 1381 he served on the Consistory, and in 1380 on the Biccherna. The participation of practising artists in the political life of the city continued in the following century. Taddeo di Bartolo, for instance, served on the General Council on at least three occasions and also held other minor offices in the civic administration; Jacopo della Quercia was elected to the General Council in 1409 and to Consistory in 1420; and Francesco di Giorgio Martini served on Consistory in 1486.

Such full civic participation may have been mutually beneficial to commune and artist, but it did, on occasion, create practical difficulties. His civic duties could interrupt an artist when he was engaged on a commission and so delay the completion of important projects. Certainly the demands of civic office conflicted with that clause, which normally appeared in all contracts, requiring an artist to work constantly and solely on the one particular commission. When, for instance, in 1438, and again in 1444, the name of Piero della Minella, who was at the time supervising the building of the Loggia della Mercanzia, was drawn for castellanships in the *contado*, the whole progress of the prestigious building works at the Mercanzia was threatened and he had to be excused from serving.

It was obviously more convenient to use practising artists in those areas of the administration for which their talents were peculiarly well-suited. Chief among the posts largely reserved for them by the commune were those which involved the design or the inspection of fortresses. Simone Martini served the commune in these areas while in the fifteenth and sixteenth centuries he was followed by Jacopo della Quercia, Vecchietta, who was concerned with fortifications at Sarteano, Orbetello, Montacuto and Talamone in 1469 and 1470, Cozzarelli, who worked on those of Montepulciano in 1496, and Francesco di Giorgio Martini. In the sixteenth century the foremost examples are Francesco di Giorgio's disciple, Anton Maria Lara, Baldassare Peruzzi, appointed in 1528 as inspector of bridges, roads, and fortifications, and Giovan Battista Peloro. Although the demands of fortresses and fortifications were considerable and time-consuming, and necessarily diverted the attention of artists from other matters, such work was not always unrewarding. Several Sienese, and notably Francesco di Giorgio, were among the most important theorists of the new science of fortress-design in the renaissance, and Francesco's experiences in this area were to lead him to formulate new ideas about the relationship between fortresses and towns. This, in turn, led him to a fundamental re-evaluation of the importance of the urban environment in creating and fostering the *vita civile*.

Other areas of civic life in which practising artists played an active role have already been alluded to: the various committees concerned with the building of the cathedral, for example, and the perennial problem of Siena's water-supply. Duccio was given responsibility for searching for water as one of his first civic offices, and the supervisory committee for Jacopo della Quercia's Fonte Gaia, appointed in 1408, included a goldsmith, Tommaso Vannini and Domenico di Niccolò—Domenico of the Choir. The first civic office of Francesco di Giorgio in 1464 was that of supervisor of *bottini* and, thereafter, whenever he was resident in Siena, he tended to be involved in one way or another, either with the water-supply or with the fountains of Siena. In 1469 the General Council commissioned him, together with Paolo d'Andrea, to work for three years on the city's fountains, *bottini* and aqueducts, their commission being so to improve the system during this period as to increase the flow of water into the fountains by at least one third. During the same period they were given the additional responsibility of creating special fountain displays for the annual celebrations of the Assumption in mid-August. In 1480 Antonio Federighi held a similar supervisory position over the *bottini*, a post for which he was paid an annual salary of 80 florins.

Such examples of integration into the civic life of Siena provide an accurate indication of the status of the artist in the Sienese community. He was regarded as a useful but unexceptional member of society. Even in the fifteenth century when in the rest of Italy the artist began to be held in higher esteem, and to be in a certain sense a privileged person, in Siena he continued to enjoy the kind of position held by other Sienese craftsmen, from whom indeed he was largely indistinguishable. His working methods and customs were very much the same as theirs. Like other craftsmen, he worked from his own shop, which might be either owned or rented, and it was here that he trained his apprentices. The apprentice who had successfully completed his training within the standard guild system would then set up his own workshop, either alone, or more usually with a partner, for partnership was a common and distinctive feature of the Sienese artistic community.

Lacking high status, and rarely providing wealth, the artistic life was in no way an avenue for upward social mobility in Siena before the sixteenth century. Even the more successful Sienese artist could not hope to earn much more than a respectable competence unless he were remarkably fortunate, for as one painter put it 'the rewards of our art of painting are scarce and limited, so that there is little to do and less gained.'[1] In the fourteenth century, individual paintings such as Duccio's *Maestà*, which was paid for at the rate of two and a half florins a panel, occasionally brought to an artist rewards of a quite exceptional nature, but this was due more to the expense of materials and to the value of the painting in symbolic terms than to the prestige or merit of the painter. Even in the fifteenth century this remained true. Sassetta, for example, was a successful artist with a large workshop and a number of important pupils, including Sano di Pietro, Vecchietta and Pietro di Giovanni Ambrogio, yet he died a poor man. His last illness, pneumonia contracted while he was working on the prestigious and highly important government contract of the *Coronation of the Virgin* for Porta Romana, lasted for over a month; during this time he not only used up all his capital but contracted debts of 187 florins for doctors' fees and medicines. His funeral, therefore, had to be paid for by mortgaging his only remaining piece of property.

The evidence provided by the tax returns of fifteenth-century artists is quite unequivocal. Even making allowance for the established convention that in making such returns the citizen should paint as dark a picture of his circumstances as possible, artists were not wealthy men. Despite his fame and his abilities, Vecchietta in 1465 owned only one small house in Via de'Fusari; another, unprofitably rented out; a piece of unproductive land in the commune of Certano; and half a house and vineyard in the commune of Ginestreto. He complained that his wife was usually in ill-health and that he also had been ill for six months and unable to work. In order to stay alive he had been forced to sell all of his household goods.

Throughout his whole working-life, Sano di Pietro grumbled about his poverty and showed himself willing to accept almost any kind of commission provided it paid. He was, fortunately, remarkably skilled at reproducing his own best efforts, since his over-ready acceptance of commissions meant that he was forced to pour out altarpieces by the dozen; forty-two are preserved in the Pinacoteca of Siena alone. Despite such prodigious productivity, Sano's tax returns do substantiate his claim that he was not a wealthy man. In 1453 he owned no more than the house he lived in at Camporeggio, valued at 340 florins, an uninhabited and unfurnished house in Salicotto, and a vineyard worth 100 florins, while his debts amounted to 150 florins. Neither of the subsequent returns which he made in 1478 and 1481 suggest that his wealth had increased substantially by the end of his life.

The precarious existence of the artist in material terms is also suggested by Matteo di Giovanni who, in 1453, declared that he owned:

> the undivided half of a number of materials appertaining to his profession as a painter, not worth 20 florins, of which the other half belong to his partner, the painter Giovanni di Pietro. They have them in the house where they live, which they lease from Guiccardo Forteguerra in the palace of the Forteguerra; they lease it as a house and not as a workshop; otherwise he owns nothing in the world. . . . He would like to remind your worships that

he earns nothing but is merely passing the time in learning at the expense of his uncle.[2]

In a similar position was Priamo della Quercia who, in the same year, described himself as:

> a poor beggarly painter, without any means of living ... and with a number of debts to various persons ...[3]

and Ventura di Giuliano who, in 1478, described himself as a wood-carver and architect, forced to live away from Siena:

> because of my debts; and I am currently in Naples. I still owe money for three forced loans and am too afraid to return to Siena.[4]

On the other hand, the cumulative evidence of such tax returns and of other records does suggest that, provided he made some insurance against the normal accidents of life and was not encumbered by too many marriageable daughters for whom he had to provide dowries, the competent Sienese artist did not need to starve. Even from the returns we have already considered it is clear that, in the course of their working lives, most artists, even those from very humble backgrounds like Francesco di Giorgio or Beccafumi, managed to accumulate a little property: a house in the city and a small vineyard or farm in the *contado*. The community of Siena did have a positive attitude towards its artists and craftsmen and was anxious to encourage their skills, acknowledging that: 'Men of skill always increase the honour of republics.'[5]

Thus, in order to encourage them, the commune often granted its most skilled artists either immunity from communal taxation, as in the case of Giovanni Pisano, or communal employment or pensions. Domenico di Niccolò, for instance, was given a communal pension so that he could impart his skills in wood-carving and inlay to others, although it has to be confessed that:

> because there is little money to be made in this business, none ever wanted to continue with it, save Master Matteo di Bernardino who studied the craft so assiduously that he became a great master as all or the majority of the citizens well know.[6]

And even after he was too old to work, Domenico continued to be paid a communal pension of two florins a month, in recognition of his former great services to the commune.

As a community Siena was, in fact, remarkable in being able to support an exceptionally large number of artists and craftsmen throughout the middle ages. Between the twelfth and the sixteenth centuries, such large communal projects as the building of the cathedral and the Palazzo Pubblico, lesser government-sponsored works, ecclesiastical patronage, including that of the religious orders, the patronage of the guilds, of hospitals and especially Santa Maria della Scala, of the *contrade*, of families and of individuals all provided certain and continuous opportunities for artistic employment. But over the centuries it was above all the Sienese commune that required the services of artists. The major works of communal patronage, which have already been described, and the continuous works on the fountains of the city continued to provide many opportunities. The city-gates were built, enlarged and decorated with important frescoes, largely at communal expense. Churches were built to honour communal religious vows or in thanksgiving for graces previously bestowed on the city. The church of San Giorgio was enlarged and given its *campanile* in thanksgiving for the victory of Montaperti; the chapel of St. Paul was added to the Mercanzia on the Campo to show:

the great and due reverence in which this regime holds St. Paul, as the only patron and prosperer of many happy events in our city.[7]

The church of the Madonna of Fontegiusta was built in 1482 as a thanksgiving for the defeat of the Florentines at the battle of Poggio Imperiale. The commune also contributed to the cost of other ecclesiastical buildings, paying, for example, for their decoration or furnishing; as a result there is scarcely a church in Siena which was not at least partially financed by the civic authorities. Such patronage was often a response to popular pressure. In providing for the city's religious buildings, the communal government was providing a social service, just as it was in maintaining a hospital, providing doctors and teachers, maintaining the University, caring for the poor, or fixing the prices apothecaries might charge for their medicines.

Another explanation of the commune's willingness to act as a generous patron of the arts was the necessity of maintaining the city's reputation abroad. Petitions to the commune asking for assistance frequently point out that the present state of a building brings shame to the city when it is seen by foreign visitors. This, in turn, it was argued, injured Siena's reputation abroad and so was detrimental to the interests of her bankers and merchants. Such considerations were particularly important in the context of the rivalry of the Tuscan and Umbrian communes, fought out not only on the battlefield, but also in the embellishing of churches, as if, by such embellishment, the commune in question could win the support of heaven. Thus the Carmelite friars could be fairly certain of a favourable response from the communal authorities when they petitioned in 1365 for assistance in paying for their new tabernacle; it had cost 900 florins less than a similar one at Orvieto and yet was judged, 'far more beautiful than the one at Orvieto by those who have seen both the one and the other.'[8]

The maintenance of the whole decorative paraphernalia of Sienese civic life required further communal artistic patronage. Many distinguished artists, including Simone Martini, were, for instance, employed to paint special banners or flags. Others were employed to make or to decorate furniture; Andrea di Bartolo, for example, in 1378 painted the casket now in the Palazzo Pubblico, with the four patron saints of Siena. And distinguished artists were regularly employed to paint the *tavolette* for the Gabella and the Biccherna. Festivals and festivities with all their attendant ephemera were also a regular source of employment. The celebrations of mid-August were frequently arranged by artists. Festivals and state banquets frequently required expensive and elaborate stage-props of which we may take as a type those produced for the visit of the Duchess of Ferrara in 1473 when the decorations included:

> a column . . . decorated with a Lion and a She-Wolf, and the Lion gave out white wine and the She-Wolf red, and from a spout between them flowed water . . .[9]

However, the commune was far from being Siena's only source of artistic patronage. All the major churches had within them family altars which were elaborately decorated by the families concerned, just as they were in the cathedral. Other altars were the property and concern of the guilds who, particularly during their period of relative prosperity in the fifteenth century, became important patrons of the arts. The statutes of the Stonemasons Guild of 1441 fined each member 15s for non-attendance at their annual festival of Santi Quattro Coronati, and directed that the money should be used for a building fund for their chapel in the cathedral. In 1447 the Grocer's Guild commissioned from Giovanni di Paolo an altar-piece for their chapel in the church of Santa Maria della Scala; in 1478 the Bakers commissioned the altarpiece of Saint Barbara for their altar in San Domenico from Matteo di Giovanni; and Cozzarelli's *St. Catherine of Alexandria* was painted for the Guild of Doctors and Apothecaries, the saint in the painting being surrounded by symbols of their trades. Eventually some guilds came to build their own churches; the prettiest, built to a design of Riccio in 1617, was that dedicated to St. Joseph by the Carpenters' Guild.

Throughout the later middle ages another important source of employment for artists was the great civic hospital of Santa Maria della Scala. It enshrines within its walls works by many Sienese artists and is, in consequence, surely unique among hospitals in that its patients are still treated beside walls and under ceilings covered by renaissance frescoes. The church of the hospital, dedicated to the Virgin of the Annunciation, is a positive show-piece of the Sienese renaissance, despite the fact that many of the works which once enriched it have been removed. The rebuilding of this church, undertaken in 1466 by Guidoccio d'Andrea was only one of a handful of new ecclesiastical architectural projects undertaken in fifteenth-century Siena, and as a result its decoration provided unparalleled opportunities for some Sienese artists. Giovanni di Paolo's *Presentation in the Temple*, which is now in the Pinacoteca, was originally commissioned for the high altar in 1447. In 1471 Francesco di Giorgio was working on the church, constructing a new choir and ceiling, assisted by Cozzarelli, and painting a *Coronation of the Virgin*. From 1441, when he first painted a major fresco for the hospital, Vecchietta was to devote most of his working-life to its embellishment, and it therefore came to contain all of his major work. His relationship with the institution was so close that, in the end, in 1476, he asked the hospital to grant him a chapel in their church to be entirely designed by him and dedicated to the Saviour. This chapel, where he arranged to be buried and for which he intended the *Risen Christ*, which now stands on the high altar, he endowed with a piece of property in the *contado*.

By the fifteenth century the *contrade* of the city were already beginning to develop that important role as patrons of the arts which they have maintained until the present day. It was in fact in the late fifteenth century that the inhabitants of Fontebranda completed their building of the church, dedicated to St. Catherine, which they had announced their intention of building in 1465:

in such a way and so well ornamented, that it will be an honour to God and to Saint Catherine of Siena ... and a consolation to all the city. ...[10]

By the early sixteenth century the *contrade* were more and more actively involved in maintaining the fabric and the monuments of their own areas of the city, taking on responsibilities which had previously been shouldered by the commune, such as the maintenance of the city fountains. It was, for instance, the inhabitants of the *contrada* of Pian d'Ovile who decided to restore and improve the frescoes which decorated their city-gate.

The public display of wealth and splendour which was a necessary part of the life of the religious confraternities also led them to act as very progressive patrons of the arts, particularly during the renaissance. The banner painted by Sodoma for the Confraternity of Saint Sebastian, for instance, which was carried in their processions, is still preserved in the Pitti Palace in Florence, and among the surviving works of the Sienese High Renaissance master, Girolamo del Pacchia, is a banner made for the Company of Corpus Domini. Pacchia also painted for the same company a bierhead showing a *Madonna and Child holding a Goldfinch* and the production of such bierheads became common: Matteo Balducci, a pupil of Pacchiarotto, painted three for the confraternity of St. Catherine della Notte, showing *St. Catherine receiving the stigmata*, *St. Catherine and four flagellants*, and a *Risen Christ*; Beccafumi painted one for the Company of St. Anthony Abbot in San Martino, and one for the confraternity of the Misericordia; Francesco Vanni painted one for the Company of the Blessed Ambrogio Sansedoni, and Cozzarelli one for the Misericordia.

Wealthy confraternities also invested money in providing themselves with beautiful surroundings for their meetings and their religious services and one of the most important commissions given in the sixteenth century was that of the Company of San Bernardino for the decoration of their Oratory; Sodoma, Girolamo del Pacchia and Beccafumi all contributed to this project. The furbishing of such oratories and chapels also provided other commissions, and an additional source of employment for artists may be illustrated by the commission given to Giovanni di Paolo d'Ambrogio by the Company of St. Anthony Abbot in October 1526 for miniatures to illustrate:

> our chapter book which we have recently had made ... with four stories from the life of our glorious protector, St. Anthony ...[11]

The patronage of the confraternities was corporate and ostensibly, at least, democratic in its nature. Decisions about such commissions were taken by the confraternity officials, together with the whole company, who could vote on a number of designs submitted to them either by one or by a number of artists. Perhaps surprisingly, this led not to conservatism but to experimentation. The confraternities were always remarkable for their willingness to employ previously untried artists. In 1400, for instance, Taddeo di Bartolo painted a triptych for the Company of St. Catherine della Notte, and this was among the first of the works he painted in Siena. Similarly, one of the earliest commissions given to Francesco di Giorgio was from the Company of St. John the Baptist, or of Death, who paid £12 for a relief of their favourite saint, while among the earliest works of Francesco Vanni were a Crucifixion for the Company of the Sacred Nails, painted in 1585, and an altar-piece for the Company of the Blessed Ambrogio Sansedoni which dates from 1589–91.

The Sienese commune, supported by a network of other ecclesiastical and secular groups, thus provided Sienese artists with an enduring structure of patronage. Inevitably there were periods when the fortunes of artists stood higher or lower than normal. In the early years of the Nine, for instance, the available opportunities were unusually good and, in terms of the curtailment of patronage, the Black Death was an obvious disaster. None the less, after the Black Death the arts continued both to flourish and to be well-supported by the Sienese community; in 1363 an estimated population of 25,000 still contained at least thirty master-painters, twenty-one master goldsmiths and sixty-two master-stonemasons, and these numbers were on the increase. By the 1370s there were sixty-four master-painters in Siena, a figure that rose to about a hundred at the turn of the century. It was not until the 1430s that the number again dropped to thirty-two and, by that date, the population of the city as a whole had probably fallen to little over 15,000.

These artists and craftsmen formed a tight-knit and distinctive social group within the city. Both at a professional and at a private level the Sienese artist tended to enjoy a close relationship with other artists. Most ran their workshops as family businesses, many inter-married, many more entered into partnerships, and all seem to have found their closest friends among other members of the artistic community. Duccio, for instance, had strong family links with other painters; three of his sons were to follow him in his trade and his cousin was Segna di Bonventura, a painter who was frequently employed by the commune. Simone Martini, whose brother, Donato, was also an artist, married in 1324 the daughter of another painter, Memmo di Filippuccio, who was also the father of Lippo Memmi, with whom Simone subsequently set up a workshop. Francesco di Piero de'Giovannelli, a painter who worked on the cathedral in 1380, had a daughter who was married to Lorenzo di Vanni, and his two sons were also painters. Jacopo della Quercia's father had been a Sienese goldsmith and wood-carver, and his son was to become a painter. In 1468 Francesco di Giorgio took as his second wife, Agnese, the sister of Neroccio di Landi. Francesco then entered into a partnership with Neroccio until 1475, but he meantime enjoyed close personal and professional relationships with both Sano di Pietro and Vecchietta. Similar patterns of relationship could be found among all the known artists of Siena throughout the fourteenth and fifteenth centuries.

Such a structure of relationship between individual artists was not without an effect on the development of the arts. It seems to have encouraged a certain homogeneity and stylistic conservatism, for it tended to confirm the Sienese quality of each artist's work. It also meant that within the community, artists were particularly prone to borrowing and learning from each other. An outstanding example is the work produced in the workshop of Francesco di Giorgio and Neroccio di Landi, where the constant interplay of ideas led to a stylistic unity which frequently makes the work of the two artists almost indistinguishable. Such borrowings clearly contributed to the creation and sustaining of the Sienese tradition in painting.

It is also likely that such close-knit relationships encouraged that marked ability shown by most Sienese artists to excel in more than one of the visual arts. Few Sienese painters were just painters; most also turned their hands to sculpture, to architecture, or to miniature-painting. So Vecchietta like his pupil, Neroccio di Landi, was as distinguished as a sculptor as he was as a painter; Francesco di Giorgio was an engineer, an expert on hydraulics and fortifications, an architect, a miniaturist, a sculptor and the author of many treatises covering all aspects of the arts, as well as a painter; and Peruzzi, who was both an architect and a painter, actually began his career as a jeweller and goldsmith. Indeed, it is in Siena, rather than in Florence or Rome, that we find the many-sided genius who has been held to represent 'renaissance man'.

Related to this multi-faceted quality of so much Sienese art is the high standard of craftsmanship and the technical ingenuity which found expression in all artefacts. In some ways, therefore, the most characteristic Sienese works of art are the ones which display these varied skills to the full; the inlaid marble floor of the cathedral, Domenico di Niccolò's *intarsia* work, or the elegant ironwork which separates the chapel and the ante-chapel of the Palazzo Pubblico, and which may well have been designed by Jacopo della Quercia. Work of such a quality could only be produced in a society like that of Siena; one where the guilds, backed by the communal authorities, succeeded in imposing high standards of craftsmanship, skill, and finish; where the artist was well-integrated into a craftsman-dominated society which respected and valued his skills; one, above all, in which the arts were readily and publicly accessible.

All the evidence which we possess suggests that, certainly, in the later middle ages, and most probably in the early renaissance, all the great works of art in the city were known, seen, appreciated and even loved. The city's mystics and saints, her preachers and her chroniclers, constantly refer to and comment upon those works of art as one of the passionate concerns of their lives. Just as Siena's artists were closely involved with the life of society as a whole, so that society was deeply involved with the works of art those artists produced. Their paintings, sculptures and works of architecture were seen as a manifestation of the worth of the city to the outside world—an expression, that is, of Siena's urban values. It is this framework which has to be borne in mind in turning from a consideration of the role of the artist in society, to an account of the works of art which the artist produced.

II

Throughout the complex history of their relationship, one concern seems to have been shared by Sienese patron and Sienese artist alike: a search for beauty. To a degree which would have been remarkable elsewhere in the middle ages, and even during the early renaissance, the Sienese patron was prepared to reward an artist for work of a particularly beautiful nature. A famous but by no means untypical example of this is to be found in the career of Vecchietta who, in 1467, was commissioned by the hospital of Santa Maria della Scala to make a bronze tabernacle for their church, for which the agreed maximum price was to be 1,200 florins; when the work was completed in 1472, Vecchietta was given not only 1,150 florins, but also a house rent-free for the rest of his life because the tabernacle was:

> a most notable work, and more beautiful, and ornamented, and greater than he had promised.[12]

A concern for the beautiful remains the first and most striking characteristic of the Sienese tradition. A Sienese painting is, invariably, a delight to the eye and the emphasis within it is normally on decoration and decorative qualities. The essential interest of the Sienese artist, therefore, was often in a beautiful but two-dimensional surface, rather than in the three-dimensional illusionistic world which absorbed the interest of the Florentine renaissance painter. The unity of a Sienese painting is normally created by decorative patterns, and it is no accident that the painters of Siena were influenced far more than were those of the rest of Italy by patterns in textile design; such influence is reflected in the loving care and attention which they always lavished upon the dress of the figures in their paintings. This compelling love of decoration remained characteristic of Sienese artists and their patrons throughout the centuries and is the most striking feature of Sienese art in all periods. Thus, even Baroque art in Siena, whose decorative elements are often exquisite, both rich and delicate, blends rapidly into work which we can more easily identify as *rococo*, a style eminently suited to the Sienese tradition.

The love of decoration also explains the passionate interest of the Sienese artist in colour, an interest so characteristic that it is often through the purity and the clarity of its colours that a Sienese painting can most easily be identified. This love of colour is there in the breathtaking, jewel-like colours of Duccio's *Maestà*; it is the chief charm of Sassetta's major works; it distinguishes Francesco di Giorgio's striking *Nativity* in San Domenico and his even more remarkable *Coronation of the Virgin*; and it is one of the most admirable qualities of Rutilio Manetti's Baroque *Infant Christ blessing the Infant St. John*. But it is also present in all minor works as well; the 1344 Gabella *tavoletta* which shows *The Good Government of Siena*, for instance, or the Biccherna cover, painted by Giovanni di Paolo in 1436, showing *St. Jerome caring for the Lion's Paw*.

Until a very late date, Sienese painters also made extensive use of decorative gold-leaf which they used to cover large areas. They delighted in the elaboration of engraved and punched patterns on the *gesso* surface of their panel paintings, and they made the embossed architectural mouldings of such paintings an integral part of their design. Sometimes they would even continue the carved decoration of a frame and its mouldings over into the picture. A typical example of the use of such techniques can be found in the work of the painter Paolo di Giovanni Fei, with his profusion of rich, decorative detailing in gold, his punched haloes, borders and materials. His *Madonna Lactans*, now in the Metropolitan Museum of Art in New York, still in its original frame, elaborately decorated with gold and semi-precious stones, is an outstanding example of this tradition from the Middle Ages.

The demand for this kind of work remained constant in Siena until well into the period of the High Renaissance. Many of the major works of the Sienese renaissance, like Matteo di Giovanni's under-valued *Saint Barbara*, painted in 1478, continue to employ a gold background, and as late as 1529, the Sienese government was still finding it necessary to ban the import of 'Madonnas . . . worked in gold',[13] since this threatened the livelihood of practising Sienese artists.

Another means frequently employed by Sienese artists to achieve a desired decorative effect was the use of the curve and the curvilinear pattern. Simone Martini was among the first to adopt such formal patterning, the finest example being his *Guidoriccio* where the whole picture is built upon the repetition of an S-shape which gives the image its sense of movement. Paolo di Giovanni Fei was another artist to follow in this tradition; his *Visitation*, in a recess of the right wall of San Francesco, is based entirely on a similar curvilinear pattern, and the consummation of this trend is to be found in the works of Sano di Pietro, whose Madonnas are always so gracefully bent that they inevitably invite comparison with Oriental paintings.

In a search for an explanation of its distinctive qualities, commentators on Sienese painting have frequently spoken of its mysticism and other-worldliness, and it is true that Sienese painters are typically concerned to portray a transcendant rather than mundane reality. From the very first period in the second half of the thirteenth century when we can distinguish a distinct Sienese school of painting, centred around the earliest Sienese painter whose name is known to us, Guido da Siena, until the time of the High Renaissance, Sienese art remains highly symbolic and persistently stresses spiritual qualities at the expense of realism. Indeed, one of the best examples of this other-worldly quality of the whole Sienese school, dates from the time of the renaissance: Francesco di Giorgio's lovely *Annunciation*, where the artist, desiring to dispel any sense of an objective or earthly reality, deliberately makes use of a perspective distortion to achieve an expressionistic effect that would have been anathema to any contemporary Florentine painter.

This painting of the *Annunciation* therefore epitomizes the vast gulf which in the last analysis always separated the Sienese and Florentine traditions in painting. Rarely can there have been two major artistic centres, as close to each other as Florence and Siena, constantly in contact, always open to each other's influence, sharing artists and craftsmen, which none the less developed such distinct traditions in the visual arts. How distinct they are is shown by the way in which all late medieval Tuscan art can be interpreted in terms of a continuing dialogue between two opposed yet complementary currents, one centred on Florence, the other on Siena.

This dialogue was, no doubt, fuelled by the natural antipathy of Florence and Siena. It is certainly significant that Sienese art flourished in those areas which were subject to Sienese dominion, and Florentine art in those areas subject to Florence, with crucial meeting-points at Certaldo, Poggibonsi, Castelfiorentino and Montepulciano, since a deliberate cultural imperialism was used by both Siena and Florence as a unifying force within the territories each ruled. When Siena recovered Montepulciano from Florence in 1496, for instance, the first concern of the new Sienese commissioner for Montepulciano, Antonio Bichi, was to have Cozzarelli sent to him. He required the presence of a major Sienese artist not only for the rebuilding of the defences of Montepulciano, but also to obliterate all traces of Florentine rule and to replace them with Sienese symbols. In particular he was anxious to replace the Florentine coats-of-arms on the city-gates by a *Balzana* and a Lion and a *Libertas*. The *Balzana* was so important that he wanted it made in Siena, and even for the other two shields he specifically requested the dispatch of a Sienese sculptor, 'who knows how to make them'.[14] In the main square, he was anxious to erect a column surmounted by a She-wolf, to replace the Florentine *Marzocco*, and again he requested that Siena should send him a 'master who will know how to make it well'.[15]

An even more explicit example of Sienese cultural imperialism can be found in 1540 with the building of Grosseto cathedral, when Siena expressed her intention of retaining complete control over the design and execution of the building. The citizens of Grosseto were to have no say in the design:

desiring that the fabric of the cathedral ... shall be brought to completion according to the good order and design of our architect, the excellent master Antonio Mario Lari ... we forbid anyone to continue the walls or the fabric according to any other design ... or to employ masters of any kind, either masons or sculptors or any others, unless with the consent and agreement of the same.[16]

The political differences between Siena and Florence gave to the two cities a distinctly different cultural orientation. In the early middle ages, Florence was the greatest of the Guelph cities, for most of the time allied with Naples, France and the Papal court, deeply influenced by the culture of these three centres and particularly by the organizing and rationalizing capacity so characteristic of medieval French culture. The Sienese were intensely suspicious of this Guelphic culture, and, in the fifteenth century, their poet, Il Saviozzo, spoke for them all in describing the Florentines as a:

Detestable seed,
Enemies of peace and of charity
Who have 'Liberty' always in their mouths
But devastate the world with their tyranny.

Even at this late date, Siena remained obstinately Ghibelline in all her cultural assumptions.

The chief artistic beneficiary of the Ghibelline traditions was Simone Martini whose paintings are best understood as the supreme expression of the sentiments and the aspirations of the native Tuscan nobility and the Italian chivalric tradition of the thirteenth and fourteenth centuries. Decorative and poetic in their inspiration, his works are inhabited by knights in burnished armour, prelates in ornate robes, holy virgins, clad in graceful gowns, and ethereal angels. In his paintings we thus discover a world of refined beauty, in which all is perfect harmony and joy, and from which sorrows, sin and vulgarity are permanently banished. It is, in fact, the idealized world of the medieval courtly tradition.

Paradoxically, however, these same Ghibelline ideals which fired the imagination of Simone Martini, also fed rather than opposed another dominant theme of all Sienese art and architecture: civic idealism. For one important consequence of the battle of Montaperti was the forging of even closer links between the great Ghibelline cities of Tuscany—Pisa, Arezzo and Siena; as a result, until well

5

into the fourteenth century, Siena had closer cultural relationships with Arezzo and Pisa than she had with Guelph Florence. It was, therefore, from Pisa that in 1265 the Sienese summoned Nicola Pisano to erect the pulpit of their cathedral, and, as we have already seen, under the stimulus of Pisano's influence, there subsequently emerged an independent school of Sienese sculptors, whose best representative is Tino di Camaino. The work of these sculptors was remarkable for its blending of the religious and the civic ideal into a uniquely Sienese art-form, characterized particularly by its expression not just in stone, but in carved and painted wood.

Sculpture in turn had a direct impact on fourteenth-century Sienese painting, in the period which saw the emergence of the great Sienese school, of which Simone Martini is so prominent a representative but whose founder-member and most creative genius is, of course, Duccio di Buoninsegna. Born shortly before the battle of Montaperti and dying, probably, in 1313, when the rule of the Nine was at its height, Duccio did not abandon the tradition of Byzantine painting which had dominated Sienese painting until his lifetime, and of which Guido da Siena had been so fine an exponent. Duccio's works continued to emphasize the divine mysteries and the value of hierarchy and order, and indeed his paintings can be seen as the crowning glories of the Italian-Byzantine tradition. Nevertheless, Duccio is much more than a great Byzantine painter; he is a true innovator. In his *Maestà*, in particular, he emerges as the first great painter of masterpieces in an unmistakably Sienese manner. This is not just a question of brilliance of colour, of flowing line, and decorative qualities, but is inherent in the very subject-matter of this great painting. For it is the *Maestà* which establishes the tradition which was to become so insistent in Sienese painting, and which finds its fullest exposition in Lorenzetti's *Good and Bad Government*, in which there is a synthesis of the civic and the sacred through the lay celebration of divine themes.

In Duccio's *Maestà* there is also a specific concern for the urban environment and, particularly, the urban environment of Siena. Duccio's Jerusalem is, quite recognizably, an idealized Siena, and it is Duccio's experience as a citizen which assists his observation of reality. It is thus no accident that Duccio is the first painter of the western tradition who tries to present a near view of a scene which actually takes place in a town. Towns had, of course, appeared in late Byzantine paintings, but the relationship between man and such urban backgrounds is always a hesitant one, represented uncertainly by figures who are set either against isolated buildings or against a town which is depicted as a whole and from the outside. It is significant that the first questioning of this tradition is to be found in the work of Guido da Siena, whose *Crucifixion* in the Pinacoteca shows a real innovation in the presentation of architecture, with high buildings set on a slant, which indicates a dawning concept of perspective recession. Building upon these insights of Guido, Duccio was to take the matter even further, setting his figures in close and intimate relationship with their urban landscapes, as in the panel from the *Maestà* of the *Healing of the Blind Man*, which is now in the National Gallery in London, where, on the right of the scene, a typical Sienese fountain reaches to the very foreground of the picture.

After Duccio, we rarely get away from the urban theme in Sienese painting, although it may be very diversely expressed. At its simplest, the civic tradition may be overtly alluded to as in Simone Martini's lyrical Uffizi *Annunciation*, in which the figure of St. Ansano, probably painted by Simone's partner, Lippo Memmi, carries the Sienese standard. At a more sophisticated level, it found expression, as in Guido and Duccio, in the interest shown by Sienese artists in man and his relationship to an architectural environment. The finest exponents of this tradition were the two Lorenzetti, but their followers all continued to be obsessed by the way in which man inhabits the buildings he constructs. Thus, a concern with the exploration of architectural interiors in relation to figures, comes across clearly, for instance, despite its Gothic emphasis, in Paolo di Giovanni Fei's *Birth of the Virgin*, modelled on Pietro Lorenzetti's treatment of the same subject; and very many Sienese narrative paintings, including Ambrogio Lorenzetti's *Effects of Good Government*, show a great interest in the actual building process by which the urban environment was created.

Architecture as a whole, and its relationship to human figures, were thus predominant concerns in Sienese paintings at a time when the Florentines seem to have been largely unaware of their significance, and such interests were often developed by the Sienese artist into a loving and detailed exploration of the city and of its topography. The subject of a painting may be Jerusalem but it is Siena which is always depicted. Some of these paintings we have already encountered, but there are a great many others; Bartolo di Fredi's highly-stylized *Adoration of the Magi*, for instance, shows a rich procession winding

its way through the conical Tuscan hills, piled up towards the sky
and ending in a Gothicized Siena; and Sano di Pietro, throughout
his work, conflates the cities of Siena and Jerusalem, localizing the
biblical stories firmly within the context of fifteenth-century Siena.

Yet, for all its concentration upon urban values, we should not
lose sight of the fact that Sienese art was not isolated from the natural
world, whose landscape and topography the artist often delineated
with the greatest care. Siena as a city was, as it still is, in direct and
continuous contact with a landscape of quite exceptional beauty.
Even today the land surrounding the city is farmed right up to the
city walls, while from almost anywhere in the city it is possible to
catch evocative glimpses of the countryside roundabout. It is from
just such a perspective that the countryside is presented in the work
of such sixteenth-century artists as Beccafumi and Fungai. The
majority of citizens, even those of modest means, continued to maintain direct relationships with the *contado*, while there was also something
of a rural dimension to a city whose citizens turned the tops of demolished nobletowers into roof-gardens, and where, even at the height
of urbanization in the fourteenth century, the city-walls enclosed
orchards, gardens and vineyards.

Through their concentration upon urban values, balanced by those
of the natural world, the Sienese artists arrived at the third consistent
theme of their paintings; an emphasis upon humanity. A great boost
was given to this theme in the thirteenth and fourteenth centuries
through the teachings of the friars, particularly the Dominicans and
Franciscans. Both orders were, from their very inception, extremely
popular in Siena, and their two great churches, among the most
important brick constructions in central Italy, exercised a profound
influence on the culture and the urban development of a city whose
sky-line they still help to determine and whose limits they partially
define. Both date from the early thirteenth century. In fact, as soon
as the news of the death of St. Francis reached Siena, the commune
decreed that a church should be built in his honour, and that first
building was already complete by 1255. It bears little relationship,
however, to the present San Francesco which was begun in 1326
and completed, probably to the designs of Francesco di Giorgio,
only in 1475. After a disastrous fire in 1655 it was again altered and a
number of Baroque additions were made; these, however, were
removed in accordance with the dictates of neo-Gothic taste in the
restoration made by Giuseppe Partini between 1885 and 1892. Even

then, the church still lacked a façade until as late as 1913 when one was finally added by Vittore Maini and Gaetano Coccarelli.

The Dominican order made an equally early impact on Siena. The great, gaunt, red-brick church, built on a vast substructure to crown the hill above Fontebranda, was constructed over an original building, which today forms the crypt, and was already under construction by 1220. By the end of the thirteenth century the new church was already so important and so popular that the commune was forced to build a new street so that the inhabitants of Camollia might reach it with ease, and it was found necessary to enlarge the original building. The present massive and unadorned San Domenico, so impressive in the stark simplicity of its line, was begun in the fourteenth century and was to a large extent financed by contributions from the commune. The *campanile* was completed by 1340, but the whole building was not finished before the end of the fifteenth century.

The vast investment by the Sienese community in these two great friary churches over so many centuries, confirms the great appeal which the friars made to the Sienese, and their consequent ability to attract over the centuries the patronage of commune, guilds, confraternities and individuals. The influence of the friars in a city where already by 1280 the *Fioretti* of St. Francis were a part of the common cultural heritage, was all-pervasive. Their churches even came to rival the commune as civic centres and it was within their walls that many leading Sienese citizens chose to be buried. Thus, the walls of San Francesco shelter the bones of Provenzano, the great hero of Montaperti, and also those of that most characteristic of Sienese saints, Pier Pettinagno. Again, many of the city's leading confraternities were directly attached to either San Domenico or San Francesco; family altars indicate the relationship between the friars and leading Sienese families; and the squares in front of both churches soon became important focal points of Sienese civic life.

As is clear from the essential nature of these two great churches, the friars saw art in entirely functional, almost prosaic, terms. It was a means of introducing the truths of the Christian religion to the illiterate. Their churches were therefore serviceable; they were not built as arcane celebrations of divine mysteries, but as areas of open, rectangular space where the people might hear their preachers. The walls of these churches were large and visible and were used to further the purposes of religion through frescoes which could clearly narrate the Christian message.

The message which the friars wanted to impart was essentially a humane one, for their primary aim was to bring heaven and earth closer together. The teaching of St. Francis, in particular, emphasized the humanity of all things, from God to animals and birds. The regal and aloof saints of Byzantium were meaningless to Francis of Assisi. He saw Mary not as the Virgin in Majesty, but as a tender mother suffused by human suffering; Christ not as the Divine Judge, but as the Man of Sorrows; the saints not as principalities and powers around the throne of the Almighty, but as human and humane figures. Such ideology the friars sought to have reflected in contemporary art and literature; the divine truths should be presented in familiar and down-to-earth forms. Thus, painters no longer showed Christ on the cross as erect, but rather bent and curved, in a manner most sympathetic to the Sienese style, his suffering emphasized and even over-emphasized. The Virgin was no longer portrayed as the majestic Queen of Heaven, familiar in the Byzantine tradition, but through the human episodes of her life; there was, for instance, in Siena a distinct vogue for paintings which illustrated the *Marriage* or the *Birth of the Virgin*. Again, the divine and the sanctified were presented in new attitudes. Paintings emphasized the playfulness of the infant Christ, or the resignation and patience of the aged St. Joseph. And, in Siena in particular, the teaching of the friars led to an emphasis on the small and domestic miracle, a *genre* in which the Sienese excelled, and which culminates in Francesco di Giorgio's enchanting *Miracle of the Sieve* in the Uffizi gallery. Human interest became all-important in painting, so much so that at times the divine message almost became subordinate, and the history of redemption, which such art was designed to illuminate, tended rather to become obscured. This is, for example, clearly the case in the numerous Sienese paintings which represent the Virgin trying, almost by violence, to prevent the events of the Passion.

There are, of course, many ways in which human interest can be conveyed in a work of art. The one most commonly favoured by the Sienese was the careful suggestion of human emotion. This was the technique of Duccio, for one, who virtually begs the viewer to identify with the emotions displayed by the figures in his paintings. Thus, in the *Deposition* from the *Maestà*, the mourners press around the dead body of Christ, all expressing an intense, passionate concern, while the Virgin, Mary Magdalen and St. John simultaneously embrace and support the dead body. Another means of conveying human interest was through the use of naturalistic figures and backgrounds which could be easily identified by the viewer. Simone Martini, stongly influenced by the work of Pisano who had introduced such techniques into Sienese sculpture, was a keen observer of reality and shows a conscious interest in natural phenomena. Such a concern is seen at its best in the paintings done for the church of St. Augustine in Siena of the *Blessed Augustino Novello and the Story of His Life*. Associated with this humanizing impulse was the common tendency to elaborate in paintings the most human incidents in the bible story. An example is Simone's painting in the Walker Art Gallery of Liverpool, which represents Mary and Joseph admonishing Christ in the temple. The greatest exponents of these traditions were, of course, the two Lorenzetti, both of whom were profoundly sympathetic to the teaching of the friars.

A primary reason for the success of the friars in achieving the desired humanization of religion within Siena was the close connexion which they developed with the religious confraternities. The confraternities themselves were a means of popularizing, vulgarizing and extending the Christian message among all classes of Sienese society. The confraternities, therefore, in association with the friars helped to give guidance and direction to the creative and artistic life of Siena in the fourteenth and fifteenth centuries. Thus, within the circle of St. Catherine, who numbered among her close friends the artist Andrea Vanni and the poet Nari di Landoccio dei Pagliaresi, a follower of Dante, the same emphasis upon humane and humanized religion is to be found as in the visual arts. And similar religious values are expressed with particular strength in the poetry of Niccolò di Mino Cicerchia, whose *Passion of Our Lord,* written in 1364, was to have a vital impact on the cultural development of all Tuscany.

A parallel and connected development, whose spiritual impulse also ultimately derives from the teaching of the friars, was to be found among the Gesuati, founded by the Sienese patrician, Giovanni Colombini. Colombini urged his followers to sing at all times as they went about the business of preaching and spreading the gospel of love and reconciliation. The resulting *genre* of spiritual song or laud, written by Colombini and his followers—the most famous of whom is Bianco da Siena—is yet another example of the popularity of the new, humane and often highly emotional Christianity in this period of European history.

The same religious circles, by making Dante available to a wide

Sienese audience, provided Sienese culture with another new and constant source of inspiration. Readings aloud from Dante, for example, formed a part of the proceedings of the *cenacolo* of St. Catherine and those of other confraternities. Such readings helped to popularize his works among the public story-tellers of Siena and, by such means, Dante became so universally known that by the end of the fourteenth century he was virtually public property. It is indicative of his great importance in Sienese civic life that from 1396 Buccio da Spoleto was lecturing on Dante in the University, and giving public expositions of *The Divine Comedy* from a pulpit outside San Vigilio on the major feast-days of the church.

The popularity of the Florentine but Ghibelline-orientated Dante among the Sienese is not really surprising, for it is a confirmation of the humanistic impulses in their culture. *The Divine Comedy*, like the other major works of the *Dolce Stil Nuovo*, is a major example of that humanization of culture which we associate with fourteenth-century Tuscany and to which the friars made so great a contribution. The success of this religious and cultural movement within Siena was such that Dante inevitably made a direct appeal to the city's major artists. It is probable that he influenced Simone Martini, who was to become a close friend of Petrarch, and very likely that he had a very profound effect on Paolo di Giovanni Fei. The works of Taddeo di Bartolo, Sassetta, and Giovanni di Paolo also all contain direct or indirect allusions to *The Divine Comedy*.

What emerges from this account is that the Sienese tradition in painting, both in theme and style, was well-established by the end of the fourteenth century. Sienese art grew naturally out of the society of the city and was a clear expression of its civic culture, which it also helped to shape. In the following centuries, the nature of Sienese society altered radically and a reflection of this change were the new styles which are associated with those movements we call the Renaissance, Baroque, and Neo-classicism. But, in Siena, there was never to be a major break in the continuity of artistic development. Change took root but slowly and, as we shall see, the themes and styles which had characterized Sienese art in the past, rather than being abandoned were only modified or elaborated in the creative consciousness of the future.

7

City of the Virgin

Maria advocata
Mediatrix optimum
Inter Christum
Et Senam suam.

THE INFLUENCE of religion on the civic life of Siena has always
been all-pervasive. The 1355 statutes of the Painters' Guild open
with a clear statement of faith:

In the beginning, in the middle and at the end of all that we do or
say, our regulations will be made in the name of omnipotent God
and of his mother, the Holy Virgin Mary. Amen.[1]

But such an affirmation of the ultimate and all-embracing significance
of religion need not have been restricted to the painters' guild, for the
city's entire corporate life was structured according to religious norms.
Religion provided the firmest foundation and the most authoritative
title to political power in Siena, and no area of life in the city escaped
its influence. The family, economic life, commerce, education, all
were equally subject to its control, while religious ceremonies played
a crucial part in the city, by uniting basically disparate groups in common moments of civic participation.

Of course, such general comments about the role of religion can be
made with equal accuracy about almost any other pre-industrial town.
Peculiar to Siena, however, are the intensity of its corporate religious
life and certain specific forms of piety, characteristically exemplified
by the development of the idea of Siena as the special city of the Virgin.
Official recognition of the Virgin as the Queen of the city is normally
dated from the battle of Montaperti in 1260. According to tradition, in
the anxious hours which preceded the battle, Bonaguida Lucari, who
had been chosen as ruler of the city with full powers for the duration
of the war, led the populace in surrendering Siena into the Virgin's
hands. Bareheaded and barefooted, a halter around his neck, he

5*

headed a procession of citizens to the cathedral. Here he was met by all the clergy of the city, and, at the foot of the choir, the Bishop and Buonaguida embraced, in pledge of the complete union of Church and State for the defence of the city. Then, after silent prayer, Buonaguida, who had prostrated himself before the high altar, formally made over the city and the *contado* of Siena to the Mother of Heaven.

Thus, according to the chroniclers, did the Virgin become the Queen of Siena and SENA VETUS CIVITAS VIRGINIS—Siena City of the Virgin. From 1262, in commemoration of this event, two candles burned night and day at communal expense before the altar of the Madonna in the cathedral. The special relationship between Siena and the Virgin was to be reaffirmed on the occasion of many crises in the city's history. In 1483 exiles from a regime overthrown in the previous year invaded the Sienese state and appeared to be about to capture the city. The communal officials panicked and decided to rededicate their city to the Virgin. This occasion is illustrated in a *tavoletta* of the Gabella of 1483, in which the Virgin is shown leaning forward from the altar to receive the keys of the city. An official contract was actually drawn up by a government notary in which it was expressly stipulated that no one, 'of whatever rank, dignity or eminence, ecclesiastical or temporal, should acquire or be held to have acquired any right, by reason of the ceremony, save only the Virgin' who was thereby made the 'true feudal lady, guardian, defender and safeguard'[2] of Siena, while the magistrates of the city, for all time, were to be deemed her immediate vassals and representatives, and to hold their offices directly from her. On this occasion, as in 1260, the Virgin responded to Sienese prayers. The attack of the exiles failed and they were driven from Sienese territory to take refuge in the Church State, although it must be confessed that, only four years later, they returned in triumph to Siena.

The next rededication of the city occurred in 1526 when papal and Florentine forces invaded Sienese territory, advanced to the very walls of Siena, and encamped outside Porta Camollia. The Sienese once again entrusted their city to the protection of the Virgin. Then the city militia, with a hundred cavalry, made a surprise sortie from the gates of Fontebranda and Camollia, and the enemy were, miraculously it seemed, put to flight. Some years later, when Charles V threatened to build a fortress in the city, and the Sienese came to believe that their traditional liberties were under attack, it was therefore natural that they should have recourse to the Virgin in a ceremony:

like that which was held at the time of the battle of Montaperti, so that all-powerful God and his immaculate mother, the Virgin Mary, should hear the city, and maintain its liberty and preserve it from the threatened fortress.[3]

A solemn procession wound its way through the streets to the cathedral; the officials of the city 'all dressed as if it were Good Friday',[4] headed by the Captain of the People, Claudio Zuccanti, were accompanied by fifty unmarried girls. The keys of the city, in a silver basin, were presented to the Virgin by Zuccanti, who, on behalf of the Sienese people, implored her to effect a change of heart in Charles V. A solemn vow was made, not only to marry the fifty virgins with a dowry provided by the state in that year, but to do the same for fifty others every year that Siena remained an independent republic. However, despite a further rededication of the city during the last tragic days of independence, on this occasion Sienese prayers were without avail, and, within five years, Sienese liberties were at an end.

Yet the intensity of Sienese religious experience survived the collapse of the independent republic. In many ways, indeed, it was further deepened, since this was one of the few remaining ways in which Sienese identity as a corporate unity could be asserted. The most remarkable expression of the search for a fresh expression of Sienese identity was the development of the popular cult of the Madonna del Provenzano at the end of the sixteenth century. In 1594, confronted once more by disaster—on this occasion, famine and plague—the Sienese resolved to have recourse to their traditional advocate, the Virgin. Unfortunately, their pleas to Heaven could not take the traditional form of a ceremony in the cathedral for the somewhat unedifying reason that the Archbishop* of Siena was in open conflict with the Rector of the cathedral. The Sienese were therefore forced to resort to the popular icon of Our Lady of Provenzano. The Provenzano Madonna, supposedly set up by St. Catherine herself, stood between two windows in the humble area of the Via dei Provenzani di Sotto, traditionally the red-light district of Siena. In 1552, a Spanish soldier had had the temerity to fire an arquebus against this statue, a sacrilegious act sufficiently horrifying to ensure the development of the cult of an image which rapidly gained a considerable international reputation for miracle-working. So it was to this icon that, as the Biccherna cover of 1592–94 illustrates, the city authorities made their pilgrimage and devotions in 1594

---

* Siena was raised to the status of an archbishopric by Pius II in 1459.

vowing to build the great church which today houses the miraculous image and which was completed in 1611. The feast of Our Lady of Provenzano, on 2 July, has remained one of the principal holidays in the Sienese calendar.

Throughout the seventeenth and the eighteenth centuries, the Sienese continued to believe that they were under the special protection of the Virgin to whom they had particular recourse on many occasions, most notably during plague epidemics and earthquakes. Popular religious sentiment remained as strong as ever, and was therefore deeply offended by the anti-ecclesiastical reforms of Grand Duke Leopold I at the end of the eighteenth century not to mention the anti-Christian sentiments of so many Jacobins. It was, then, hardly surprising that the anti-Jacobin revolt of 1799 with its slogan of 'Viva Maria and Death to the Jacobins' should have taken on the aura of a religious festival. The counter-revolutionaries saw their success in traditional terms declaring that:

> It has pleased the most Blessed Virgin Mary, our particular Advocate and Queen, who has so often protected us at times of public disaster, to hear our most fervent vows, liberating us from a foreign yoke, and restoring to us . . . our laws and our customs.[5]

Archbishop Chigi-Zondadori of Siena chose to authenticate this view of the counter-revolution by ordering that the miraculous image of the *Madonna del Voto* from the cathedral be exposed to the faithful as a thanksgiving for the victory over the French. At the same time he did nothing to prevent the horrendous scene on the Campo where in the name of the Virgin the counter-revolutionaries built a great bonfire and burned alive nineteen Jews, including six women.

The shame of the terrible events of 1799 remained with the Sienese for many years and did much to fuel a certain anti-clericalism among the city's liberals; yet, paradoxically, it did little to dampen Sienese religious ardour. Siena remained as it remains today, the city of the Virgin, irrespective of the good or bad deeds committed in her name, and as recently as 1944, when Siena seemed in danger from Allied bombardment, the city was once more solemnly rededicated to the Queen of Heaven, the text of that rededication being hung today at the entrance to the Capella del Voto in the cathedral. So great was the crowd at this ceremony that it spilled out into the cathedral square where the citizens listened to the *podestà* renewing the compact first made with the Virgin in the thirteenth century, 'proud of a faith that does not diminish with the centuries', and addressing the Queen of Heaven as: 'the voice of our conscience, the light of our spirit, and the inexhaustible fount of that love for our neighbour which alone can save our beloved city.'[6]

There is no doubt that the relationship of the city of Siena as a collective body to the Virgin, as expressed in such ceremonies, has always puzzled the outsider, for it can ultimately only be understood, as it were, from the inside. Certain characteristics of the relationship, however, do lend themselves to description and of these the most striking is its curious familiarity. In the middle ages, after all, no inhabitant of Siena could enter into even the simplest commercial transaction without being reminded of the Virgin, for Sienese coins all bore the inscription, *Sena Vetus Civitas Virginis*. And, when the great bell of the Mangia was rung to assemble the magistrates of the republic, its summons commenced with three distinct and separate strokes, commemorating the angelic salutation; again, the bell of the cathedral which sounded the *Ave Maria* each evening recalled the Madonna for this was the bell which bore her name.

The sense of familiarity in Siena's relationship with the Virgin in no way diminished its passionate intensity. One reason for its emotional depth was that since the city was seen as the child of the Virgin it became, in the imagination, conflated with the Christ-child, for the Madonna's maternal care was, in both cases, identical. It is this fact which explains the perdurable influence of the *Madonna Lactans* in the tradition of Sienese painting. This image, whose richness of meaning was heightened for the Sienese by its visual allusion to the traditional motif of Lupa and the twins, acted as a constant inspiration. Of all Ambrogio Lorenzetti's paintings, the best-loved and the most popular, both in his own life-time and through all succeeding centuries, has been his *Madonna del Latte* which was painted in about 1340 and hangs in the seminary of San Francesco. Although this was a subject already popular with sculptors, it had never previously been painted but Lorenzetti's altarpiece was so well-attuned to Sienese religious sensibility that it became an immediate success, inspiring countless variations on the same theme.

The warm relationship, which is portrayed in paintings which illustrate the Virgin nursing the Christ-child, was subsequently used by Sienese mystics and preachers to symbolize the relationship between Christ and His people, or between the church and the devout. So St. Catherine represents Christ as saying:

What I say of the universal and mystical body of the Holy Church
. . . I say also of my ministers, who stand and feed at the breasts of
Holy Church, and not only should they feed themselves, but it is
also their duty to feed and hold to those breasts the universal body
of Christian people.[7]

From here it was but a short step for the Sienese to see themselves in
the uniquely privileged position of the child at the Virgin's breast, and
they saw no theological impropriety in claiming in a popular song in
praise of the Virgin:

> You . . . in order to give your milk to Siena
> Deprived the heavenly-child of his share.

In such ways, the Sienese were constantly being invited or encouraged to dwell upon the humane and gentle qualities of the Madonna.
San Bernardino, for example, told of the happiness of the Virgin in
caring for her new-born son:

> how sweet she found it, caring for him, washing him, feeding him,
> and doing all those things. . . .[8]

And Sienese painters elaborated upon the same qualities. Indeed, no
school of painters has ever portrayed with such lyrical care, the mystery
of gentleness inherent in the Madonna's relationship with the infant
Christ. At the very beginning of this tradition stands Duccio's *Madonna
da Crevole* in the Opera del Duomo, in which the Christ-child fixes his
mother with the tenderest of regards, as he lifts her veil with his right
hand. Towards the end of the fourteenth century, to take another fine
example, there is Paolo di Giovanni Fei's decaying *Polyptych* in the
Sienese Pinacoteca, which builds directly on this tradition. In an overt
statement about the tender relationship which exists between mother
and child, the infant Christ is raised on his mother's hand, so that his
cheek rests against hers. At the same time, his hand lovingly caresses
her chin, and he gazes affectionately into her eyes. A typical renaissance
version of the same theme is represented by the Pienza *Madonna and
Child* of Matteo di Giovanni, in which this time the Christ-child
stands upon his mother's knee and softly strokes her face.

The tender qualities of the Madonna are also emphasized in the
vision of her as the Queen of Humility. Her humility was for San
Bernardino Mary's greatest quality since:

> We are told that the Devil fell from Heaven because of his pride and
> so Mary, because of her humility, rose to glory.[9]

In consequence, another much-loved Sienese iconographical image was that known as the *Madonna of Humility* in which she is portrayed seated upon the ground and in which her humane qualities are overtly emphasized. Paolo di Giovanni Fei, for instance, was to paint this subject at least twice, and Giovanni di Paolo's justly-famed *Branchini Madonna* of 1427 is, in fact, a very beautiful *Madonna of Humility* but one who, in this case, is surrounded by cherubs whose wings seem about to lift her from the ground on which she sits.

These paintings are not merely of interest, then, to the art historian. They are also important historical documents, illustrating, with remarkable fidelity, the highly-charged religious atmosphere which the cult of the Madonna produced in Siena. Given this atmosphere, it is hardly surprising that the most loved images of the Virgin became more than paintings and took on a kind of living reality. This was always true at the personal level; various miracles related down the centuries involved punishment or reward by some particular religious image. But it was equally true at the collective level. Such paintings were expected to rejoice when the city rejoiced, to weep when Siena mourned and so, in 1550, the Duccio *Maestà* from the cathedral was carried in solemn procession to view the Spanish fortress, so that the Virgin might see for herself 'the ancient walls and the tall palaces, now reduced to ruins'.[10]

On such occasions, an overtly political use was being made of a sacred image. Just as possession of the Palazzo Pubblico gave to any regime the power to govern within Siena, so possession of the religious icons around which so much of civic life revolved, gave to any regime divine authentication. So, among the first acts of the group of men who overthrew the Petrucci in 1524, was the parading of the familiar Duccio *Maestà* through the streets of the city.

Such incidents serve to illustrate the essentially magical power which any religious painting enjoyed to an accentuated degree in Siena. For, while today we regard these paintings essentially as works of art, throughout the middle ages their function remained a magical one. This explains the Sienese custom of cutting out uninjured portions from any paintings which happened to be damaged by fire, placing them in tabernacles, and setting them up at street-corners. Here, they would soon attract offerings from the faithful and they frequently became centres of popular cults or sources of miraculous cures. Many of these tabernacles still decorate the walls of Siena to this day and not all, by any means, are neglected.

The political dimension which is so marked a feature of the relationship between the Virgin and the Sienese is connected with the idea of the magical power of paintings, since that power was most commonly invoked for political ends. Paintings of the Virgin on the city-gates, like those at Camollia and Porta Romana, were placed there to provide a magical defence at the city's weakest points, for, if the Virgin was Queen of Siena she had certain obligations towards her city, including that of defending it from its enemies. She was, as the painting by Sano di Pietro of the *Virgin Commanding Pope Calixtus III to protect Siena* makes quite clear, the city's advocate both with God and with man, and in such terms she is always addressed in official documents. Her role, in this respect, was carefully spelled out by San Bernardino:

> ... she places herself between us and danger, she stands up to temptation, saying and commanding—away you evil one, get you behind me with your ill-fortune. Leave this city of mine alone, in which live so many of my devotees.[11]

The political relationship between the Virgin and Siena also involved both parties in a series of contracts and mutual obligations such as are laid out in the 1321 report concerning the rebuilding of the cathedral. The Sienese are urged to build an harmonious and beautiful edifice which:

> ... should be finished with artistic decoration befitting such a famous cathedral, wherein our Lord Jesus Christ and his most blessed Mother and their celestial assembly will be praised and worshipped, and consequently they will guard the city of Siena from any danger.[12]

The Virgin is to have her cathedral. In return she is expected to protect the city from all enemies. More succinctly, but no less powerfully, the same idea is expressed in the words written in the halo of Sassetta's *Madonna of the Snows*: 'If you trust in me, Siena, you will be full of grace', and it is made completely explicit in a petition by the inhabitants of Fontebranda in 1470, when they reminded the civic authorities that:

> It is an obligation on the Republic to take care to increase the spiritual devotions and the number of divine temples in the city; and it is particularly an obligation for you because of the heavenly gift of most sweet liberty, such as we and only a few other cities in the world enjoy.[13]

Interior of the Cathedral

Ambrogio Lorenzetti, *The Madonna del Latte*

Sassetta, *Madonna of the Snow*

Francesco di Giorgio, *The Madonna sheltering the City during the earthquake*, Biccherna Cover 1467 [1]

Virtually everything that was done in Siena can, therefore, be seen as part of a perpetual and complicated bargaining with heaven. Prisoners were released in honour of the major festivals, in order that:

> God and the . . . Virgin Mary may conserve the city and people of Siena in a good and pacific state.[14]

Alms were given to the poor, 'for the good of the city and the preservation of its present free status',[15] while in 1427 when the threat of war with Florence was averted, the General Council ordered that thanks be rendered to the Virgin by increasing the expenditure on the celebrations of mid-August.

A consequence of such a world-view was that any crisis in Siena was likely to be confronted by attempts to renew the city's contract with Heaven by a restatement of history in terms of a series of divine rewards and punishments for the virtues or sins of Siena. A committee would be appointed to draw up a kind of heavenly balance-sheet which would then be presented both to God and to the Sienese for joint approval. Thus the decision by Charles V to build a fortress in the city in 1550 prompted the creation of a committee whose sole remit was to appease the wrath of Heaven by pacifying all family feuds. One of Siena's leading citizens, Lelio Tolomei, made a number of suggestions all designed to further the same end: the hospital should be supported, the Archbishop and his vicar should be asked to report on those areas of Sienese morality most in need of reformation, and the state should lend its support to seeing that reformation was effected, while the price of salt ought to be reduced, 'out of compassion for the poor.'[16] When, during the same crisis, the looked-for miracle occurred and the Spanish were driven from the city, the first meeting of the General Council was asked to consider, as a matter of urgency, ways of fulfilling Siena's debt to heaven:

> by considering what alms should be offered to religious and mendicants as a thanksgiving for our recovered Liberty.[17]

Even today, a survival of such overtly commercial religious relationships survives among the Sienese, and may be seen at its clearest in the relationship which the inhabitants of a *contrada* enter into with their patron saint for the Palio. A clear contract is made, the *contradaiolo* declaring: 'If I give you a candle, you must give me the palio', and a patron who then fails to fulfil his side of the bargain will be punished by having his candles extinguished.

In the middle ages, in such a contractual context, sin was seen as important by the commune, not because of the effect of the sin on the individual, but because that individual's sins threatened the whole community—the Common Good—by attracting the wrath of heaven. Contemporary law taught citizens that each was responsible for the whole community, and for each of his fellow-citizens; the debt or the crime of one, was the debt or the crime of all. Thus, the delicately balanced world of Lorenzetti's frescoes of *Good Government* was one in which a single sinner might contaminate the whole city since:

He who is not corrected and does not correct others, becomes like a limb which putrefies and corrupts the whole body.[18]

In consequence, so San Bernardino told his Sienese:

As refuse is taken out of the house so as not to infect it, so wicked men should be removed from human commerce by prison or by death,[19]

and he taught that the whole duty of rulers lay in preserving the Common Good, in encouraging goodness and virtue, and, above all, in restraining sinners and preventing sin. The Sienese would then be victorious over all their enemies and be protected from hail, pestilence, thunder, storms, lightning, famine and plague, 'which God sends to the world in order to punish our sins'.[20]

In such a context, morality and religion were intimately related to civic concerns, were indeed themselves civic concerns, and the fate of the Cities of the Plain had a peculiar relevance for the Sienese. In consequence, in the framing of legal statutes, we find the elaboration of a criminal code in which the worst crimes were those which seemed most to threaten the religious fabric of society. 'Adulterers, patricides, rapists, those guilty of sexual relations with nuns, sodomites and blasphemers of God, of his Son, of the Virgin, the protectress of this city, or of any saint,'[21] violators of sumptuary laws, and destroyers of images, were those against whom the fullest rigours of the law were directed. The Jews, known as 'despisers of the Most Glorious Virgin Mary',[22] were hounded, persecuted and outlawed, and anti-sodomite legislation was specifically introduced in 1324 in the hope that:

because of these . . . holy provisions, the Lord our God Jesus Christ, and his purest mother and always glorious Virgin Mary, the special advocate and defender of the city, commune and people of Siena, by their piety and mercy ... will remove scandals from the same city and take away perils, and the more swiftly lead that same city and its citizens to a state of tranquillity and peace, and ... conserve it in the same state.[23]

Despite the frequent conflicts throughout the middle ages between the city and her bishop, there was in Siena no division between church and state but a normal identity of interest, symbolised by the lamp which, after 1262, always burned in honour of the Virgin before the *carroccio*, just as if that war-cart had been an altar. Again, for important civic works the commune taxed the clergy without compunction, since it could see no distinction between the lay and the religious when such works were: 'made for the universal good of all'.[24] On the other hand, the church's festivals were civic holidays, their observation enforced by the communal authorities and the guilds. There were by the late fourteenth century seventy-one such feast days, not including Sundays, in which the religious and the secular were blended together in public celebration.

A similar identification of interest may be found between the Sienese and their many saints, who, however ascetic their personal lives, never entirely rejected the secular life. Indeed, as far as one can tell, it was the practical miseries of life in the urban community—plague, poverty, famine, political and social strife—which acted as the catalyst in their spiritual lives, awakening their religious impulses. They devoted their lives to the solution of urban, social problems and the alleviation of those ills which seemed concomitant upon life within the city-walls. Similarly, Siena's saints saw their role as the sanctification of the urban life, their preaching and teaching, a means of creating the new Jerusalem on earth in Siena, the chosen city of the Virgin. It was, in fact, these saints who elaborated most clearly a justification of civic life and taught the Sienese to think of it not apologetically but as a better and higher form of life, by identifying the city of Siena with the holy city of Jerusalem. San Bernardino, for instance, typically conflated the two cities:

Hear what Saint Luke says in his eighteenth chapter, through the inspiration of God. . . . Jesus, seeing the city of Siena, wept over it. . . .[25]

The Sienese, in their turn, loved their saints for the affection they showed to their native city. There is, for example, the extreme case of the Blessed Ambrogio Sansedoni, for, however neurotic he may have been in his attitude towards women, and however unfortunate in his capacity to attract the pressing attentions of the Devil, he was beloved not for his ascetic qualities but rather for the sterling services he had rendered his city. In 1271 he persuaded Pope Gregory to lift an interdict, and it is in recognition of this achievement that the Blessed Ambrogio is always represented in Sienese painting as holding in his arms the city he rescued from the realm of the Devil.

An equally popular saint is the Blessed Agostino Novello, who, born of a Sienese father, entered the Augustinian order, and lived during the latter part of his life as a hermit at San Leonardo al Lago, close to Siena, where he died on 19 May 1309. He was beloved by the Sienese for the intimate concern he showed with the details of their daily lives. Whereas the Virgin was resorted to in times of need on the grand political scene, it was the Blessed Agostino Novello who came to their aid on more mundane occasions. In the altar-piece which Simone Martini painted for the church of Sant'Agostino four such incidents are depicted: that of the child killed by a wolf, that of the child who fell from a balcony, that of the baby dropped from a hammock, and that of the knight thrown from his horse.

At first glance, it seems more difficult to accept a third Sienese saint, the Blessed Giovanni Colombini, founder of the Order of the Gesuati, as an urban saint, for he came to reject the secular life entirely. Described by his biographer, Feo Balcari, as 'a man of nice, kind expression and of short, slight build',[26] he was a leading member of the Sienese ruling élite and belonged to the Wool Guild. He was a merchant and a banker with branches of his banks in Perugia, San Giovan d'Asso and in Castello della Val d'Orcia. He held high office at the time of the Nine and may even have been a member of the governing executive. In 1355, however, just before the fall of the Nine from power, he seems to have suffered some kind of religious conversion. He abandoned all of his businesses and gave away all his property; the convent of Saint Bonda and the hospital of Santa Maria della Scala were the chief beneficiaries.*

The way of life subsequently adopted by Colombini seems to be an overt rejection of the urban experience, and yet, paradoxically, it is only comprehensible within an urban context. To Colombini the

---

* His wife is supposed to have reproached him for such excessive zeal. When he replied that she had always prayed for greater charitableness on his part, she pointed out: 'I prayed for rain, not for the Flood.'

worst sins were wealth, exploitation, and above all, usury. To atone for his own former failings in this area, he had himself scourged in front of the Palazzo, while entreating his companions to accuse him of such quintessentially urban sins as having sold grain at inflated prices and making profits out of famines.

The constant reiteration in Siena and other medieval urban centres of the theme of the evil of usury derived from the main economic strands in Sienese life and, in particular, the predominance of banking in her economy. Filippo Agazzari, another wealthy Sienese who had retired to a hermitage at Lecceto, in his *Assempri*, a collection of moral tales written towards the end of the fourteenth century, reverted again and again to the subject of the evil of usury. His usurers inevitably die a miserable death, devoid of all hope of eternal life, the corruption of their bodies which he recommends, 'should be buried in the ditch with dogs and beasts; not in churches and holy places',[27] symbolizing the corruption of their souls.

This particular strain in Sienese piety was as prevalent in the sixteenth century as in the fourteenth and is epitomized in the preaching of that strange religious fanatic, Bartolommeo Carosi da Petroio, known to the Sienese as Brandano, whose opposition to urban values was as staunch as that of any medieval saint. His hatred of the market knew no bounds and he attributed all human misery to banks and to the usury they engaged in, telling bankers and merchants that: 'The earth brings forth abundance and you have created famine.'[28]

Nevertheless, the origin of such ideas, for all of their animus against the urban life, lies in a distinctively civic Christianity, well-rooted in a flexible but robust tradition. Religion in Siena was far from being the preserve of a separate priestly or clerical caste, and, in fact, the most characteristic expressions of religious piety were essentially lay-orientated ones. The *Arti* or guilds were one such manifestation. The origins of all guilds were religious and their statutes show a marked religious orientation; they oblige their members to observe religious festivals; to keep their shops shut until after the daily sermon throughout Lent; they fine their members for blasphemy. In fact the original functions of the guilds were more related to that perennial medieval problem of ensuring the saying of prayers for the soul in purgatory than they were to craft needs. By requiring all the guild members to attend the funeral of one of their number, they were also a means of easing the passage between this world and the next by providing ceremony and corporate prayer and mourning. For such purposes the guild was better suited than the parish, simply because of the nature of urban society, which meant that, even in a town like Siena where local ties were strong, men still tended to associate by occupation. As religious institutions the guilds were each associated with a particular church, or with a particular altar within a church, and, around one or the other of these, the corporate life of the guilds revolved, reaching an annual climax in the great Corpus Christi day processions, which in Siena, as in so many other towns in western Europe, was the great guild-festival.

Another important manifestation of urban Christianity were the religious confraternities, made up of groups of like-minded men and women who met together for various pious purposes. There were a very large number of these confraternities in Siena; at the beginning of the eighteenth century, when they were already in decline, they still numbered some fifty-four. Many were of medieval foundation, dating particularly from the period immediately following the Black Death; many more date from the troubled early sixteenth century, but some were still being founded in the seventeenth and eighteenth centuries. Although often locally-based and largely concerned with the religious life of the *contrade*, the confraternities all originate in a common impulse—they are a practical response to the problems which were created in attempting to adjust the traditional feudal structures embodied in the institutions of the church to the looser and less hierarchical life of the town. In social terms the confraternities proved to be of immense benefit to Siena. Each reflected in microcosm the social structure of the city, for, within each, the various classes of the city could be found working together. As a result, a new avenue of communication and control between the ruling élite and the poorer members of city society was opened up. The primary purpose of the confraternities was also, like that of the guilds, to provide a link between the living and the dead. As a secondary purpose, they had the obligation of penance and existed as a defence of their members against the wrath of God. This was particularly true of the flagellant confraternities like the Disciplinati di Santa Maria della Scala, the Compagnia dei Penitenti, and the Disciplinati di San Michele.

But the confraternities also came to act as great charitable institutions, for this was something which grew naturally out of their more purely spiritual life. Criminals and prisoners were a frequent object of concern and the Company of St. John the Baptist, known as the Company of Death, specialized in providing care and comfort for condemned criminals who were buried in their oratory. In the eighteenth century the Company still regularly distributed bread, salt and coal to prisoners in the communal gaols, who, without such assistance, would often have been left to starve or freeze to death.

The poor of the city were another universal concern. The lay confraternity of St. Anthony Abbot in San Martino, for instance, took as its special charge the extreme poor of the city, devoted time to nursing in the hospital of Santa Maria della Scala, organized elementary schools, and assisted beggars. The Congregation of St. Peter was likewise founded in 1522:

> to provide generous alms and continual assistance, both to the dead and to the living, particularly to poor and marriageable girls, to the sick, and to the poor of all kinds, at all times, but particularly in times of famine.[29]

And a very common charitable concern of the confraternities were those, like distressed gentlefolk, too ashamed to beg. In this latter case, spiritual concern coupled with social custom occasioned a particular type of charity. This was also true of the common practice of providing dowries for young girls. Thus matrimony was encouraged and fornication discouraged.

Another whole range of general charities was aimed at the temporary alleviation of poverty. Some of this charity was distributed on a regular basis; on 16 January, for instance, the Company of St. Anthony Abbot regularly distributed money and bread to 350 paupers, and on 12 June the Congregation of the Pious Gentlemen of San Onofrio provided a dinner for thirteen of the city's poor. Much charity, however, was purely occasional: payments to mothers who had given birth to twins, to foreigners in need, to accident victims, to the relatives of persons too poor to pay for a funeral.

To their own members, however, the confraternities exercised a more systematic charity, providing for the sick, the old, the infirm, the orphaned, or for other victims of the accidents of life. Thus, for instance, the Company of Death regularly provided alms to sick brothers and sisters in the form of money, food or medicine, or to paupers who were members of the confraternity. Small loans to members to tide them over temporary difficulties were also common.

It is through this world of active charity and a civic Christianity manifested in the guilds and confraternities that we can best approach St. Catherine. With a characteristic sense of occasion, Catherine Benincasa was born on 25 March, Annunciation Day, 1347, in the district of Fontebranda, together with a twin sister who died shortly after birth. Catherine was thus the youngest of twenty-five children, born to a prosperous dyer, whose family was extremely active in Sienese politics. Catherine's own brother, Bartolo, was deeply involved in the turbulent upheavals of the later fourteenth century and her entire family were to be ruined by revolution in 1368.

It is significant, therefore, that despite her personal asceticism, having felt a religious vocation, Catherine in 1364 should have chosen to enter not a nunnery but the third order of the Dominicans. As a tertiary, she could live in the world while not being wholly of it, and her choice indicates a positive and reasoned rejection of the monastic ideal which she saw as largely irrelevant to urban life. A major feature of St. Catherine's thought, and one of her most original contributions to the whole Catholic tradition, was her emphasis upon the value of the lay and secular experience. She saw the diversity of life, the manifold occupations and designs of men, as a manifestation of the 'greatness of God's goodness'.[30] Nor did she have that fear of wealth and riches that was experienced by so many other Sienese mystics. Although she at one time prayed that her own family might fall into poverty since she believed that their temporal prosperity was a primary cause of their evident spiritual inadequacies, she did not see property, worldly possessions, and position in the secular order as a bar or even a hindrance to salvation:

> because everything is good and perfect and created by Me, Who am the Supreme Good, for the service of my rational creatures . . . wherefore, in whatever condition a man may choose to be, he may have a good and holy will and be acceptable to Me. . . . Those wishing to remain in the world, can do so, possessing riches, retaining their dignities, living in the state of matrimony, bringing up their children and striving for them in whatever condition they may choose.[31]

The condition which Catherine herself chose was to continue to live in the house of her father. Here, much to the annoyance of her family, who would have preferred her to make a good marriage, for three years she lived the life of a recluse, speaking only to her confessor and teaching herself to read. By 1370 her reputation as a mystic was already considerable and she began to gather around her a group of young Sienese who met regularly for discussions in the chapel of the crypt of Santa Maria della Scala where, today, the Brethren of St. Catherine still meet for their devotions.

In 1374, Siena was visited by one of the many fearful plague epidemics by which the city was devastated in the second half of the fourteenth century. During the epidemic, Catherine, who had personally buried eight of her nephews and nieces, together with a few of her friends selflessly devoted herself to the care of the sick and the dying. For weeks this group of young men and women were the only people who moved about the empty and desolate streets, helping to bury the dead and comforting the stricken, the dying and the bereaved. 'Never', wrote a friend of Catherine at this time, 'did she appear more admirable', and for the following five years she continued to pursue a life of active charity within Siena, caring for an old, sick, prostitute, visiting hospitals, prisons, and the dreaded leper-hospital which lay just beyond the city gates.

Catherine constantly emphasized that love of God and love of one's neighbour were inseparable:

... because love of Me and of her neighbour are one and the same thing, and, so far as the soul loves Me, she loves her neighbour, because love towards him issues from Me. ... The soul, enamoured of My truth, never ceases to serve the whole world in general, and more or less in a particular case, according to the disposition of the recipient and the ardent desire of the donor.[32]

Yet she also made it plain that the physical well-being of the Sienese was by no means the first of her concerns. Her ultimate interest was in their spiritual welfare, and, in particular, their preservation from those peculiarly urban related sins which seemed so characteristic of the Sienese. Avaricious men called forth particularly scathing comment, since in her view they acted:

like the mole, who always feeds on earth till death, and when they arrive at death they find no remedy.[33]

Avariciousness is evil because it is the direct denial of charity. In consequence, just as charity is the chief binding force of the community, so avariciousness is its primary destroyer:

... how many are the evils that come of this cursed sin ... how many homicides and thefts, and how much pillage with unlawful gain, and cruelty of heart and injustice! It kills the soul and makes her the slave of riches, so that she cares not to observe My commandments.[34]

Injustice was also bitterly condemned and was seen by St. Catherine as originating in false divisions of class and caste within society. Although her own disciples were drawn from the Sienese ruling élite, she had a fundamental belief in the value of equality within the city-state, since, 'virtue is the only thing that makes us gentlefolk.'[35] In accordance with these views she roundly condemned the order founded at Monte Oliveto by a number of Sienese noblemen in the early fourteenth century, because it accepted only legitimately-born aristocrats within its walls.

Such views gave to Catherine her abiding passion for politics, whether Sienese, Italian or European. In relation to Siena, her concept of the nature of the ideal state was essentially a medieval one. All her emphasis lay upon the corporate nature of the state, an idea vividly expressed through her image of a person's vine:

> joined directly to their neighbour's vine, so closely that no one can do good or harm to his neighbour without doing it to himself, and all of you together make up the universal vine which is the whole congregation of Christians, who are united in the mystical body of Holy Church from which you draw your life.[36]

Given such a corporate vision of society, factionalism and strife are evil, manifestations of bad government, undoubtedly meriting divine censure. In consequence, St. Catherine urged the Sienese to pursue the virtues of unity and concord, which alone could bring them good government and justice.

This latter aspect of the message of St. Catherine was taken up, amplified and preached with even greater intensity by the fiery Observant Franciscan, San Bernardino. A native of the city since the age of eleven San Bernardino had a great affection for Siena and could name with love its every street, alley and building. The direction of his spiritual life towards an outgoing, charitable, piety, was indubitably the fruit of a Sienese experience, in the home of the two aunts who brought him up; one was an Augustinian, the other, a Franciscan tertiary, whose life was devoted to the seven works of mercy and who told Bernardino, 'when a beggar comes to your door, put a loaf under his cloak but so secretly that you are hardly seen, even by yourself.'[37]

This early exposure to standard manifestations of urban piety was built upon subsequently by every aspect of Bernardino's typical upbringing in Siena. It was at the University of Siena that he chose to study and it was here in 1400 that he and a group of twelve of his University companions followed the example of St. Catherine and devoted themselves to the care of the sick during a plague epidemic. At the age of eighteen, like many of his fellow Sienese, he joined the aristocratic confraternity of the Disciplinati di Santa Maria della Scala. Later he entered the Franciscan order and had a distinguished career as a preacher and teacher. He was often sent to preach in Siena: in 1405 in the Oratory of San Onofrio, in 1410 in the cathedral, in 1425 on the Campo; and, the most famous occasion of all, on the Campo on 15 August 1427 when he began a long and famous series of sermons, first capturing the attention of his audience by recounting a vision of Siena, its four gates, and:

> the glorious Virgin Mary standing before her Son, beseeching Him with humble prayers, to protect the city of Siena, which has taken her for its advocate in every peril and adversity.[38]

At the Virgin's request four angels were immediately dispatched to guard the gates of Siena.

These sermons were both great civic and great religious occasions, the entire population of Siena being gathered together to listen to the man who, however he might castigate them, still showed himself imbued with a love of the city which, like St. Catherine, he compared to the soul and called a 'demi-paradise'.[39] He showed nothing of the traditional medieval antagonism to the urban experience. On the contrary, for Bernardino the life of the city was entirely good, seen, as it had been in the Lorenzetti frescoes of which he was a great admirer, as a means of bringing great prosperity, civilization and learning to the world. Inevitably opposed, like all the Observant Franciscans, to any form of usury, Bernardino yet urged the value of trade and industry and recommended the turning of money and precious objects to productive use through commerce. Prosperity, provided it was enjoyed with temperance, was good not evil; trade and industry contributed to the Common Good in that they produced wealth, and it was wealth alone that permitted the exercise of charity and the survival of the state. For Bernardino one of the most important of charitable objects was the University, for it was the seat of learning. Without learning, no truly Christian community could exist, for study and learning were fruits of the spirit and beloved of God. Bernardino therefore impressed upon the Sienese the necessity of maintaining their University, and declared its care and support to be an act of piety. Equally important were the hospital, 'one of the eyes of the city',[40] and the other, the Cathedral.

City-life, therefore, was good in Bernardino's eyes because it allowed a higher form of existence. But he was also aware that city-life brought its own dangers. In particular, like St. Catherine, he exhibited a deep hatred of factionalism:

> Hold this as a certain truth that there is no more sinful a people nor one more mad, than that which permits party-strife . . . hold this as a certain truth that there is no worse nor more evil a sin than that of supporting a party . . .[41]

Throughout his career, he urged the Sienese to substitute the holy monogram—YHS—for the badges and symbols of party, and no visitor to Siena can remain unaware of the fact that, at least in externals, the Sienese *did* try to follow their beloved preacher's behest. Apart from the great symbol on the Palazzo Pubblico, there are to be found many houses, even of quite recent date, still decorated with the holy monogram.

The reiterated insistence by all such saints and preachers that the evils which befell Siena were the result of party-strife and factional fighting also had a deep psychological impact. No people so divided against itself has ever advocated or pursued unity as relentlessly as the Sienese; they came to see the abolition of faction as the only political reform ever necessary in their city. They singularly failed to reflect that factionalism and division might actually result from genuine problems within the body politic, and, in consequence, never addressed themselves to such problems. Thus, as late as 1552, when it was clear that the real conflicts and divisions within society were hastening the demise of the republic, the *Balìa* or executive committee set up to reform the city did little more than mouth traditional platitudes, advising the abolition of factions and parties without beginning to consider the conditions which made such factions and parties inevitable.

Another consequence of this Sienese view of the world was a more constructive one. Since factionalism was endemic in Siena, the wrath of Heaven was permanently threatening the city. In an effort to ward off the divine judgement which they saw as inevitable, the Sienese therefore threw themselves into charitable works. The belief in Siena as the Virgin's own city also had an humanizing effect upon government, impelling it towards practical good works. San Bernardino but repeated a Sienese commonplace when he told his fellow-citizens that alms were a greater defence of their city than were its walls.

Charity consequently became an important arm of the state in Siena, where the government made many regular payments towards the upkeep of religious houses both in the city and in the dominion, 'in order to render thanks to God for his benefits to the republic'.[42] The beneficiaries of such charity were, for their part, required to pray 'for the salvation of our city and the preservation of our liberty'.[43] Dowries were provided for poor girls and alms were regularly distributed to the poor. Even during the appalling financial crisis of the 1530s when the whole future of Siena hung in the balance, the government, 'for the love of God', refused to pressurize its debtors. The University was maintained and encouraged as was that institution whose existence was interwoven into the daily life of the city to such an extent that it completely exemplifies all the civic values of Siena—the famous hospital of Santa Maria della Scala.

The buildings of this hospital date from the end of the thirteenth and the beginning of the fourteenth century. They are still in use and occupy the whole side of the Piazza del Duomo, opposite the cathedral façade, and, like the cathedral itself, they reflect the unity of the religious and the secular in the life of the Sienese community. It is impossible to disentangle the spiritual and secular interests of the hospital. Control by the commune over its activities was more or less complete, symbolized by a decision of the General Council in 1309 that a large stone plaque, bearing the communal arms, should be fixed to the main doors of the hospital to show that it belonged to the commune. This control became absolute in 1404 when, for the first time, the hospital's rector was not elected by the religious of the Cathedral chapter but chosen by Consistory. A communal point of view of its origins and the services provided by the hospital subsequently appeared in Vecchietta's *Vision of the Blessed Sorore*, painted for the hospital, and giving a distinctly lay version of the story.

Vecchietta's painting illustrates the pious legend, the very quintessence of traditional Sienese piety concerning the foundation of the hospital. According to this legend the hospital was founded towards the end of the ninth century by a cobbler named Sorore, who began by lodging pilgrims who passed through Siena on their way to Rome. At first he merely mended their shoes, then he began to nurse those of their number who fell sick on the way, and eventually he founded an order to carry on his work; the hospital Friars. The legend goes on to relate the dream of a woman, sometimes described as the mother of the Blessed Sorore, who saw upon the spot where the hospital was to be built a ladder reaching up to Heaven, and little children passing up it into the arms of the Virgin. In consequence a foundling hospital came to be added to the hospital.

The only truth in such legends is a metaphorical one. The hospital in fact began its life as a simple lodging-house for pilgrims, one among several founded in Siena in the early middle ages. It was originally created by the canons of the cathedral who were obliged to devote a part of their revenue to the relief of the poor, and who chose this means of fulfilling their obligation. It was already a hospital institution in 1090, nursing all diseases except leprosy. Success bred success, and the hospital was rapidly enriched by gifts and bequests from citizens. By the twelfth century, therefore, after the commune itself, the hospital was the most important corporate body in Siena.

For all social and economic disasters, as the six large frescoes painted by Domenico di Bartolo between 1440 and 1444 for the hospital illustrate, Santa Maria della Scala could offer some kind of relief; it buried the dead, gave shelter to foundlings, provided night shelters for homeless adolescents, 'lest they die of cold',[44] apprenticed orphans, provided dowries for young girls, provided free bread in time of famine, and, above all, cared for the sick.

This wide range of activities and services demanded, of course, extensive premises and, by the early fourteenth century, the hospital was already cramped. In 1336, therefore, it began a great programme of expansion by the construction of a large new hall, purpose-built for the care of the sick and foundlings. Construction work on this project continued until the early sixteenth century and was itself a major source of employment for many among the poorest classes of the city.

Every aspect of life in Siena was thus, in some way or another, connected with the hospital. It was among the most important property-owners, both in the city and the *contado*. Individuals, guilds, families and confraternities lavished patronage upon it. Among important confraternities that met in its crypt were the Company of the Blessed Virgin Mary, that of St. Catherine della Notte, and that of S. Girolamo, and the Guild of Weavers also at one time had a chapel in its crypt.

The importance of the hospital in the civic development of Siena would thus be impossible to over-emphasize. For centuries it was the civic institution in which the community took the greatest pride. So vital was the relationship that the survival of the hospital and of the state were seen as going hand in hand. Even in periods of great difficulty and stress, therefore, the authorities never forgot their obligations. Although on occasion they might shamelessly use the hospital as a source of capital liquidity to tide them over temporary difficulties, they did all in their power to uphold, maintain and embellish it. Even in 1553, when Siena, virtually bankrupt, was making an all-out attempt to refortify her state in preparation for the last great struggle of her independence, the *Balìa* would yet write to the Sienese commissioner in Grosseto:

> You will know how, at all times in the past, the magistrates of this city have always kept in mind the safety and the security of the affairs of the hospital of Santa Maria della Scala. They have kept these things in mind, since the hospital is a sacred foundation. Because we have always done so, we daily witness miraculous demonstrations of God's favour towards our city and so we are obliged to keep its interests constantly in mind.[45]

Thus, in the last years of Siena's existence as an independent republic, we find the governing impulses of her ruling élite to be what they had always been in the past: a recognition of the necessary union of the sacred and the secular within the urban community; a belief in the necessity of upholding the city's traditional urban institutions; but, above all, a continuing awareness that a Sienese citizen was distinguished by his ability to render unto Caesar the things that were Caesar's and unto God the things that were God's.

8

The Sienese Renaissance

Sta adonque, come fior sciolto da l'erba
Languida, nuda e scalza tra le spine
Negletta al mondo e povero e superba.

Il Saviozzo

THE BLACK DEATH has traditionally been seen as having as great an impact on Sienese cultural life as on the city's economy, society and government. It is held to signal the end of the most creative period in Sienese civilization, subsequent artistic developments simply marking the decline from the marvellous years of the early fourteenth century. An elaboration of this argument results in the image which modern-day Siena projects of itself: the city had no experience of the Renaissance of the late fourteenth, fifteenth and sixteenth centuries; it remained a medieval city, lost in an isolated Gothic dream, impervious to all subsequent developments in European thought and culture. Furthermore, we are told, when at last Siena's painters became aware of the new renaissance modes, which reached the city from Umbria and Tuscany, they still preferred the Gothic traditions, so that theirs are old-fashioned works whose only positive merits are naivety, charm and mysticism. The implication is that after the mid-fourteenth century the cultural life of Siena is no longer of importance, and that we would do better to shift our attention to Florence, Rome, or even Venice.

It is, of course, true that the Black Death was a disaster for Siena. Not only did the economic crisis which the epidemic exacerbated virtually end all major building operations in the city for some two generations, the Black Death also affected the cultural development of the city simply because it carried off so many major artists: Ambrogio and Pietro Lorenzetti, Giovanni d'Agostino, Lippo Memmi, Agostino di Giovanni and Agnolo di Ventura were probably all its victims. It is also true that this group of major artists was succeeded by another of younger painters, principally Bartolo di Fredi, Luca di Tommè and Andrea Vanni, who were all less gifted than the giants of the early Trecento and who abandoned many of the more recent pictorial innovations to re-adapt and explore the conservative elements present in Sienese art. This conservatism found expression in both style and content, as artists turned away from the realism of the early fourteenth century to articulate a renewed concern with hierarchy and the 'exaltation of God, the Church and the Priest'.[1] The humanizing of the religious experience that had meant so much to Duccio, Martini, the Lorenzetti brothers and their circle, seemed no longer a major concern.

Despite such changes, however, a traditional delight in the arts, and the structures that supported the city's cultural life, survived the plague epidemic. Sienese culture cannot be said to have been brought to an end by the Black Death. And, if we consider the problem of the renaissance not from a Florentine but from a Sienese viewpoint, we can see that Siena experienced just as important a cultural change between the late fourteenth and the early sixteenth centuries as did any other Italian city; that while this change may have differed from that which occurred in Florence, it was no less a significant one; and that while it may be true that Sassetta and his fellow fifteenth-century Sienese artists failed to approach the problem of perspective with the typical calculation of the Florentines, preferring to employ a naturalism which was but timid and episodic, they are, in no sense, medieval or Gothic painters. In fact, far from undergoing a cultural decline at this period, Siena actually produced some of the really great names of the Renaissance: Peruzzi and Francesco di Giorgio, and Beccafumi, not only the first, but the greatest of all the mannerist painters of Europe.

Perhaps there is still a tendency to assume that Siena is a medieval town because the lay-out of its streets and open spaces is indeed a medieval one. As we have seen, the relationships between the organic parts of the city were a creation of the fourteenth century. And it is true that within Siena some flamboyant examples of a prolonged attachment to Gothic traditions do exist. The most important Gothic palace in the city and certainly the most beautiful, that of the Salimbeni, was not built until the fifteenth century, nor was the Palazzo Marsili in Via di Città, designed by Luca di Bartolo Lupani, nor the Palazzo Tegliacci which today houses the Pinacoteca. But, while paying all due regard to such evidence, it remains true that, if the articulation of space within Siena is medieval, the definition of that space is often of the renaissance. Siena contains a few great works of renaissance sculpture:

6

Jacopo della Quercia's Fonte Gaia will stand comparison with any of
the works of Donatello and Ghiberti, who were his contemporaries;
Vecchietta's *Risen Christ* is, by any standards, an outstanding work,
while his *Tomb of Mariano Sozzini* of 1467 is among the greater examples of Italian renaissance portraiture. More important still are the
great works of renaissance architecture within the city: the papal
Logge, and the Palazzo dei Diavoli, both the work of the fine Sienese
architect, Antonio Federighi, the chapel on the Campo, Peloro's
church of San Martino with its fine and delicate sense of space, the
exquisite and decaying little Oratory of Santa Maria delle Nevi, the
centrally-planned Oratory of San Sebastiano in Valle Piatta, built in
the early sixteenth century, Santa Maria dei Servi, built between 1471
and 1528, Santo Spirito, begun in 1498, and, of course, the great renaissance palaces.

Our view of the renaissance in Siena is inevitably affected by the
sad fact that, for the most part, the renaissance palaces have subsequently been stripped of their furnishings and the works of art that
once decorated them; frescoes, for example, by Pinturicchio, Sodoma,
Beccafumi, Matteo Balducci and Peruzzi. Yet some idea of their
vanished glories can still be gleaned from the beautiful cycle of frescoes,
painted by Beccafumi on classical themes for Marcello Agostini in
what is now the Casini-Casuccini palace. Another major loss is that of
the painted façades with which many of the major palaces were decorated, such as the façade of the Palazzo Borghesi, decorated with 'many
figures of ancient Gods', which, according to Vasari, was Beccafumi's
first major commission in Siena. To see examples of such façades today,
it is necessary to visit Pienza or Colle Val d'Elsa.

For many other important renaissance developments in Siena the
vital physical evidence is lacking either because it has not survived or
because it has been so badly damaged as to make it difficult to interpret.
The most important work of sculpture in renaissance Siena was obviously the Fonte Gaia, but this has deteriorated so as to be almost un-
recognizable, and its present location in the Loggia of the Palazzo
Pubblico gives but a feeble idea of what it must once have looked like.
The most crucial painting by Paolo di Giovanni Fei is his *Polyptych* in
the Pinacoteca; it is the artist's only signed work, and therefore the
basis for determining the authenticity of every other work assigned to
him. Yet this painting is in poor condition and visibly disintegrating.
Over the centuries, once again, acts of vandalism have meant that
altar-pieces have been broken up. The re-assembly, even in theory, of

some of these is a matter of guess-work and dedicated detection. In addition, there is scarcely a renaissance altar-piece in Siena which retains its original predella. The loss of a predella is always regrettable, since it was more often there, rather than in the formal, main part of an altar-piece, that an artist's imagination was given full rein. In the case of Giovanni di Paolo the loss is particularly hard, since his greatest contribution to the art of renaissance painting was made in his predellas, and only one of these, that for the church of S. Stefano alla Lizza, to go under the polyptych painted by Andrea Vanni, is still in the position for which it was commissioned.

However, despite all such difficulties, sufficient evidence survives from the late-fourteenth, fifteenth and sixteenth centuries to convince us that, during this period, a distinct cultural shift took place in Siena, transforming the style both of the city itself and of the works of art within it. The difference in style which we have already noted between the Palazzo Pubblico and the Chapel at the foot of the Torre de Mangia is evidence of this, and it might be said that the transformation in style to which the chapel bears mute witness is the Sienese Renaissance.

The principal features of this new style are exemplified in painting by what we may take as a typical fifteenth-century work: Sassetta's *Madonna of the Snows* of 1430, the first Sienese painting to show the direct influence of the new font for the Baptistery which was completed in 1427. Much of the grace of the *Madonna of the Snows* derives from traditional Sienese traits: the hieratic and strict line, the verticality, the elaborately ornamented and embroidered clothes, the Simoniesque faces and the very formal pose of the Madonna and Child. The *genre* touch on the left of the Madonna of an angel making a snowball derives from the Lorenzetti, the scroll in the Child's hand from Martini. The frame is a traditional Sienese Gothic frame, but for all its traditional emphases, this is not a Gothic painting. It has a novel sense of volume and space, described by the flights of angels who are wheeling and turning against the traditional gold background and emphasized by the Christ-child whose right foot is moving him out from his idealized world into that of the spectator. Such a painting, therefore, implies the existence of a new concept in Siena about the relationship between man and his environment, no less real than that to be found in contemporary Florence. That same concept is also expressed through the new naturalism and realism of Sienese sculpture, in particular the works of Vecchietta, Neroccio, and Francesco di Giorgio, and through the new classically-inspired architecture, which,

however, remained true to Sienese elegance, and was never taken to
the purist extremes of Florentine and Roman classicism.

Why then did such stylistic changes occur in Siena? The answer to
such a question would traditionally be seen as involving both artist and
patron, yet, in Siena, there are very strong reasons for supposing that
the patron was the dominant influence. Until well into the sixteenth
century, commissioned works in Siena were still produced to a set of
most detailed instructions. Patrons not only prescribed the subject of a
painting, but sometimes even the style in which it was to be painted.
In 1447 the Guild of Grocers commissioned an altar-piece for its chapel
in the church of the hospital of Santa Maria della Scala from Giovanni
di Paolo. The subject of this painting was to be *The Presentation in the
Temple* and the contract specified that not only the subject but also the
composition and its treatment should be dictated by the rectors of the
guild. What the rectors demanded and what, to all intents and purposes, they got, was something very like Ambrogio Lorenzetti's *Presentation*, painted over a century previously for the Spedaletto of
Monna Agnese. In the following year, Sano di Pietro was commissioned to paint an altar-piece with a predella whose five compartments were to tell the story of the *Life of the Virgin*, 'like those on the
façade of the hospital.'[2] Sano, in other words, was to imitate the frescoes
which had been painted on the hospital by Ambrogio and Pietro Lorenzetti in 1335. Another typically conservative commission was given by
the Baker's Guild in 1477 to Matteo di Giovanni for their chapel of
Saint Barbara in the church of San Domenico. Detailed instructions
were indicated not only about its size and quality, but also about its
contents:

Item, that in the middle of the said picture, there shall be painted the
figure of Saint Barbara, seated on a gold throne, and she shall be
dressed in a robe of crimson brocade.

Item, that in the said painting there shall be two flying angels, holding
a crown over the head of the said Saint Barbara.

Item, that to one side of the said Saint Barbara, that is on the right
side, there shall be painted the figure of the German Saint Catherine;
and on the left the figure of Saint Mary Magdalene.

Item, that at the top of the said painting there shall be . . . the story
of the three Magi, who will be approaching by different routes, and
at the meeting of these three routes, these Magi will come together
and go to make their offerings at the Nativity: it shall be understood

that the Nativity will contain the Virgin Mary and her Son, Joseph, the donkey, and the ox, as it is customary to paint a Nativity. . . .[3]

Instructions so detailed left little real room for originality, although they did not prevent Matteo from producing a remarkably beautiful painting. The result of the gifts of Matteo and close supervision and control by the Bakers' Guild is a highly typical work of the Sienese renaissance.

Strong evidence of the power of the patron is also to be found in the kind of work often produced by foreign artists working in Siena. Spinello Aretino's work in the Sala di Balìa of the Palazzo Pubblico is, as we have seen, very close to Sienese tradition, and that produced by Niccolò de Naldo di Norcia and Gualtieri di Giovanni di Pisa in the sacristy of the cathedral is indistinguishable from traditional Sienese. Matteo di Giovanni was Umbrian in origin and had trained under Piero della Francesca, yet his paintings show little of this background and much of the influence of Domenico di Bartolo, with whom Matteo studied from 1450 to 1457. All the Sienese traits of aristocracy, mysticism and hierarchy predominate in his paintings, despite their additional monumentality, restraint and mastery of contemporary techniques. The paintings of Sodoma also suggest that in response to the demands of his patrons, he too came, in the end, to be more Sienese than the Sienese themselves.

The power of the patron affected stylistic developments in another way, for it was always the patron who chose the subject-matter of paintings, and it was often the challenge of new subjects which led artists to change their style. But in this area Sienese patrons seem to have been quite astonishingly conservative. In the first place, although we know that Sienese fifteenth-century artists were interested in portrait-painting from life, there appears to have been virtually no demand for portraits from Sienese patrons until the very end of the century. In the second place, the demand for any other kind of secular painting was equally limited. Surviving secular works from the period before the mid-sixteenth century fall for the most part, into two distinct groups. The first of these is made up of painted marriage pieces, especially salvers and *cassoni* or marriage chests. The second are peculiarly Sienese and of such a nature that they need not concern us greatly in this context. These are the political subjects which were painted for the Gabella and Biccherna covers. As with the *cassoni*, it is clear that these were commissions which were occasional and extraordinary, rather than the norm.

In consequence, the emphasis within Siena was still on religious paintings. But even here the patrons seem to have demanded a narrow range of subjects. At least half of all the paintings commissioned between 1350 and 1550 from Sienese artists were for paintings of the Madonna in one guise or another. Yet the very brilliance of Siena's early fourteenth-century masters meant that virtually every possible elaboration on the theme of the Madonna had already been explored by 1350, and the Sienese renaissance artist could do little more than imitate, copy, vary or comment upon the works of the Lorenzetti or Simone Martini. Thus, at the very beginning of the fifteenth century we find the artist, Andrea di Bartolo, turning out endless variations on a now-vanished *Madonna Lactans* of Simone Martini, and Taddeo di Bartolo producing a cramped version of Simone's great Uffizi *Annunciation*, and even at the very end of the century Matteo di Giovanni producing his own version of the same painting. A good run-of-the-mill high renaissance painter, Girolamo del Pacchia, could still produce an *Annunciation* Madonna which echoes that of Simone as she shrinks from the angel, her veil pulled over her face. Similarly, at a distance of a hundred years, Sano di Pietro's *Nativity of the Virgin* is closely modelled on the great painting of the same subject by Pietro Lorenzetti. It is no wonder, given such problems, that the paintings of the Sienese in this later period sometimes appear wooden and devoid of inspiration or that when these artists were at last given a new theme —the *Massacre of the Innocents* or the *Madonna of the Snows*—they should have done it to death.

The power exercised by Siena's patrons was clearly very great. Hence, in relation to the innovations of style, their influence must have been of paramount importance. The principle question, then, is the degree to which those changes in style in Sienese art that do occur, are themselves reflections of changes in the structure of Sienese patronage. As we have seen, in the period before the Black Death patronage of the arts in Siena had been largely corporate and communal. Even family palaces were built, not in order to honour an individual, but for strictly utilitarian reasons: defence and the encouragement of family solidarity or to celebrate the power of the family clan. The largest single employer of artists and craftsmen was the commune of Siena itself. Since, however, the commune was only as wealthy as the sum-total of the wealth of all its citizens, the decline of the economy after the mid-fourteenth century meant the impoverishment of the commune which found it increasingly difficult to finance prestige projects.

The face of a city where in the later fourteenth century plague and famine became endemic must have been desolate indeed. The decline in population had led to the abandonment of more recent areas of settlement; in 1385 the commune decided to sell its property 'outside the gate of Val di Montone which has long remained unused'.[4] A church which had been erected in the same area was by 1402 in ruins and much regretted for it had been 'so very lovely and well-proportioned'.[5] The city was full of empty and decaying houses and by 1380 of the number of large buildings which had been erected by the Wool Guild in the early fourteenth century only three were still in use. By 1422 the economy of the city was so decayed that the commune was forced to admit that 'all the guilds of Siena are idle and, in general, reduced to the worst possible condition'.[6]

Throughout the fifteenth and the sixteenth centuries the situation remained much the same. The public water-supply, created with so much optimism in the thirteenth and early fourteenth centuries, was, by the end of the latter century, too expensive for the commune to maintain adequately, with the result that by the early sixteenth century the city's fountains were only 'half-full of water'.[7] The street-system fared no better. By 1394 the streets were in so bad a state that their complete repair and repaving was ordered. Four years later the Francigena was still in such a condition that 'it was unusable in bad weather'[8] and the Via dei Banchi:

> which runs from Piazza Tolomei to Porta Solaia and than which there is no street more beautiful, neither in Florence, nor in Venice, nor in any other city in Italy,[9]

could be described as completely ruined, fronted only by the shops of cobblers and tailors, where once had stood the *botteghe* of merchants, bankers, goldsmiths and drapers.

Such money as the commune could find was, for the most part, necessarily allocated to one particular cause—the refortification of Siena and its dependent towns, since, with the virtually continuous warfare of the period, and the increasingly effective use of cannon, this was believed to be the imperative need. So vital was it that there was scarcely a charge on the communal revenues which was sacrosanct when it came to finding money for fortification purposes; less important building-projects inevitably suffered. Thus, for instance, we find that in 1412 the £1,400 which had been allocated to the Fonte Gaia project was being diverted to the fund which financed the building and maintenance of the city-walls. The importance of such fortification projects explains why the city did continue to employ state architects who were known to be of proven ability as military engineers, even though artists on the grand scale, working within the established Sienese tradition, like the mural painters Barna and Bartolo di Fredi, had to leave Siena to find work. But because they did work mainly on fortifications, two of the greatest renaissance architects, Francesco di Giorgio and Baldassare Peruzzi, have left but scant evidence of their activity in Siena despite having given many years of service to the city. Fortification works by their very nature tend to be ephemeral and, today, only one of Peruzzi's beautiful curved bastions survives to illustrate the work which he undertook in 1528 in strengthening the city's walls. Equally transitory in its nature was the work of Anton Maria Lari, il Tozzo, who was created communal architect in 1537, but whose entire working life was devoted to the design of fortifications.

Despite all the difficulties the community faced in the wake of the Black Death, Siena was not prepared to abandon all concern for its cultural life. The communal authorities were as interested as ever in the appearance of the city and always anxious that it should be embellished. Nor did the sources of civic patronage dry up completely. Individual government offices and officers continued to commission important works: Sano di Pietro was employed by the Biccherna to produce a fresco of San Bernardino in their offices and it was for the office of the *Biado* that he painted his famous *Virgin commending the city of Siena to Calixtus III* in 1456. In fact, in the fifteenth century, when the economy had recovered slightly and there was new civic enthusiasm, resulting from the expulsion of the Visconti, the commune began to spend heavily on the arts once more. As we have seen, Taddeo di Bartolo, Paolo di Giovanni Fei, Andrea di Bartolo and Spinello Aretino were all commissioned to execute frescoes either in the cathedral or in the Palazzo Pubblico. It was at this time also that the cathedral was embellished with the stained-glass windows of Fra Ambrogio Biondo, while for thirteen years Domenico di Niccolò was at work on the choir-stalls of the Palazzo Pubblico. On the Campo Jacopo della Quercia erected the Fonte Gaia, while in 1417 the Loggia della Mercanzia was commissioned.

The citizens of Siena remained deeply concerned about the appearance of their city and bombarded the General Council with petitions like that of 1397 which proudly maintained that:

Your city has always been the most beautiful and the most clean of any in Tuscany and possessed of the most beautiful fountains. For this reason, all the foreigners who visit it want to see the Fonte Branda . . .[10]

Citizen concern thus continued to be part of the collective will shaping the city. As we have seen, Domenico d'Agostino's original Orcagnesque design for the chapel on the *piazza* had to be abandoned in the face of popular complaint, and the original plan of the Fonte Gaia had to be modified from fear of citizen reaction. The continued commitment of the citizens to the fabric of Siena even led in 1413 to the creation of a new communal office, the three *Ufficiali sopra l'Ornato,* who for more than half a century were to direct their efforts towards maintaining and improving the appearance of Siena, 'continually thinking of anything that may embellish the city and particularly the road to Rome along which foreigners pass'.[11]

Subsequent disputes over the building of the Loggia della Mercanzia reveal a continued and widespread involvement in the city's image. On 21 November 1421 Consistory was asked to put its mind to the problem of the design of this Loggia, since the three architects and master-masons who had been commissioned to design and build it were in basic disagreement over the form the new building should take, with the somewhat ludicrous result that:

on one day they build in a certain way and on the following destroy and rebuild in a different manner.[12]

Consistory referred the matter to the Council of the People who, in turn, elected a committee to make the final decision. This committee then widened the debate still further, asked the opinion of 'a great many citizens and craftsmen'[13] and looking at 'many designs by skilled masters'.[14] Even when a final decision had been made the designs were displayed 'for very many days in front of the Merchants, Palace, and . . . in the Council Hall, for the better information of everyone'.[15]

However, despite such wide public involvement and concern, all the works of art financed by the commune in this period were, essentially, minor projects, the completion of works which had originally been conceived in the early fourteenth century. The commune's role as a patron was, therefore, essentially a conservative one, and the dynamic of artistic change is to be found in the private domain which was becoming increasingly important.

6*

Art was now used for the first time for the aggrandisement and delight of the private individual rather than for that of the community as a whole, and it is significant that it is in the fifteenth century that we can begin to identify individual patrons in the works of art which they commissioned. The outstanding example, of course, is that of Aeneas Sylvius Piccolomini—Pius II—for, to this day, Siena bears more the stamp of Aeneas Sylvius than it does of any other individual. Throughout the city we come across Piccolomini half-moons on walls, monuments, ceilings and even floors; the Logge raised by Pius and dedicated to his family in 1462, and the Piccolomini palaces, dominate the city both by their size and by their elegance. Pius's impress even lies heavily on the communal records; among the *tavolette* is one from the Biccherna of 1460 by Vecchietta, illustrating the coronation of Aeneas as Pius II, and another from the Gabella of the same year shows him investing his nephew, Francesco Todeschini Piccolomini, with the cardinal's hat. The archives of the cathedral also preserve a constitution granted by Pius, who raised the status of Siena from a bishopric to an archbishopric, with an illuminated frontispiece showing the Pope enthroned, and, kneeling before him Agapito Cenci di Ruspoli and Antonio Piccolomini.

In this period when it was individual rather than collective power that dominated Siena's cultural life, the grandest articulation of private power was the great palace. It was in the fifteenth and early sixteenth centuries that all of the most luxurious of the Sienese palaces were built: the Palazzo del Magnifico, designed by Cozzarelli for Pandolfo Petrucci and decorated by Pinturicchio, Signorelli and Genga; Palazzo Piccolomini d'Aragona, designed by Rossellino and built by Pietro Paolo del Perina da Casale, which even the eighteenth-century critics thought might 'take first place in any city in Italy';[16] Palazzo Piccolomini delle Papesse, now the Banca d'Italia, designed by Rossellino and built by Federighi and Urbano da Cortona for the sister of Pius II; Palazzo dei Diavoli; Palazzo Spannocchi, begun in 1470 by Giuliano da Maiano for Ambrogio Spannocchi, the treasurer of Pius II; Palazzo di San Galgano and Peruzzi's Palazzo Celsi.

There was, of course, still a public function to buildings whose primary purpose was to manifest to the world the power, wealth and prestige of their owners, and their foundation-stones were laid with all the solemn pomp and formality which had once attended the founding of the great Sienese public buildings. The private palaces made an immediate impact on the urban fabric very similar to that produced by the Palazzo Pubblico. Just as, in an earlier period, the style of that public palace had been immediately imitated in all buildings within the city, now these private palaces found just as enthusiastic imitators; four years after the laying of the foundation-stone of Palazzo Spannocchi, for instance, the Monks of San Galgano announced their intention of building a house in the city, 'just like the palace of Ambrogio Spannocchi'.[17] Thus the building of these great palaces tended to have an effect upon the appearance of the city in general.

The commune itself well appreciated the public dimension of such palaces whose splendours could only reflect glory on Siena and improve its appearance. For this reason, just as the commune had always given assistance to ecclesiastical buildings, now it gave judicious assistance to creators of secular palaces. Such aid might take the simple form of the granting of permission to encroach on communal property for the sake of the regularity of a façade, or the waiving of certain building restrictions. But it might also mean exempting certain building materials from the payment of Gabelles, and on occasion even the giving of direct assistance; in 1465, for instance, the *Ufficiali dell'Ornato* proposed that the commune make Tofi Sansedoni the *podestà* of Buonconvento in order to assist him in the completion of the Sansedoni palace:

> considering how ornamental the said palace will be when it is finished, and that it stands upon the main street of our city.[18]

Yet, whatever the public dimension of these buildings, their purpose was individualistic—the celebration of the patron who built them. They were private palaces. And even buildings which were public in their nature, yet had some private purpose. Thus the Piccolomini library, in its lunar extravagance, is not an integral part of the cathedral, but a celebration of Pius II and his family, whose coat-of-arms Pinturicchio was instructed to paint, 'richly and beautifully'.[19] Similarly, the other set of frescoes by Pinturicchio in the cathedral decorating the chapel of St. John the Baptist, tells us less about the Baptist than it does about the patron of the chapel, Alberto Aringhieri. And the Oratory of Santa Maria delle Nevi was largely a celebration of the wealth of Bishop Cinughi who had it built in 1470 on the site of a ruined palace of the Malavolti.

In addition, even in public patronage of the arts, the role of the individual was now often more significant than the role of a committee. In 1460, for instance, Pius II simply over-rode the artistic judgement and the wishes of the commune whose authorities requested him to employ Vecchietta as the architect of his Logge. Pius preferred to use the Piccolomini *protégé*, Antonio Federighi, and by so doing he made Federighi rather than Vecchietta the official communal architect. Equally important, as we have seen in discussing the building of the cathedral, was the influence of Pandolfo Petrucci. During his ascendancy Petrucci managed the city by getting himself elected or nominated to every key body, and acting as chairman over a number of contending groups. Significantly any committee which was in any way connected with the arts tended to find Pandolfo a member of it.

The important patron in Siena was thus no longer the commune or, indeed, any corporate body, but the individual member of the ruling élite. But the part that élite played in the life of the city between 1350 and 1550 was deeply affected by a series of profound economic, social and political changes and it is these changes that underlay the shift from an art which was essentially public to one which was essentially private.

The later years of the fourteenth century, which were years of economic decline or stagnation, were marked by increasing tension and instability in political life, typified by the disastrous year of 1368 when, between September and December, the constitution was changed four times in order to make room for new contending power groups. Noble factionalism which, to some extent, the Nine had managed to curb, revived with a new virulence to disturb the peace of the city. Externally the period also saw a series of disastrous foreign wars, though these were far less damaging than were the successive visitations of mercenary bands who either ravaged the *contado* or had to be bought off with huge ransoms or chased away by other, equally expensive, mercenary troops. In twenty years Siena paid out 275,000 florins to such mercenaries but was still unable to prevent the pillaging of the *contado*. Finally, in 1399, the Sienese were forced to resort to the desperate remedy of surrendering their city for ten years into the hands of Gian Galeazzo Visconti, the tyrant of Milan. Although the Sienese poet, Il Saviozzo, was to celebrate this event in one of the last and finest outpourings of literary Ghibellinism, to most Sienese the Visconti tyranny over their city represented its ultimate humiliation and degradation.

These political upheavals left their own characteristic impress on Sienese life, for it was in these years that the divisions hardened between the city's *monti* or *ordini*. Unique to Siena, the *monte* was originally a means of designating those families who had served in one of the city's ruling signories. There were by the end of the fourteenth century five of these *monti*, each the ultimate heir of one of the ruling regimes of the previous two centuries: the Gentiluomini or Nobles, the Noveschi or Nine, composed of all the families who had ever contributed one or more members to the office of the Nine, the Dodici or Twelve, whose forebearers had overthrown the Nine in 1355 and who were themselves overthrown by the Riformatori—the Reformers—and the Popolari or Popular party.

While, in some ways, the *monti* were useful political institutions, they inevitably tended to become ends in themselves and so to make of Siena, in the eyes of one Florentine critic, 'not so much a republic as a hotch-potch . . . or one might say, a confusion of republics'.[20] In truth, between them, the *monti* so divided the ruling citizen élite of Siena that stable government was impossible except by, at best, a broad coalition of all parties and, at worst, one between the Nine and the Popolari, the two most numerous of the *monti*. Fortunately, it was not always impossible for the *monti* to work together and successful coalitions account for periods of stability in the late fourteenth, fifteenth and early sixteenth centuries, including that of the so-called 'tyranny' of the Petrucci family.

Further evidence of political instability in Siena is provided in the fifteenth century by the development of the system of government by *Balìa*, which indicates a breakdown of traditional systems of communal government. A *Balìa* was originally a committee to which power or authority was delegated for some special and limited purpose and for a restricted period of time, but it gradually became converted into a permanent magistracy and from 1455 until the fall of the republic the College of the Balìa had supreme authority in Siena and largely replaced Consistory.

The *Balìa* was the political expression of a more generalized change in the nature of Siena's ruling-classes, by which the city's élite redefined itself and its interests, and, largely in response to external pressures, became more exclusive. Among such external pressures the most significant was that from the artisan classes trying to gain access to the power structures of the city. Such pressure was fairly continuous in Siena in the later middle ages but reached fever-pitch during the 1360s and 1370s when its most spectacular manifestation was the revolt of the Compagnia del Bruco, the first major revolt by paid workmen of the middle ages.

As we have seen, the rapid political changes in Siena after 1355 coincided with a series of epidemics, bad harvests and consequent food shortages. They also coincided with a number of disagreements over wages and conditions of work between the wool-workers and the Masters of the Wool Guild. In 1370, in the Ovile district of the city, some 300 of the lower paid wool-workers, led by the artisan Domenico di Lano, formed an association which, from the emblem of their *contrada*—the caterpillar or *bruco*—was known as the Compagnia del Bruco. In July 1371 motivated largely by hunger, a number of the company forced their way into houses where grain was known to be stored and seized it for their own uses. The War Captain of Siena was called, seized three of the leaders, put them to torture, and condemned them to death. Immediately the entire Compagnia del Bruco rose as one man, joined with others of the lower working classes of Siena and, resolving to liberate their leaders, attacked the Palazzo Pubblico. Having captured the palace, where they displayed the banners they had seized from the Gonfalonieri of the Terzi in order to testify to the legality of their actions, the rebels expelled four of the Twelve and three of the Nine from the ruling magistracy, substituting instead seven of the *popolo*.

A temporary and uneasy peace came to the city, which was broken by the leaders of the Twelve and some of the Salimbeni who aimed to use the situation to further their long-standing feud with the Tolomei. Unwilling to accept their expulsion from the regime, the Twelve planned to seize the government on 1 August. However, their plot came to light and they were forced to act prematurely on 29 July. They failed to capture the palace but they virtually destroyed the district of Ovile where they attacked the carders and wool-workers, hunting them as if they had been wild animals up and down the narrow streets and alleys. Then they fired eight houses, starting a conflagration which rapidly spread until it had engulfed the whole quarter of Ovile.

There are many ways in which these incidents can be interpreted, but, for our purpose, their significance seems to lie in the novel threat which the whole episode seemed to present to the traditional ruling classes of Siena. During the fighting, all law and order broke down, threatening the complete social fabric of the city. In addition, the Compagnia del Bruco had been able to enforce its will on Consistory fairly easily and had its own nominees, men who did not form part of the traditional ruling structure, imposed on the government. It then took between ten and twenty years for the traditional ruling classes to recover a dominant position in city life and to enjoy it with an assurance of continuity.

Once the ruling class had recovered its position it made sure it would never again be threatened. In the end, rather than risk such a threat, it was willing to preside over the annihilation of Siena as an independent state, for the response of this élite to the crisis of the late fourteenth century was to close ranks. As we have seen, in the past, Siena internally had been divided more by territory than by rank, class or occupation. In the fifteenth and sixteenth centuries this position was reversed as the ruling class came to identify their interests as lying with their own class in much the same way that, however fleetingly, the wool-workers demonstrated a nascent class-consciousness during the events of 1371.

Increasing restrictions were placed upon admission to this élite. Traditionally, admission to the citizenship of Siena and so to political privilege had been given fairly freely. But, from the late fourteenth century, it was far more difficult to become a Sienese citizen. Full citizenship and participation in government was now restricted to men who belonged to one or other of the *monti* and, eventually, in 1497 was legally reserved to 350 named houses, known as the Nobili Reggenti or Riseduti. Membership of this body became a jealously guarded privilege and citizenship came to be granted but rarely and then only to such men as Julius II, ambassadors of Charles V, or after 1552 to Henri II, Thermes, Lansach, Piero Strozzi and Montluc.

The nature of this ruling group was also changing as its membership narrowed. The Sienese aristocrats, as we may now begin to call them, began to become more like aristocrats elsewhere in Europe with a wealth based primarily no longer on trade, commerce and industry, but on agriculture. This did not, of course, happen overnight: the Salimbeni were still actively engaged in commerce in the fifteenth century and in the sixteenth century there were still a number of important Sienese banking families, particularly in Rome, where the Chigi, the Spannocchi, Alessandro Bichi, the Ugurgieri, the Tolomei, the Venturi, Pietro Borghesi and Stefano Chinuccio all had branches. Other aristocrats were still actively engaged in trade in the early sixteenth century; in 1509 Leonardo di Nanni Marsili together with Marcantonio Tolomei formed a company 'to trade with Rome';[21] the Buoninsegni, the Tancredi, the Marsili and Mino della Gazaia were all silk merchants and others, including the Bichi and the Petrucci, traded in wool. Nevertheless there was a shift of interest among the aristocracy as a whole, away from trade and commerce. Pride in a mercantile career was no longer a possibility; the social ideal of the new kind of Sienese aristocracy had become the leading of a leisurely life, its economic ambition to become a *rentier* class. When agricultural rents proved insufficient to support their chosen way of life, the aristocrats no longer turned, as they had in the past, to trade, banking or industry to create wealth for them, but to traditional feudal sources: the profits of office-holding or the church. Thus Pius II, who played a major part in the restructuring of Sienese society by insisting on the restoration of the nobility to a full political life, is reputed to have enriched many of the Sienese upper class by the grant of wealthy ecclesiastical benefices.

The withdrawal of the ruling élite from their traditional occupations and the change in their way of life was inevitably reflected in the cultural life of the city. The whole nature of Siena as an urban centre was changing. Without aristocratic participation, trade and industry languished. The aristocrats might make valiant efforts to restore their city's fortunes; the deliberations of the General Council in 1417, for instance, which resulted in the construction of the Loggia della Mercanzia, suggest that the major motive for its construction was a desire to foster trade. Any suggestions for the development of trade or industry were received very favourably. Government encouragement, however, was no substitute for active aristocratic involvement and even regulations like that of 1441 which ordered that:

> all citizens aged less than forty-five shall either work at something or else personally farm their lands in the Maremma, Valdichiana or Valdorcia; and any who do not do so . . . will be ineligible for any communal office. . . .[22]

proved to have no long-lasting effects on aristocratic ways of life.

In the middle ages the city had been the main creator of wealth, the pace-maker in the economy of the region into which wealth flowed from the capital. But, from the time of the Renaissance, Siena became instead a consumer of wealth produced, not within her walls, but in the surrounding countryside. Rather than the hive of industry which Lorenzetti had illustrated, it became a centre of conspicuous consumption, inveighed against in a series of ineffective sumptuary laws.

In former centuries, much of the vitality of Sienese culture had sprung from constant contact between the ruling élite and the mass of the urban population. Much that was important in the life of the community took place in the streets; art was public and common property.

But, from the mid-fourteenth century onwards the whole impulse was towards withdrawal and privacy, a withdrawal of the aristocrats in particular either into their new private palaces opening on to a central courtyard rather than on to the street, or into their country villas where they now tended to reside throughout the summer months.

The new world being created was one of a host of mini-courts. For, in his household, each aristocrat tended to maintain a number of retainers and clients, among whom were to be found the musicians, writers and artists whom fashion dictated he maintain. The artist, therefore, began to leave the commercial workshop and to become attached to the noble household. It was often in this way that he was launched on the world; Sodoma, for instance, was introduced to Siena by the Spannocchi, Antonio Federighi by Pius II and Beccafumi by the patron who even gave him his name. Writers, too, detached themselves from their traditional civic, clerical or monastic environments, to become an integral part of noble households. The strange chronicler and historian of Siena, Sigismondo Tizio da Castiglione, for instance, was the dependent of Niccolò Borghese, 'who maintained him in his household and considered him one of his clients.'[23] Here, too, was to be found the source of protection enjoyed by the large number of sixteenth-century heretics and Protestants, for, within the noble household, they became virtually immune from the penalties of the law. The inability of the authorities to control Brandano, for instance, is largely explained by the privileged position he occupied as a client in the Buoninsegni household.

Another important structural change in the cultural life of Siena, related to the changing mode of life of her aristocrats, was the creation of that totally novel institution, the Tuscan academy. These academies were pioneered in Siena where, by the early years of the sixteenth century, there already existed some kind of aristocratic gathering which included Claudio Tolomei, an early enthusiast of the Tuscan language, Gabriel Cesano, Bartolommeo Carli de'Piccolomini and Giovanbattista Puliti, and which was dedicated to the study of Latin, Greek and Tuscan and the promotion of poetry and eloquence. By 1525 this informal gathering had probably already been formalized into the Accademia degli Intronati, the earliest modern European academy. Later records of the sixteenth century, looking back to the founding of the Intronati, emphasize its aristocratic ethos and, in particular, that retreat from the active and committed life which we have noted as a characteristic feature of the economic and social development of the Sienese ruling élite in this period. In the records we read that:

> There met together in our city a group of noble souls, outstanding in various branches of learning, who . . . desired to found a society . . . which leaving aside all troublesome and wearying problems, and every other worldly care . . . should devote itself solely to the study of literature . . . and from their firm intention neither to intervene in nor to concern themselves with anything else in the world they took for their name the Intronati.[24]

Aristocratic in its aims, the Intronati was symptomatic of a new age in that membership was restricted. The non-aristocrats could only participate in this new world by creating their own academy, that of the Rozzi, from whose membership aristocrats were in turn excluded. This was, indeed, a totally novel situation in a city where in the past rich and poor of all classes had traditionally shared in all cultural activities.

Such structural changes in the cultural life of Siena had a varied but decisive impact. One significant feature of the new aristocratic way of life was that palaces now tended to be lavishly decorated and furnished, as men of property began to invest heavily in artistic objects for private use and enjoyment. Such aristocratic practices were quickly imitated, particularly among the professional men of Siena. Thus a petition to the *podestà* recorded that in 1476 Prospero Poccio, a doctor of law, had commissioned painted bed-hangings 'for the customary adornment . . . of the nuptial chamber',[25] and the Sienese doctor, Bartolo di Tura Bandino, had several paintings in his bedroom, including two devotional images, one of Saints Cosmas and Damian and one of a Madonna and Child with Angels.

Such small, portable images are to be found with increasing frequency in Siena after the mid-fourteenth century. A typical triptych at that date would consist of a central gabled panel on which was painted the *Madonna Enthroned with the Christ-child* with a scene—most commonly *The Crucifixion*—in the gable. The Madonna's throne would normally be surrounded by angels and saints. The wings of the triptych depicted single or paired saints and often the Virgin and Angel of the Annunciation in the gable. Diptychs did vary more widely in their subject-matter, but normally depicted the *Madonna*, *The Annunciation* or *The Crucifixion*. All of these altar-pieces were still elaborately cusped and ornamented in gilt.

The fact that one can stereotype Sienese altar-pieces in this way shows how derivative they were. Their production was clearly a major source of income for Sienese artists, and thus was of benefit to the community for it meant Siena could continue to support a large number of artistic workshops. On the other hand, such workshops tended not to be innovatory in the period between 1350 and 1550, but to turn out popular and repetitive pieces. Few of these are of any real artistic interest although all are pleasant and some are very beautiful. Paradoxically, in this case, the creation of works of art for private rather than public consumption produced artistic conservatism rather than change.

A more positive feature of the new cultural environment, and one manifested in the Academy of the Intronati, was the enthusiasm with which the aristocrats embraced the new humanism in letters. The general decline of the Sienese economy was never reflected in a general decline in the city's cultural vitality. The first half of the fifteenth century was probably the University's greatest, when the city was enlivened by the presence of students, drawn from all over Europe, but particularly from Germany and Spain, to study under the great masters of the Sienese Studio. The University was as actively supported by the community as ever, and particularly in law and medicine, had a reputation second to none in Europe.

Siena, where the humanist Antonio Panormita was given a communal reception in 1434 and where Francesco Filelfo was appointed to the Chair of Oratory in Greek and Latin literature in the same year, was also one of the great centres of the new humanism, and Sienese humanists mixed with their fellows as equals throughout Italy. Aeneas Sylvius Piccolomini is, of course, the outstanding example of the successful Sienese humanist, but there were many others. In the Piccolomini family alone, besides Aeneas, there were to be found Bartolomeo Carli, author of certain Ovidian verses and translator of the *Aeneid*, and Alessandro who was one of the most distinguished philosophers and classicists of his age. The Sienese Neoplatonist Pietro Cennini was much admired by Ficino, Filelfo trained a fine pupil in Agostino Dati, and Bartolo di Tura Bandini was a friend and correspondent of Lorenzo dei Medici.

The rich library which Bandini left after his death in 1483 revealing a wide range of interests was probably typical of those belonging to many contemporary Sienese. It included philosophical and classical texts, among them a copy of Caesar's *Commentaries*, 'decorated with

miniatures in gold'.[26] Another inventory, made of the library of
Niccolò di Bartolommeo Borghesi in about 1500, lists more than 400
volumes. These included virtually all known Latin literature as well
as a few translations from the Greek, Valla's *Elegantiae*, the works of
Filelfo, Agostino Dati, Flavio Biondo and Platina, Pier Paolo Ver-
gerio's *De liberis educandis*, and Marsilio Ficino's *De vita studiosorum*.
Other libraries contained the works of the major Italian writers. Between 1438 and 1444 Vecchietta and Giovanni di Paolo decorated a
beautiful edition of *The Divine Comedy* and in 1461 Stefano di Luigi
of Milan undertook to copy and illuminate Petrarch's *Triumphs* for
Francesco di Facio Belliarmati, 'with my own hand and as beautifully
as I can'.[27]

Although such an emphasis on the beautifully illustrated and decorated manuscript is characteristic of the Sienese, it is a measure of
Sienese interest in the literary changes associated with the renaissance
that Siena should have made an early appeal to the entrepreneurs of
the new printing industry. As early as 1484, with the active support of
the professors of the University and the communal authorities, the
first printers were at work in Siena. The worlds of humanism and
literature were therefore as vital in Siena as they were in any other
Italian city and were in no sense isolated from the artistic community.
Siena was a small world in which everyone who mattered, including
scholars and artists, knew everyone else. Yet, despite the new enthusiasm for classical literature, the impact of humanism on the arts in
Siena was, compared with Florence, but slow and faltering.

The difference was not a question of simple ignorance. Sienese
patrons and artists were fully aware of contemporary developments
in the arts in the rest of Italy. Indeed, one considerable consequence
of the change in patronage structures within Siena was the opening up
of the Sienese to the experience of other centres. Many of the aristocratic patrons, such as Pandolfo Petrucci and the Piccolomini, displayed
an almost conscious cosmopolitanism, welcoming and encouraging
the works of non-Sienese artists. Such patrons were anxious to be as
up-to-date as possible. Pius II introduced the Florentine architects
Bernardino Rossellino and Giuliano da Maiano to Siena, and his sister,
Caterina Piccolomini, clearly took pride in the fact that her new
palace had been designed by 'a most excellent modern master'.[28] In a
contract made with Pinturicchio for the Piccolomini library in 1502,
Cardinal Francesco Piccolomini displays a conscious desire for artistic
innovation in his insistence that the design must include those elements

'which today we call grotesques',[29] and a similar attitude of mind is apparent in his contract with Michelangelo who was required to make fifteen statues for the Piccolomini altar which were to be 'finished with greater modern perfection than is even to be found in these days at Rome'.[30]

Their desire to be in advance of the times meant that these patrons brought many new artists to work in Siena for quite extended periods. The Piccolomini were responsible, for instance, for introducing to Siena the highly influential miniaturist, Girolamo da Cremona; he worked on the antiphonals for the Piccolomini library between 1468 and 1473, along with the equally influential Liberale da Verona. The Piccolomini were also responsible for the presence of Pinturicchio in the city almost continuously from 1503 to 1506.

The conservatism of Sienese art in the renaissance cannot therefore be explained in terms of Sienese patrons' or artists' unawareness of contemporary styles. What is in question is that conscious rejection of the Florentine manner which has so often perturbed commentators on Sienese art. Sassetta, for instance, clearly knew and understood Florentine painting. His *Last Supper* from the Arte della Lana altar-piece, painted between 1423 and 1426, shows a renaissance interior which could have come from the brush of any contemporary Florentine, and his *Adoration of the Magi* in the Chigi-Saracini collection is evidence of his perfect understanding of the laws of perspective and foreshortening. Yet, by and large, Sassetta remained wedded to the Gothicizing tradition in Sienese painting. Similarly, the Sienese painter most closely associated with Sassetta, Sano di Pietro, was also clearly aware of the new Florentine developments as a glance at the faces of his Madonnas will confirm. Yet Sano, who was exceptionally good at decorative effects, also made a very conscious use of traditional Gothic modes, even reverting to the convention of varying the scales of figures within a painting to indicate their relative importance in the divine hierarchy. The same could be said of his contemporary, Domenico di Bartolo. A study of his frescoes in the Pellegrinaio of the hospital reveals an artist who, while aware of contemporary Florentine innovations, of which he makes a veritable parade in his paintings, willingly reverted to Sienese norms: the two-dimensional image, a dependence on harmonious line, the filling of space with decoration, the confusions of heaped bodies and a profusion of colour. Domenico's ambivalence of attitude is particularly evident in his architectural backgrounds which are a curious, ill-matched medley of Gothic and renaissance styles.

Vecchietta, who died in 1480, for all his up-to-date borrowings from the Florentine and Sienese architectural renaissance—shell-topped niches, coffered roofs, classical columns and garlanded friezes—reverts to the Sienese type in his figure painting and landscapes, and in the conscious patterning of his work on the frescoed vault of the Baptistery. Giovanni di Paolo toyed briefly with the Florentine idiom and remained much under the spell of Uccello, but he uses Uccello's techniques to create a dreamlike or unreal landscape, and it is clear that his basic inspiration derived from Sienese models. Not only did he constantly echo Sassetta, he even looked back to Duccio, to Simone Martini, of whose work he was intensely aware, and to Ambrogio Lorenzetti, whose landscape painting lies behind Giovanni's *Flight into Egypt.* Even at the very end of the fifteenth century, Neroccio di Landi and Francesco di Giorgio are remarkable as painters, not because of their often rather heavy-handed Florentine classicism, but for a suavity and grace which is all Sienese, for a willingness to abandon the tyranny of the laws of perspective when it suits their purpose and, particularly in the case of Francesco, for a truly Sienese delight in jewel-like and striking colours. They succeed, in essence, in holding the classical and the Gothic worlds together in suspense.

In the creation of altar-pieces there may, of course, be solid functional reasons for Sienese conservatism. The majority of Sienese churches were dark and badly-lit, excepting always the cathedral, San Domenico, San Francesco, and Santa Maria dei Servi. If images were seen at all they were seen largely in candlelight. In such a context the continued use of a gold background was almost a necessity, since all paintings must have appeared largely as silhouettes against the gold of such a background. The three-dimensional image of the renaissance was often extremely difficult to see even in a church like San Martino where only fore-knowledge and the eye of faith enable one to make out Lorenzo Cini's *Madonna of the Victory of Porta Camollia*. Yet, despite such functional needs, a surprisingly determined Sienese preference for the two-dimensional and decorative treatment must be acknowledged. This, no doubt, explains the Sienese enthusiasm for that grisly subject, *The Massacre of the Innocents*, which Matteo di Giovanni alone was to illustrate four times, for it is a subject which lent itself well to decorative treatment, to the instant transmigration from one figure to another, and so to a reading from side to side rather than from front to back, as Florentine renaissance conventions demanded.

The fundamental cause of the rejection of such Florentine conventions by the Sienese lay in the different nature of the culture of the two cities, and, in particular, in the fact that, whereas in Florence there was a natural emphasis on the written word, in Siena the emphasis was all upon the visual image. The Sienese were always more impressed by what they saw than by what they heard or read. In a certain sense they thought with their eyes, and St. Catherine, who actually speaks of 'the eye of the intellect',[31] expresses her ideas through a series of images. It is abundantly clear that much of her spiritual life drew inspiration from actual paintings, as did that of the Blessed Andrea Gallerani and San Bernardino, who reminded the Sienese that 'we remember far more readily what we have seen than what we have heard'.

Despite therefore the major contribution made by the Sienese to the revival of humanism, dependence on the visual image remained the crucial factor in their cultural experience. In such a context it was inevitable that Sienese artists and, for that matter, Sienese patrons, should be responsive to and influenced by, not only their Florentine and Umbrian contemporaries, but also their own great artists whose works they had always before their eyes. Ghiberti noted with surprise that in 1450 the Sienese still regarded Simone Martini and Ambrogio Lorenzetti with admiration, and Sienese paintings confirm such a view. It was clearly difficult for the Sienese artist to escape from traditional styles and indeed doubtful that he even wanted to. Largely because the Sienese did think with their eyes they eschewed the radical, which the Florentines positively welcomed. It was this which gave to Sienese culture a sense of continuity, of a single development pursued by the whole community, and it was for this reason that Sienese humanism remained a largely academic exercise, whereas in Florence it found practical application in painting, sculpture and architecture. Thus at the very moment that Florence and Siena were to become involved in the greatest political and military struggle in their histories, their cultural traditions remained as aloof as they had been throughout the middle ages.

9

The Fall of Siena

Where is the Commune, there is the City.

UNTIL THE sixteenth century the political and commercial importance and the cultural strength of Siena clearly derived from the wealth and self-confidence of her ruling élite, for the characteristic style of Sienese civilization was nourished by a ruling-class which provided the material basis of the city's life, ran and manned its government, created and supported its charities, controlled its church and University, and patronized its culture. The urban artefact of Siena was essentially the creation of that élite. It is, then, not surprising that the most serious difficulty in the life of the city should have coincided with a profound political, economic and social crisis experienced by her ruling class. To a superficial observer in the first half of the sixteenth century Siena's rulers might have appeared as powerful as ever. In their own households and extended families the cultural dominance of the aristocrats was still supreme, their word law. In government they successfully maintained their monopoly of power, and the same names dominated Siena's councils as had dominated it for centuries. Nor was there any apparent erosion of aristocratic authority in the *contado* and state of Siena.

Yet the idea that all was well in this aristocratic world would have been essentially false. Familiar political alignments were crumbling, the consensus by which the aristocrats had maintained their position was breaking down. There was a revival of factional strife between *monti*, a complete collapse of governmental structures which had to be reformed ten times between 1525 and 1552, and, most serious of all, a breakdown of traditional allegiances to the *monti*. One manifestation of this last phenomenon is to be found in the formation of cross-party groups like the *Libertini*, a group of ardent republicans drawn from the Popolari, the Nobility, and the Riformatori. Another was that even the Nine were increasingly subject to internal dissensions.

In 1524, for instance, a contemporary distinguished four groups among them: those who were supporters of Fabio Petrucci, those who opposed Fabio but favoured his brother, those who opposed the Petrucci altogether since, during their ascendancy, 'they had been kept too low', and those who were in favour of a policy of 'quiet and just government'.[1]

On 18 September 1524 it was, in fact, a conflict between protagonists and opponents of Fabio Petrucci which heralded the outbreak of the series of rebellions and unstable governments which were to mark the next quarter of a century. The Petrucci were exiled from the city, authority was restored to the traditional communal councils and some three months later a new ruling Balìa of sixteen was created with the dual and unenviable task of reforming the city government and combating a French invasion threat. At the start the new regime was dominated by Alessandro Bichi, one of the Nine, a man of the highest probity and integrity, but, on 7 April 1525, Bichi was murdered by a group of the *Libertini* led by Mario Sallustio Bandini.

Under Bandini's guidance, a new constitution was devised by which power was shared equally between the Nine, the Popolari, and the Riformatori. Despite a series of difficulties, particularly in the *contado*, this regime lasted until May 1527 when the Sack of Rome by the imperial troops of Charles V created a general instability from which Siena could not hope to remain immune. The Sack depressed trade even further, and so sparked off unrest and attempted revolution within Siena. Factionalism revived with open opposition to the Nine; in July their houses were attacked and Piero Borghese, one of their leaders, was killed. The popular party being now in the ascendant, the *monte* of the Nine was deprived of any share in the government; soon, however, troops of the Emperor Charles V had to be dispatched to the city to quell continued street-fighting, and in 1530 these troops restored the Nine to the city.

Thereafter, largely at the instigation of the Nine, an imperial garrison remained in Siena, and it was in response to imperial pressure that a new reform of government was now attempted. Again, as in 1525, the main feature of the new constitution was enforced coalition through power-sharing, the offices in the city being equally divided among the *monti*. But despite this outward show of equality it was well known that the local imperial representative, Don Lope di Soria, was lending support to the leaders of the Nine who were rumoured to be plotting to seize exclusive power for themselves

by using the imperial garrison of 200 troops. In consequence serious
riots and street-fighting broke out, and the imperial garrison had to
be strengthened with another 200 men.

During the next decade the situation remained fairly stable, but in
1541 there came a fresh imperialist-inspired attempt to reform the
government of Siena. There was little that was novel about the new
scheme which remained true to what had by now become a traditional
model—a constitution based on power-sharing and government
through a Balìa. In this case the Balìa was to consist of forty men,
drawn equally from all of the *monti*, but at least eight of its members
were to be the nominees of the permanent imperial representatives
in Siena. Criminal and civil justice were taken out of the hands of
the Sienese altogether. Henceforth all legal cases were to be judged
by a Spanish-nominated Captain of Justice.

Initially, this particular constitution proved surprisingly successful.
The first Captain of Justice, Francesco Grasso, was a man of great
integrity who won universal respect as a dispenser of ruthlessly
impartial justice. By common consent the years 1541–43 were years
of 'good government' in Siena during which a careful balance was
maintained between contending power groups, and justice was
equitably administered. But, by 1543, it was already being rumoured
that the imperial representatives now permanently resident in Siena
were favouring the Nine at the expense of the other *monti*, and in
1545 these less-favoured *monti*, supported by the populace, revolted
and drove the imperial garrison from the city.

There followed the sixth attempt in twenty years to stabilize the
government of Siena. The Nine were exiled and some 300 exiles
were recalled by a hastily-summoned Council of the People which
proceeded to entrust the government to a Balìa of ten, composed of
the Captain of the People and nine priors, three from each of the
remaining *monti*. This attempt to equalize the distribution of offices
was not, however, maintained in the rest of the magistracies and
councils of Siena. Here the numerical strength of the Popolari, which
could only be balanced by the equally-numerous Nine, now excluded
from office, worked against the equitable division of power. Thus a
situation was created which would have produced instability within
Siena even without imperial intervention.

Imperial power in Siena was, in fact, re-asserted in 1547 when a
garrison of 300 troops returned to the city. In the following year,
despite open Sienese opposition, the constitution was changed once

more by the imperial representative, Don Diego Hurtado da Mendoza. He recalled the Nine, chose his own hand-picked Balìa, and appointed another non-Sienese Captain of Justice. Under very direct imperial surveillance, this constitution was to last until the dramatic changes of 1552. But, within twelve months, it was apparent that severe strains existed within the governing classes which threatened the breakdown of even this Spanish-inspired regime, and that it would only be a matter of time before this constitution too, like its predecessors, ended in failure.

The effect of such violent political oscillations on the cultural life of Siena was profound and marked. Since it was during these years that Beccafumi was creating some of his finest works, that Orlando Malavolti, the Sienese historian, was being educated, that the Academy of the Intronati was founded, and that the city produced in Lelio and Fausto Sozzini two of the most creative thinkers of the Protestant reformation, it would be difficult to suggest that all cultural vitality had left the city. The cultural institutions of the city still existed and the commune's concern with the appearance of Siena was as real as ever. Nevertheless, all contemporaries are agreed that the political situation seriously weakened Sienese cultural life, for in the 1530s and 1540s many of Siena's best scholars, writers, artists and craftsmen either left the city voluntarily or were exiled. The University was also brought to a state of complete disruption between 1530 and 1540; it had few good instructors, no economic resources, and a very unruly student population. As a result of Spanish and papal pressure, decrees against heresy were introduced in 1541, together with censorship of the Press. The number of permitted activities during carnival was severely restricted. Letters in and out of Siena were very effectively censored. Freedom of speech became impossible in a city where a momentary expression of exasperation could lead to arrest and imprisonment or exile. Freedom of association became impossible after 1535 when all popular assemblies, with the exception of those of the confraternities, were banned, and when any private gatherings, even for social purposes, were treated with acute suspicion. All in all, one is forced to respect the judgement of the great humanist scholar Paleario, who visited Siena in October 1530 and stated that the social and cultural life of the city had completely collapsed because of the unstable political situation.

Given such depressing consequences, the political instability of Siena, which was the despair of Charles V and his servants in Italy, seemed often to contemporaries to be an expression of deliberate Sienese perversity, while the Sienese themselves regarded it gloomily as a punishment for their sins and therefore irremediable. In fact political instability really stemmed from the crisis of the Sienese ruling-class, a crisis which was itself a reflection of fundamental changes in the economy of Europe. In the middle ages the power of the Sienese ruling-classes had derived from their great wealth, but the substructure which had created that wealth no longer existed. The wars of the sixteenth century, for instance, had seriously affected agricultural production in the Sienese countryside, doing long-term damage of such a nature that, in some areas, it was only repaired in the twentieth century. Devastation of such a nature, coupled with climatic changes and a declining population, produced a situation in which year after year bad harvests produced famine.

This agricultural crisis naturally affected the economic position of the aristocracy for, as we have seen, by the early sixteenth century the majority of the Sienese élite had most of their wealth invested in land. This, in turn, weakened the commune because it led directly to increased rivalry between the *monti*. As their economic position weakened, the aristocrats became far more interested in the potential profits of office. Governmental posts, particularly the lucrative positions in the *contado*, were becoming so important that all the *monti* were competing to make them exclusive rights for their members. Any political pacification in Siena, therefore, which involved the full restoration of political rights to any one of the *monti*, inevitably resulted in the loss of profitable office to members of others. Equally, the dominance of any one of the *monti* gave it a virtual stranglehold on the best and most lucrative posts. Therefore, the tendency of the imperialists to favour the Nine led to the fear that eventually the Nine would have a total monopoly of both power and profit within Siena.

In previous centuries, the collective wealth of the aristocracy had underwritten the prosperity and solvency of the commune. Now that collective wealth was declining just at the time when communal solvency was threatened by new demands upon available resources. Whenever famine struck, for instance, grain had to be imported from abroad, for the aristocrats knew that their survival as the city's élite was dependent on preserving the stability of the city's institutions. Equally they knew that nothing was more likely to threaten that stability than a revolt by starving labourers or peasants driven to take refuge in the city during a famine. Thus Siena continued to accept responsibility for feeding her starving subjects, but this involved the city in mounting expenditure. Equally costly were the largely unsuccessful attempts to solve the food-supply problem on a more permanent basis. These included projects for the creation of artificial lakes near the city where fish could be farmed, drainage schemes for the Maremma, and attempts to compel farmers to grow grain. The almost permanent warfare of the sixteenth century also strained communal finances. Of course, as we have seen, medieval war-making, particularly when it depended on the hiring of mercenaries, had been costly for Siena. Yet warfare and defence had then been intermittent rather than permanent expenses. The development of renaissance fortifications, designed to provide defence against the new artillery, meant now not only an initial capital outlay but also the cost of their garrison and maintenance.

Like other Italian states at this time, Siena also experienced an upsurge in the incidence of banditry and for Siena this had a particular and direct effect on the finances of the city-state. For it meant that, since banditry was worst in the Maremma, Siena lost the greater part of the valuable income she had always derived from rented communal pasture rights there. Under bandit influence and protection, cattle-stealing became a virtual way of life for many border communities, souring relationships with all of Siena's neighbours. Homicide and assassination were almost as common, and life and property could barely be protected within the walled towns of the dominion. Outside those walls armed might prevailed. In May 1530 the Sienese were even powerless to prevent a murderous attack on the guard of one of Charles V's emissaries, barely a few yards from the gates of Pienza. Nor could the safety of travellers on the Francigena any longer be guaranteed within the Sienese state.

Another major problem as far as the finances of the city-state were concerned, was the decline in population both within the capital city and in the dominion, for this meant a smaller group of persons from whom revenue could be raised. After the demographic disasters of the fourteenth century, the fifteenth century had witnessed a gradual increase in the number of births within Siena itself, but in the six-teenth century this trend was once more reversed. Even so, by com-parison with many parts of the dominion, the capital city was positively flourishing, for in the country areas depopulation was already a serious problem in the 1520s and was having an adverse effect on agricultural production. As the commune of Piancastagnaio explained to the Balìa in February 1530:

> because of the great shortage that there is here, the few men that remain have been forced to go elsewhere in order to earn a little money.[2]

Similarly in May of the same year, a Sienese representative at Casole reported that:

> almost all the young men capable of bearing arms have gone either to Volterra or to San Gimignano.[3]

And, in the same month, the community of Grosseto had to seek help from the Balìa, since although the grain was standing ripe in the fields it could not be harvested for lack of hands. Poverty lay at the root of the problem, but the situation was not improved by banditry and the associated activities of Sienese exiles in the *contado* where they seem to have lived a totally lawless life with virtual impunity.

The income of the Sienese state was therefore declining at a time when new and old obligations were imposing fresh financial demands upon it. Cumulatively, these demands were bankrupting Siena. In 1530 payments on the public debt were suspended for a year, the gabelles were doubled, and the coinage debased; but by the following year the situation had so far deteriorated that the Chigi and the Ugurgieri bankers, who came to the rescue of the state with a massive loan, refused to accept any security other than the personal obligation of each individual member of the Balìa. In order to function at all the government of the commune had increasingly to resort to the most hand-to-mouth expedients. It was so impoverished that it became heavily indebted to the imperial representatives in Siena and, even so, in order to send an embassy to Rome in 1531, the Balìa had to borrow money from one of their own number. Matters did not improve in the succeeding two decades and in 1552 the Balìa grimly spelt out the situation to the General Council:

> We find that everything has already either been pawned or committed and that money is so short that we cannot make the kind of provision the situation demands. . . . without help from your excellencies it is quite clear that we shall be unable to provide for the defence of our city as it is both our desire and our duty to provide.[4]

The burden of the Balìa's remarks was that it was no longer possible to remedy the city's bankruptcy. From the later fifteenth century every option had been closed as the commune began indulging in dubious methods of revenue raising: the sale of communal lands, of offices, vicariates, *podestà*ships, castellanships and benefices, state lotteries, frequent forced loans, debasement of the coinage, and increased salt-taxes. Virtually everything that could be was taxed, and such a very high level of taxation, combined with rising prices, had inevitable social and political consequences: popular discontent, manifested in riots and disturbances.

These sixteenth-century riots had interesting new features, suggestive of important changes within traditional Sienese society. It is true that certain members of the ruling élite, most notably Aeneas Piccolomini delle Papesse, and Mario Bandini—to whom the state was so heavily in debt that they could never discipline even his worst excesses —attempted to manipulate these riots towards their own political ends in a time-honoured Sienese manner. But there are also indications that the artisan class itself was becoming more articulate and moving towards an organized opposition to this élite who appeared to them to have betrayed their city. 1534, for instance, was a year of famine, and food-riots were only to be expected, but these particular food-riots bore a disturbing resemblance to the medieval revolt of the Compagnia del Bruco, for they had an organized artisan leadership. This leadership was provided by the Bardotti, a genuinely revolutionary group of artisans, artists and shopkeepers who, encouraged by some leading citizens, including Piccolomini, had been meeting together to discuss the works of Livy and Machiavelli and used the riots to demand admission into the closed circle of the governing body of Siena.

Nor were the Bardotti the only group of malcontents with whom Piccolomini concerned himself. In the mid-sixteenth century he emerged as the leader of the Giovani, a pressure-group which may be compared to similar groups in Florence and Venice, an alliance of young men anxious to break the oligarchic stranglehold on government. Their views were summed up in 1552 in the General Council of Siena, when it was argued that the exclusion of the majority of citizens from most areas of government had alienated them from the regime and so weakened the body politic:

because it may reasonably be believed that there are many in the city in every *monte* who, although qualified to sit there, are excluded from the Council. They are bound to be dissatisfied since they are denied that which their birth entitles them to. It is a received truth in all republics that all those who are truly citizens thereof should have a voice in the government.[5]

Meanwhile other Sienese citizens, like the Tolomei and the Bandini, were patronizing the activities of preachers of the Augustinian order or crypto-Protestants like Bernardino Ochino. In 1544, along with other Sienese aristocratic intellectuals, Basilio Guerrieri and Lelio Sozzini were actively encouraging artisan groups to adopt a fully Calvinist theology. These were organized in the lay confraternities, like that of the Trinity in the crypt of Santa Maria della Scala where an enterprising young artisan publicly denounced the role of the saints.

This heightened religious sensibility in the 1540s is but one manifestation of mounting tensions as the old order and its institutions were gradually eroded. Perhaps the most significant collapse of all was that of the system of justice, for, as we have seen, the good administration of justice had always been the binding-force of the city-state of Siena. The message of the Lorenzetti frescoes was not forgotten but was hammered home throughout the succeeding two centuries, and San Bernardino but echoed the sentiments of his fellow Sienese when he demanded:

What are states without Justice? Don't you know what they are? They are one long robbery. It is a well-known fact that cities and states always come to ruin if Justice does not reside in them.[6]

And Jacopo della Quercia showed a similarly elevated view of the value of Justice and its role in the maintenance of the state, when he recalled in 1428 to the Consistory of Siena that:

. . . . the Justice of governments does not render injustice either to the small man or to the great.[7]

By the early sixteenth century, however, the gap between such expressed ideals and the reality of the Sienese law-courts had widened beyond all credibility. Civil cases dragged on for generations unless the litigants had powerful friends in the Balìa; this situation was not helped by the recurrent plague epidemics when all the law-courts were closed down. Criminal cases were increasingly treated as political cases. Known criminals went about the city freely, if they were protected by powerful political friends, since no one had the courage to denounce them to the commune's law-officers. The growing power of the Balìa led to a blurring of the distinction between the executive and the judiciary, to more arbitrary and less open justice, and, ultimately, to justice that was simply partisan, a situation which as Ambrogio Catarino reminded the Balìa in March 1544, 'inevitably brings the ruin of kingdoms and cities.'[8]

The dangers inherent in the position were not lost on at least one impartial observer of the Sienese scene—Girolamo Morone, Chancellor of Milan. In 1525 he warned the Sienese:

If your Government ... does not see to the administration of Justice you will lay yourselves open to frequent disturbances so that you may lose the possession of your state along with the good will of the Emperor.

Morone was, in fact, expressing what became a standard imperialist view of the Sienese problem. Five years later, the Sienese representative in the imperial camp before Florence, after a series of peculiarly unpleasant interviews with the imperial commanders, warned his home government in the strongest possible terms to 'Remember Justice'.[9] Since his representations appeared to have absolutely no impact on the Sienese government, the Prince of Orange, Charles V's Captain-General, wrote himself on 8 June 1530:

Having been informed that there are daily committed in your Magnificent City insolences and disorders by some of your citizens, and that the affairs of Justice do not proceed with that order and reason which would be suitable in so ancient a republic, to the disgrace of those who govern, it has seemed that I should ... exhort your excellencies to prevent such scandals and not give cause to your enemies to complain of the government of this your city. You should consider the evils and inconveniences which occur not only to cities and republics but even to kingdoms and empires if those who govern do not care for the affairs of justice ... I thought that as a friend I would remind you of this and implore you that you will put your minds to reforming your systems of justice and government, punishing the insolent and the scandalous ...[10]

The importance which the imperialists attached to the question of restoring the administration of justice in Siena derived from the

7

belief that this was the only means by which stability could be restored to the city. Such stability was a primary concern because the constant turbulence of Siena created a kind of power vacuum in the centre of Italy from which the French might profit, and which threatened the position of the imperialists. If peace could not be imposed on Siena, it could not be imposed in Italy or, indeed, on the rest of Europe, and a lasting European peace was the primary objective of Charles V's policies.

At first Siena had maintained a strong Ghibelline stance in relation to Charles V. Of all the Italian states she alone seems to have welcomed his imperial election with positive enthusiasm and the eventual imperial coronation of 1530 was made an occasion for maximum civic celebration with processions, bonfires and fireworks. Subsequently Siena's support for Charles V's Italian policies was so marked that a contemporary suggested that Charles might command the Sienese 'as he would the inhabitants of Valladolid or of any other town in Spain'. Thus, for instance, while the imperial forces were laying siege to Florence in 1529–30 their commanders were able to use Siena as a bank, as a source of supplies and pioneers, and as a factory for artillery. However, the consequent drain on Siena's limited resources was crippling since, as the Sienese ambassador to the imperial army was to remark in 1530:

> If God does not soon grant us grace and bring this affair of Florence to a conclusion . . . we shall be forced to supply so much by way of provisions, meat and other things that we shall have nothing left for ourselves. . . . Whenever anything of that kind is needed their minds immediately turn to Siena, thinking that they have already shown us sufficient respect by not extorting money from us or molesting us directly.[11]

The coming of peace brought but little relief, for, even then, the relationship between the imperialists and the Sienese was largely an exploitative one on the imperial side. Spaniards in increasingly large numbers were placed in legal and administrative posts in the Sienese state, taught in the University, or enjoyed Sienese benefices. So many Portuguese and Spanish students were to be found in the University that in 1541 other students revolted against their dominance. Even the presence of Charles V's official representatives in Siena was very costly. They had to be given expensive presents. They had to be housed, fed, and provided with stabling and firewood at com-

munal expense—no small matter since imperial dignity demanded
that each representative should travel with a full retinue. In May 1530,
for instance, one emissary brought with him a train of:

> more than sixty ... and, although ... they were not all of his
> household, but merely in company with him, we have had to pay
> for them all since his stewards say that they are all his servants.[12]

If the visit of an imperial representative brought financial difficulties,
a visit or even worse, a threatened visit by Charles V himself was a
disaster. For, in the latter case, the city did not even have the opportunity to recoup its initial outlay on plans to welcome the emperor by
a temporary access of business to the city during the imperial visit.

Yet despite all these difficulties and strains, Siena remained firmly
loyal to Charles V and the imperial cause in Italy. Of course, one
reason for this loyalty was the imperial garrison which, as we have
seen, after 1530 was maintained in Siena permanently. Yet Siena
still remained a free city in that she was a privileged corporation,
not directly ruled by any foreign power, but controlled by her own
citizen-élite. In the view of the Sienese themselves they were also
free because in theory they lived within a framework of justice and
under their own law.[13]

Siena lost this freedom and independence for a number of reasons,
not least because the city rebelled against the satellite status she enjoyed
in the empire of Charles V. A second cause was the ambition of
Duke Cosimo of Florence to incorporate Siena within his own
principality, and so to fulfil the centuries-old ambition of the Florentines and realize the deepest fears of the Sienese. In pursuit of this
goal, Cosimo provided some of the troops with which the emperor
garrisoned Siena from 1528 to 1552, and gave considerable material
assistance in the two military campaigns leading to the fall of Siena
in April 1555. Meanwhile within Siena, by a judicious use of bribery,
flattery and reasoned argument, he succeeded in building up a body
of support among the ruling élite for the idea of the incorporation
of Siena into an enlarged Duchy of Tuscany.

Another important factor in the situation was Sienese resentment
against the kind of men who had been sent to represent Charles V
in their city, for Charles, in this case, seems to have had a flair for
picking the worst possible men for the job. In 1541 the Duke of
Amalfi, a relative of the Piccolomini, had to be dismissed for incom-
petence. He had caused trouble by his blatant favouring of the Salvi

family, and by his constant interference in judicial processes. Don
Juan de Luna, sent to the city in 1543, openly supported the Nine at
the expense of all the other *monti*, and dreamed of being given Siena
to rule as a principality under the crown of Spain. The last Spanish
representative in Siena, Don Diego Hurtado da Mendoza, was
expressly chosen because of his presumed expertise in Italian affairs.
As a young man he had studied at the University of Siena, and he
had close friends among the Piccolomini. He had been at one time
a successful ambassador both to Venice and to the papacy, but, for
Siena, he proved a disastrous choice. His rule there, all were agreed,
was arbitrary, partisan and unjust. He was a man of great pride,
little imagination, and virtually no sympathy with the pretensions
of the Sienese aristocracy. He was interfering and suspicious; when
in Siena he attended every meeting of the Balìa. In an attempt to
prevent factional street-fighting he confiscated all weapons; the
Sienese assumed that their loyalty to Charles V was in question and
took offence. Mendoza imported from Rome the cruel and partisan
Andrea Cruciato as Captain of Justice, and aroused suspicion by the
creation of two new judicial magistracies authorized to hear secret
denunciations and to take cases *in camera* and from which there
was no appeal. By 1550 Mendoza's control over the city was said
to be so complete that nothing at all could be done without his
consent.

In Mendoza's defence it must be admitted that, like all imperial
servants in Italy, he was starved of money by his home-government
and, in particular, of the necessary funds for paying the imperial
garrison. The problem of the pay of these troops had become a
running-sore in the relationship between Charles V and Siena. Charles
himself always drew a careful distinction between those soldiers
who were billeted in the city for Siena's own good, and which he
held the Sienese should pay for, and those billeted in the interests
of the empire who were, theoretically, paid from Spain. In fact, he
rarely provided money to pay any of the troops at all. Mendoza
therefore had to ask the Sienese to make up for imperial deficiencies
in this area. Although the ruling faction, naturally pro-imperial,
was usually willing enough to shoulder the burden of paying for an
arrangement, which, after all, kept them in power, it found it increasingly difficult to meet the obligation. By 1557, the garrison was costing
327 gold ducats a month for their pay alone, and the Balìa wrote in
desperation to Mendoza:

concerning the soldiers and the necessity of the Republic; that he will be pleased to intercede with His Imperial Majesty and ask him to remove this burden from the city.[14]

Not only did the disgruntled and often hungry troops, who were arbitrarily billeted on Sienese citizens, provoke incidents with civilians which increased the unpopularity of Charles V, they also sold their arms to the supposedly unarmed Sienese and deserted in large numbers, so that, when the crisis came, not one of the imperial units was up to full strength.

In such a situation Mendoza became obsessed with the need to raise money from the Sienese directly. He therefore raised taxes and forced loans without even the consent of the Balìa, let alone the traditional communal councils, fixed the price of bread to be sold to the soldiers—thus provoking a series of strikes and riots by the bakers —increased the price of salt throughout the Sienese state, and imprisoned anyone who dared to object. It was Mendoza also who first suggested that a fortress be built in Siena, partly as a means of retaining imperial control over the city, but largely because he was convinced that, without such a fortress, Siena could not be defended should the French invade Tuscany. In other words, the major reason for building the fortress had nothing to do with Siena at all, but was occasioned by international power-politics and the Habsburg-Valois conflict, in which the Sienese were involved only because of their traditional friendship with the empire.

To the vast majority of the Sienese, however, the building of the fortress presented itself in an entirely different light. They first learnt on 20 July 1550 that the familiar rumour that the emperor intended to build a fortress in their city was in fact true. To add insult to injury they were told that the fortress was to be built by their workmen and paid for by their money. Their immediate reaction was to see this decision by the emperor as signifying the loss of their liberty, the removal of all element of choice in their allegiance to the imperial cause. In addition, the proposal of Charles V offended the Sienese both in their sense of honour and their delight in their city. It was argued that if the emperor built this fortress, it would suggest to the rest of the world that he distrusted Sienese loyalty, and it was also believed that the building would destroy for ever the city's harmonious and beloved sky-line.

In their total hostility to the fortress the ruling élite found themselves more united than they had been for centuries. Yet, even at this critical moment, while recognizing the utility of doing so, they were unwilling to extend the very narrow power-base on which the state now rested and so render it socially and politically more cohesive. Throughout these last years of crisis, the aristocrats never considered extending political rights to a wider group of families within the city, or to their subjects in the Sienese state. On the contrary, this was an issue on which they found themselves perpetually in conflict with Mendoza. None of his actions had provoked more hostility than his introduction into the governing councils of new and able men who were not members of the traditional ruling-group. And when, in November 1550, there was talk of calling a special council of one man from each household in Siena to discuss the problem of the fortress, Mendoza found it easy enough to have the proposal vetoed. All he had to do was to threaten that each participant in such a council would subsequently be eligible for all government offices.

Thus the possibilities of action open to the Sienese ruling-classes were extremely limited. Their first response to the news of the intended fortress was entirely peaceful: an appeal to Charles V. Girolamo Tolomei was dispatched to implore the emperor to change his mind, and to suggest various alternative ways by which peace might be ensured in Siena. On his arrival in Spain, Tolomei was for three days denied an audience and even when he was admitted to the imperial presence, he was treated with complete disdain and told that there could be no question of the emperor rescinding his order, 'for as emperor he had decreed it and he did not want to withdraw his own commandments.'

Meanwhile, the citizens of Siena saw rising in their midst the hated symbol of their humiliation. The site of the fortress, on the north side of what is now the Lizza, had been marked out by their own architect, Giovan Battista Pelori. The foundations were being dug under the direct supervision of Mendoza who, resplendent in red velvet, came daily to inspect the work. He could not be altogether happy with its progress; Peloro had deliberately planned a fortress on such a scale that it would take years to complete, and the men who laboured on it were recalcitrant and slow.

Rather than watch the building-works go forward many Sienese aristocrats, among them Aeneas Piccolomini, left the city with their families and clients, and retired to their country estates. Here, among these voluntary exiles, an international conspiracy for the liberation of Siena was hatched, with ramifications spread through Rome, Ferrara and Venice to France where the French king finally committed himself, as part of his own struggle against the Habsburg, to the dispatch of aid to the republic of Siena.

Within Siena itself the Balìa had meanwhile appointed a new embassy to Spain, which was to carry with it a petition signed by a thousand of the more prominent citizens, and which was headed by the eminent historian, Orlando Malavolti. To this embassy, Charles showed himself more gracious, but he still refused to be deflected from his purpose. He insisted that the construction of the fortress must be hurried on.

Events were by now moving beyond the control of either Charles V or Mendoza or the harassed Balìa. On 26 July 1552 watchers on the walls and roofs of Siena observed towards evening an army of French and Italian troops, led by Aeneas Piccolomini, advancing on the city. Mendoza was at this time absent from Siena in Rome, trying to raise money to pay for the building of the fortress. In his stead he had left a young and handsome Spanish commander, Don Francisco de Alaba, whose strength of purpose at this critical moment was weakened by the very genuine affection he bore for the Sienese. Nevertheless he made what hurried preparations he could to defend the city.

During the evening of 27 July, as Piccolomini's troops waited outside the walls, the people of Siena rose, apparently as one body, shouting 'France' and 'Liberty'. Even the women joined in hurling stones from their windows onto the heads of the imperial troops who were retreating towards the high ground around San Domenico and the citadel which lay at the heart of the new fortress. As the whole city became involved in the fighting, the flaming of torches and the glow of lights in the windows were such that, throughout Siena, 'one walked as if the sun had risen'. The Sienese rebels within the city managed to open Porta Tufi while from without the French fired the neighbouring Porta Romana. Through these entrances the attacking forces burst, coming to the assistance of the rebels within. All that night and throughout the next day the fighting continued. Finally about four o'clock in the evening the Sienese managed to drive the imperial troops into the citadel.

Here they were besieged until the beginning of August when, after the intervention of Duke Cosimo, they surrendered. The imperial forces were allowed to march out to Florence with all their arms and baggage, and some at least left the city with regret; Don Francisco de Alaba shed tears when he found old Sienese friends waiting to say farewell at the city-gate. 'You brave Sienese' he warned, 'have made a most beautiful stroke; but for the future be wise for you have offended too great a man.'

With the departure of the imperialists the official French representative, Lansach, took possession of the partially completed fortress. There he summoned the city magistrates to meet him. They came in solemn procession with the banner of the Virgin unfurled in front of them and followed by all the other officials of the city, crowned with garlands of olive to symbolize the new era of internal and external peace about to be inaugurated in Siena. Behind the officials of the government came all the citizens of Siena, clergy and laity, bearing spades, pick-axes and other tools. Solemnly, in the name of Henri II, Lansach made over the fortress to the Sienese people who, without more ado, began to pull it down.

However, through the very way that their rebellion against the imperialists had been brought about, the Sienese, rather than regaining their liberty, had merely exchanged one master for another. The Sienese could only escape from Charles V by submitting to Henri II. And the position of the French in the city was to be strengthened in the following month when reinforcements arrived. Again in November the French hold on the city tightened. Cardinal Ippolito Este arrived with a guard of Swiss troops to act as Lieutenant of the King of France. But for two months the Sienese tasted what they believed to be the joys of Liberty and gave themselves up to play, giving no thought to anything but 'bird-snaring, hunting and enjoyment'. In December the blow fell. News reached the city that Charles V was already gathering troops in Naples to launch an all-out assault on Siena.

In order to strengthen the city against this new threat, Cardinal Este now ordered the building of new forts just outside Porta Camollia, and this order produced a sight rare in the annals of Italian republicanism. The Cardinal's request for volunteers for the new works was met by an overwhelmingly enthusiastic response. The Sienese voluntarily engaged in the enterprise in something very akin to a holiday spirit. Cardinal Este even ordered that music be played while the volunteers laboured and sent his own musician who 'played on the flute so sweetly that everyone stayed to listen to it as a thing most rare'.

At the beginning of 1553, however, a great imperial army of German lansquenets, Spaniards and Italians under Don Garcia de Toledo, brother-in-law of Duke Cosimo of Florence, invaded the Sienese state. The imperialists immediately occupied the Valdichiana and captured Pienza. They also took Monticchiello, after an heroic defence in which the garrison of the little castle surrendered only when the powder for their arquebuses was spent and they were reduced to fighting with stones.

Despite these initial successes, however, the first imperial attack on Siena was a failure. In the Maremma the Sienese succeeded in routing the imperial reinforcements which were landed from Sicily at Piombino, and although at the end of March the imperialists laid siege to Montalcino, the main fortified town on the route from Siena to the sea, they failed to take the town. They laid seige for eighty days but Montalcino was gallantly defended by 500 mercenaries, 1,000 Sienese volunteers, and all of its inhabitants, including the women. Then, on 14 June, help arrived; the French and Ottoman fleets were sighted in Sienese waters and the imperialists were forced to abandon their campaign.

Popular sentiment naturally attributed the subsequent withdrawal of the enemy to the miraculous intervention of the Virgin, rather than to the arrival of the French and Ottoman fleets. This assumption that heaven was on their side intensified among the Sienese a fool-hardiness, which encouraged them to prolong their struggle with Charles V to the point where negotiation was no longer possible. There were sober men in Siena who saw that the preservation of independence must now depend on permanent French aid, who reckoned that this aid would only be forthcoming for as long as the Sienese revolt was furthering the interests of the French crown, and that, in any eventual peace treaty between Habsburg and Valois, the French would bargain Italy away in exchange for substantial concessions on their own borders. Such men rightly argued that the prudent course must be to attempt to placate Charles V, but their cautious voices were completely drowned in a flood of popular rejoicing. Throughout the Sienese dominions, bonfires celebrated the imperialist departure while, in Siena itself:

all the bells of the churches rang out and the trumpets played from the roof of the Palazzo, in joy for the victory which had been won without a battle. Many old men and women were seen crying from happiness . . .

7*

This year of limited success was, however, to be followed by a year of disaster, initiated by the French king when he dispatched Piero Strozzi to Siena as his vicar-general. Strozzi, an exile from Florence and a lifelong believer in the republican virtues, was the bitter enemy of Cosimo de' Medici and although he gave a new ideological fervour to the struggle, his employment in the Sienese cause gave clear cause for Cosimo to declare war on Siena himself; the employment of a Florentine exile was an open breach of existing agreements between Florence and Siena which forbade either to shelter the other's rebels.

Towards midnight on 26 January 1554 news arrived in Siena that the Florentines had invaded their territory from the north, while an imperial army under the Marquess of Marignano was approaching from the south. The full weight of the empire of Charles V was thus thrown against the little city-state of Siena. Carrying all before it, Marignano's army first advanced purposefully upon Siena, but the imperial commander soon found that the Sienese had not been wrong to trust themselves to the impregnable site on which their city was built. Although Marignano quickly captured the new forts of Cardinal Este, he found that he could not force an entry into the city itself, nor was he subsequently able to find a traitor who would open the gates to him. He lodged himself in the elegant surroundings of Palazzo dei Diavoli and awaited events.

Although, for the present, Siena itself was secure, Strozzi knew it would be no novelty for an Italian city to be starved into submission. He was, therefore, convinced that his only chance of saving the Sienese state was to force Marignano to campaign in the open. Since he would have the unhesitating support of the local population and the mobility of a cavalry infinitely superior to that of the imperialists, Strozzi was convinced he must have the advantage. Even if he failed to tempt the enemy into open battle, he hoped that he would break the supply-line with Florence, for he knew that the imperial troops were already suffering from a shortage of food and money. He therefore begged for fresh reinforcements from France so that he might be released from the daily care of supervising the defence of Siena.

The French response was delayed until June, when Henri II at last sent fresh French and Swiss troops, under the command of Blaise de Montluc, who landed in Sienese territory on 8 July. Montluc promptly fell in love with Siena and identified completely with the city's struggle for survival. His enthusiasm is all the more admirable in that he was faced with the curiously unenviable task of trying to persuade the Sienese to co-operate together for the sake of the survival of their city. The initial unity of purpose which Charles V had created among the Sienese ruling élite by his decision to build a fortress had not lasted; by the time that Montluc arrived in Siena, discord and factionalism were as rife as ever.

As a consequence of factional struggles it had become increasingly difficult to reach agreement on elections to government office, and fewer and fewer citizens showed sufficient confidence in the regime to bother to attend the communal councils, despite the terrible danger in which the city now lay. Incredibly enough, in April and May 1554, Siena remained for a month without an Eight of War because of party discord, and, by September in the same year, it had become impossible even to get a quorum to elect the new Consistory, 'and many reckoned that the little concord of the Sienese would shortly send them all to perdition.'[15] It was only when those who were absent from the councils were threatened with a fine for non-attendance that the new Consistory could be elected. In the following month there were again problems connected with the election of the Eight of War in which Strozzi had to intervene personally; in the end the Sienese had to ask the French to choose the Eight for them.

Strozzi, then, was probably only too relieved to turn his back on the internecine squabbles of the Sienese. He entrusted the defence of the city and the management of its people to Montluc, and left Siena in order to occupy the little town of Marciano in the Valdichiana. He was followed by Marignano who drew up his troops to the right of Marciano, less than an arquebus shot's distance from Strozzi's camp. Neither commander was anxious to risk battle. The weather was stifling, the heat unbearable. There had been no rain for six weeks and the troops and horses of both armies suffered extremely from the consequent water-shortage. Marignano and Strozzi entered into a trial of nerves and pride to see which could force the other to decamp first. For four days from 29 July until 2 August Marignano's heavy artillery pounded Strozzi's cavalry which suffered many losses, but Strozzi refused to follow Montluc's sensible advice that he retreat to safety under cover of night. Instead he chose to engage in a battle which issued in his overwhelming defeat. The majority of his officers were killed along with many of his infantry. His Swiss mercenaries suffered less heavily but only because, as soon as they saw that the battle was going against them, they surrendered to the imperialists.

Altogether, between the dead, wounded and prisoners, Strozzi lost
at least 12,000 men:

> And whoever had seen so many soldiers of so many nations, without
> equipment return to Siena in the evening, wounded and depressed,
> as they threw themselves on the ground or stretched out on benches
> and low walls . . . must have wept or else had a heart of the hardest
> stone. Everyone who saw them was moved to compassion, as were
> those who heard the pathetic laments, particularly from the Germans
> and the French who besought a little something to drink or a
> little salt for their wounds, while men and women of the city
> brought them bread, wine and salt and aided them as best they
> could.[16]

So serious was this reverse that Siena was only persuaded to persevere
in its resistance by the direct pleadings of Montluc, his active measures
for the defence of the city, and his promise of more French aid. God
seemed to have turned his face against the city. The French did not
default on their obligations completely, but they failed to send
sufficient assistance to lift the siege. The arrival of the 1,000 infantry
at the beginning of July had allowed Strozzi to campaign once more
in open country, and forced Marignano to divert some troops from
the siege; but this was only a temporary advantage cancelled out
at the beginning of August when Duke Cosimo dispatched the bulk
of his own Florentine army to assist Marignano. Towards the end
of the month as many as 30,000 troops were probably engaged
against Siena.

By the end of August the blockade was complete and all attempts
made by Strozzi to break through Marignano's lines were unsuccessful.
Cut off from the outside world the Sienese morale was considerably
weakened:

> and one no longer saw young noblemen about the foot of the
> Palazzo Pubblico. . . . So it seemed to our governors that they
> had been abandoned; and each quickly made his guess at what
> the end of the war would be.[17]

The blockade meant a total collapse of all normal life and left the
Sienese idle and helpless, prone to disturbance and riot, particularly
now that hunger was added to their other tribulations. Religious
processions, encouraged by Montluc, at least provided some outlet
for civilian frustrations. So did the new hospitals which were organized

in each parish church where: 'every day the women brought the sick comforts, visiting them often.'[18] The problems of idleness and enforced leisure were also tackled by putting the whole populace to work in military capacities. All the young men of the city were drafted into the militia, and were regularly trained and exercised. Those too old for active military service, together with the women and children, were set to work improving the city's fortifications.

Marignano was by this time violating all the customs of renaissance warfare. Both sides were torturing and murdering prisoners-of-war and the imperialists executed many peasants found helping the Sienese war effort. Attacks on property, looting and burning were daily occurrences and Marignano even hired a young arsonist to set fire to buildings within the city, paying him on a *pro rata* basis for each building he managed to destroy. Outside the city, whole communities were wiped out:

> so that within a few weeks scarcely a house remained standing around the city for a distance of four to six miles that had not been burned.[19]

More serious, from the long-term point of view, was the wanton destruction of all the vines, olive-groves and orchards as well as the slaughter of farm animals.

Meanwhile, within the city a system of rationing and price-fixing was introduced. On 6 August the 'useless mouths'—those who could contribute nothing to the war effort—were ordered out of the city. On the same day, despite his earlier commitment to the struggle, the Archbishop left Siena for the comparative safety of Montalcino. This caused great scandal among the citizens 'who said that, as their spiritual head, he should never have left them'.[20] Hand-mills were built to grind such reserves of grain as remained in the city, and some brave captains of the militia led their men on effective raiding-parties outside the walls. Nevertheless by the middle of August, meat and wine were virtually unobtainable and bread was as scarce as the wood with which to bake it. At the end of the month, all those who had less food in store than could support them for three months were driven out of Siena, and, at the same time the French cavalry had to leave since there was no fodder for their horses.

The Sienese were convinced that the disasters which now beset them on every side were a divine punishment for having driven the defenceless members of their population from the city. Nevertheless

they were powerless to prevent another expulsion at the beginning
of October, for Cardinal Farnese warned them that if they did not
agree to this sacrifice they could expect no more assistance from France.
It proved to be a futile gesture in any case, since Marignano, who now
scented victory, barred the way to these refugees and drove them all
back into the beleaguered city.

The situation continued to deteriorate until December, when it was
learnt that Henri II was assembling reinforcements and a quantity of
money and supplies for Siena. This news increased the determination
of the Sienese to hold out for as long as was humanly possible. Then,
seven days later, an escort of soldiers managed to shepherd a convoy
of cattle, laden with supplies, into Siena. On 8 December, the Balìa
once more led in procession to the cathedral the fifty maidens whose
dowry was to be paid by the city that year. But there were many
who, as they returned from the ceremony, remarked that this would
be the last occasion, 'for the vow said: during our liberty'.

On Christmas Eve the imperialists launched a massive attack on
Siena which was vigorously repulsed. Charles V had ordered Marignano to bombard the city into submission and the Marquess now began
to bring up his heavy artillery for this purpose. Faced with the threat to
the fabric of their beloved city the Sienese began to waver in their
determination to resist and it took all of Montluc's considerable
gifts of eloquence to persuade them to continue with their defence.
The bombardment of the city began on 11 January but was largely
remarkable for its complete lack of success, and it was not this assault
but hunger which brought eventual surrender. By the end of February
people were beginning to die from starvation, malnutrition diseases,
and simple war-weariness and: 'one saw nothing through the streets
but biers and mourners and those who had not died envied those
who had.'[21]

Morale was further weakened by the knowledge that international
peace negotiations had been going on about the fate of Siena. In
February Duke Cosimo had offered to intervene with the Emperor,
on behalf of Siena, and Ambrogio Nuti had been dispatched to
negotiate the best terms possible. Despite a last plea to the Virgin
on the Vigil of the Annunciation, it was tacitly admitted that Siena
was defeated. The only aim of the ruling Eight of War, therefore,
was to negotiate terms which would permit the city to maintain
its own cultural identity, and, above all, prevent its being sacked.
The final capitulation of Siena in April came because there was no

alternative. The terms imposed were therefore harsh and the Sienese had to agree that Charles V might dispose of the city as he saw fit. In return he graciously consented to pardon her citizens for their revolt against him, although Florentine citizens, including of course Piero Strozzi, were not covered by that pardon. On 21 April 1555 Montluc marched his soldiers out of Siena and abandoned the city to imperial occupation.

This should have been the end of an independent Siena. As we have seen in their capitulation the Sienese had given Charles V the right to determine their future. Accordingly he gave the city to his son Philip so that for a brief period Queen Mary of England was also a ruler of Siena. Philip governed Siena directly for two years before selling it in July 1557 to Duke Cosimo. But, by a strange quirk of history, the republic of Siena survived, at least in name, until 1559. When Montluc and his French troops left, it was in the company of some 2,000 Sienese who preferred to leave the city than remain under imperial and Florentine domination. Declaring that, 'Where is the Commune, there is the City', they retired to Montalcino which still held out under French protection. They coined money with the inscription, 'The Republic of Siena, retired to Montalcino', and for some time kept the obedience of the greater part of the old Sienese state. Such actions showed a touching belief in the ideals of the ancient Sienese commune which had been at stake in the struggle with the Emperor. That struggle had finally destroyed the weakened political and economic world of Siena. Siena was ruined, its population reduced by more than half. The countryside around it had been devastated. And yet for four more years some Sienese obstinately refused to acknowledge their fate. Their destiny was finally determined by the peace treaty of Cateau-Cambresis of 1559 which imposed not only on Siena but on the whole of Italy that *Pax Hispanica* which was to endure for the succeeding two centuries. Two ambassadors went from Montalcino to Cambresis to plead either for liberty or for French rule. But they had no chance of success. The two envoys capitulated to Spain and Florence upon honourable terms in August 1559. In this obscure way, in a northern European town, the republic of Siena became a thing of the past, and Siena itself became merged with that Grand Duchy of Tuscany whose future she was henceforth to share.

10

Siena, Florence and Italy

Siena di quattro cose è piena: di cavalieri e dame, di torri e di campane.

Sienese proverb

FTER 1559 the political history of Siena is very much that of Tuscany and so eventually of Italy. In cultural history 1559 also marks a decisive break and change in direction. Previously, in terms of cultural definition, the only problem with Siena had been its corporate identity, its existence as a unified whole rather than as a collection of constituent parts. But, after 1559, the city had and has a more serious problem: the preservation of a cultural identity which is distinct from the life of larger cultural units, whether those of the state as represented either by Tuscany or by Italy, or those of class or financial, industrial or commercial interests. The previous chapters of this book have concerned to a major degree with the assertion of Siena's civic identity in the period before 1559, and with its evolution in relation to its own internal problems. The concluding two chapters must, by contrast, consider the maintenance of Siena's civic identity in the new and largely hostile world in which her citizens found themselves in 1559.

In 1561 Cosimo dei Medici made his triumphal entry into Siena. His control over the Sienese state was already assured, as was that of his successors. Siena was to be ruled directly by a Lieutenant-General or Governor, always the personal choice of the Grand Duke of Tuscany, and, save for a brief period between 1668 and 1683, from 1627 until 1731 always a member of the Medici family. The Governor was assisted, advised, and to some extent controlled by three other paid officials personally chosen by the Grand Duke: the Auditore Generale, the Procuratore Fiscale and the Treasurer. Together these were known as the Consulta and they were the ultimate authority for all matters concerning the Sienese city and state. The Captain of the People was nominated from among the members of the General Council, themselves hand-

Vecchietta, *The Risen Christ*

The Corso, Siena

The solemn entry of Violante Beatrice of Bavaria into Siena

City of Siena in 1526. Detail from *The Madonna of the Victory of Porta Camollia*, San Martino, Siena

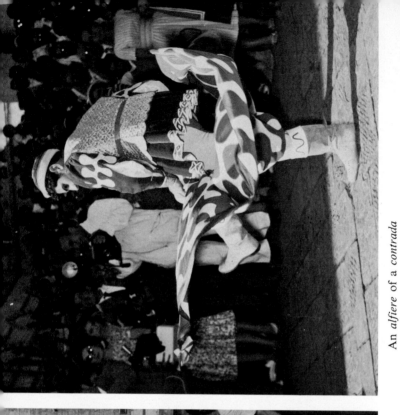

An *alfiere* of a *contrada*

The Palio:
Taking a racehorse into the church of S. Giuseppe to be blessed

picked, life-appointees. The Balìa, consisting of twenty males aged forty or over, was also chosen by the Grand Duke,★ as were the members of every other important civic office. Criminal justice was administered by eight Sienese citizens, chosen by the Grand Duke, and civil justice was placed entirely in the hands of foreign justices, also grand ducal nominees, who were warned that all cases must be decided within four months, 'lest any law-suit become immortal'.[1] The University, the Hospital of Santa Maria della Scala, and all other major civic institutions were also now directly controlled from Florence.

In 1570 Cosimo finally acquired the title of Grand Duke of Tuscany which he had so long coveted. It was an event which was dutifully celebrated by the Sienese as they dutifully celebrated a whole succession of marriages, births and deaths of that singularly uninspiring Medici family until, on 9 July 1737, Giovanni Gastone, the last Medici Grand Duke, died. Siena, together with the rest of the Grand Duchy of Tuscany, then passed to the Dukes of Lorraine, who ruled until Ferdinand III fled from advancing French revolutionary armies in 1799.

The subsequent episodes of the revolutionary and Napoleonic period had a considerable impact on Siena but did little to restore the city's autonomy or its dignity. The city continued to be a pawn of powers over which it had no control while it forfeited even that anonymity which the Florentine connexion had provided. For, under rule from Florence, Siena was maintained in a subordinate colonial role, the Grand Dukes ensuring that the main trade and commercial routes of Italy all bypassed her. While this did nothing to assist the ailing Sienese economy, it at least meant that the city remained immune from the ravages of war. From 1797 until the fall of Napoleon, however, Siena was rarely free from the attentions of either revolutionary or counter-revolutionary armies, each of which successively exacted some kind of material tribute leaving the city poorer than ever. On the fall of Napoleon, Siena was restored once more to the house of Lorraine in the persons of Ferdinand III and his successor, Leopold II. The lack of enthusiasm felt either for these or for any of Siena's previous foreign rulers is suggested by the fact that on 17 June 1859, Siena was the first Tuscan city to vote in favour of the Union of Italy under Victor Emmanuel II.

Given the Sienese experience of Florentine and foreign rule during the preceding three centuries, the attraction of a united Italy in which Siena might exist as one among other equal cities is understandable. Her

★ The Balìa was, inevitably, suppressed by Leopold I and replaced by an office known as the Magistrato dei Priori.

original loss of independence under Cosimo I had at first seemed to produce only marginal changes in her civic life. The Medici *palle* and the grand-ducal crown were added to the external decorations of the Palazzo Pubblico. In 1560 the Great Council Hall of the Republic was transformed by Riccio into the Theatre of the Rinnovati, while in 1568 the great fortress of Santa Barbara, designed by Baldassare Lanci—today the somewhat sleepy home of the national wine museum—was built behind San Domenico to dominate, overawe and control the city on which its guns were always trained. This fort, too, was lavishly decorated with mannered Medici emblems. But otherwise, as Montaigne noted during his visit to the city, Siena appeared largely unchanged.

This appearance was, however, deceptive. There is no doubt that much vitality had left Siena. What the city had lost above all was the power of self-determination, the power of choice. The Sienese were no longer able to create for themselves the kind of civic world they desired, or that urban environment which would be most beneficial to their concerns, for they had become subjects of a prince and, in consequence, Sienese culture from this time would be court-orientated, rather than civic-orientated. Yet, for many years, Siena was even to be denied the presence of that court which, to some extent, compensated the Florentines for *their* loss of liberty. It was not until 1627 that Siena obtained its first princely governor in the person of Princess Caterina, daughter of Ferdinand I and widow of the Duke of Mantua. She was succeeded by Prince Matthias, a most enthusiastic supporter of the Palio and therefore affectionately regarded by the Sienese, by Prince Leopold, the brother of Cosimo II, by Prince Francesco Maria, son of Ferdinand II, and by the beloved and highly intelligent Princess Violante of Bavaria, the sister-in-law of the last Medici Grand Duke.

The presence of these princes and princesses in the city gave frequent occasion for those festivals and spectacles which always delighted the Sienese and which were an integral part of the art of government in the seventeenth and eighteenth centuries, but they did nothing to halt the rapid decline of Siena to the status of an ordinary Italian provincial town. The decline of the city's cultural life continued. Even in the 1540s the University had begun to feel the competition of the University of Pisa, and during the subsequent war and siege many of her best scholars left Siena. Under Cosimo I the University was depressed even further in favour of Pisa, and eventually sank to the status of a small, civic university.

After the war the recovery of any kind of normal intellectual life came very slowly indeed. Matters were not helped by the positive hostility of the Medici towards Siena, especially in the years immediately after the conquest. Cosimo I, in particular, launched an all-out war on any manifestations of Sienese cultural independence. His ambition and, indeed, that of his immediate successors, was the replacement of an urban culture with a regional one, and grand-ducal favour, whether in Florence or in Siena, was reserved for those projects which encouraged a kind of all-embracing Tuscanism. In Siena this found expression in Medici support for the scholar Celso Cittadini, an exponent of the view that the Tuscan dialect was, in fact, regionally-based, deriving from both Florentine and Sienese models, and in the creation in 1570 by Ferdinand I of a chair in Tuscan in the city's University.

Under Cosimo I the Sienese printing presses were closed down and the city's academies treated with hostility. The Rozzi in 1561 hurriedly redrafted their constitution so that it opened with a sycophantic address to Cosimo. They were, nevertheless, considered too dangerous to survive, and their academy was suppressed by grand-ducal decree in 1568. It did not re-open until 1601. Even the Academy of the Intronati seems to have collapsed between 1562 and 1568 after a brief period of splendour under the Presidency of Alessandro Piccolomini in 1561. All public gatherings became so suspect that even the Company of the Virgin under the Hospital was suppressed, along with other confraternities. The demands of the Sienese that they be permitted to open a public bank in the city were persistently ignored at Florence until 1622, when permission was finally granted. Matters were not helped by the presence in the city of a new and more active Inquisition and the introduction of the Jesuit order, for these also had an overall depressing effect on Sienese cultural life.

To the suspicions of the Medici there succeeded the rationalism of the Lorraine Grand Dukes, whose policies of enlightenment were equally destructive of traditional Sienese organs of corporate expression. The government of Siena was re-organized and reformed; in 1766, under Leopold I, who was congenitally incapable of leaving anything 'unreformed', the ancient Sienese state was divided into two—Siena Inferiore and Siena Superiore, with the former ruled directly from Florence; the guilds were abolished in 1777, superfluous monasteries, hospitals and confraternities in 1783, and, despite passionate Sienese opposition, the University was disendowed and effectively shut down. Its subsequent recovery was only brought about by the united and determined efforts of all Sienese citizens in the face of constant opposition from Florence.

The decline in the status of Siena is reflected in an overall decline of the Sienese population by some twenty-six per cent between 1580 and 1769, a period in which in Europe as a whole, urban populations were growing. In 1657 the population of Siena numbered less than 15,000 and, even today, it has barely reached the high level of the early fourteenth century. Even more marked was the demographic collapse of the ruling-class of Siena, which had formerly provided leadership in all areas of civic life. Between 1560 and 1760, the number of Sienese noble families declined from some 260 to 110. It is true that the majority of the more famous aristocratic families did survive and continued to dominate civic life as they had done since time immemorial. Indeed, even in the disastrous inter-war years of the twentieth century, there was a resurgence of aristocratic power in Siena with Count Fabio Bargagli Petrucci assuming a traditional noble leadership of the city. In the first half of the twentieth century, the Piccolomini were still one of the fifteen richest families in Italy and retained their traditional power-base in the countryside outside Siena. Today the old Sienese aristocratic families still continue to play a most vital role in the life of the city. Yet, even given these remarkable examples of aristocratic survival in a supposedly democratic and republican state, in the 200 years immediately following the loss of Sienese independence a host of minor noble families disappeared completely, and those losses were never made up by the introduction of new names into Siena's ruling élite. Power instead became increasingly concentrated in the hands of a very few noble families.

Such a decline in the size of the ruling group in Siena can be linked directly to the loss of Sienese independence. In 1555 alone, some 250 families had left the city to retreat to Montalcino. Subsequently there was little to invite their return to Siena, or to encourage new recruits into the ruling group, for the loss of Siena's *Libertas* had completely destroyed the political prestige of the ruling-class which had ruled Siena since the early middle ages.

Of course, not all political power was lost overnight. Even Cosimo I was unable to get his own way quite all of the time and, in order to govern Siena, he found that he had to make substantial concessions to Sienese pride and traditions. In particular, he was forced to recognize the administrative independence of Siena from Florence, and to confirm a monopoly of the offices of state upon the Sienese aristocracy. Between 140 and 160 posts, including the coveted positions on the Balìa, remained the particular preserve of the Sienese nobility, as did a number of Chairs in the University of Siena. All these posts were conscientiously divided, as they had been in the past, among the Sienese *monti*, yet another aristocratic institution to survive the fall of the city.

Nor did Siena's aristocrats jettison their *campanilismo* after the Florentine takeover. On the contrary, they set themselves up as watchdogs, constantly monitoring all political decisions taken within Tuscany and insisting on Siena's unique position within that state. Even when laws originated in Florence, the Balìa insisted that those laws must first be registered with and passed by them, if they were to be applied to any part of the old Sienese state. The Sienese aristocrats continued to regard and refer to Florence as a 'foreign state',[2] while in 1741 a British observer noted that it was still impossible for the Grand Duke to travel from Florence to Siena with any retinue: 'by reason of the old grudges which still subsist among the inhabitants of the two cities'.[3] So fiercely devoted to their city were the Sienese aristocrats that they refused to look for brides elsewhere, and a French traveller noted in 1718 that in consequence they were all so closely interrelated that a papal dispensation was necessary before any noble marriage could take place in Siena.

For all this continued commitment to Siena on the part of the city's traditional ruling-class, a distinct sense of depression permeates the atmosphere especially in the late sixteenth, seventeenth and eighteenth centuries and seems particularly all-pervasive in the life of that ruling-class. Siena became a city of a thousand empty ceremonies of which the aristocracy themselves were prisoners. Every two months, with matchless formality, the power of the Signoria was rotated among the ruling élite. On demitting Office, the Captain of the People formally addressed his successor, recommending to him the good government of the commune and the observation of its laws, before handing over his staff of office, Siena's seals, and the two rings he wore throughout his period of office. But this ceremony was as empty and meaningless as the elaborate formality which surrounded the persons of the Signoria who were not even allowed to walk through the streets of Siena unless they wore their formal scarlet robes, their purple and red hats, and were preceded by a herald. The hollowness of it all was emphasized on public occasions when the Signoria processed with choir and band, the archers and heralds of Siena, but were preceded by standa rd-bearers who no longer bore the arms of the commune but those of the Grand Dukes. None of these elaborate ceremonies could disguise the fact that all effective power now emanated not from the Palazzo Pubblico but from Florence. A reflection of the situation is to be found in those few *tavolette* that were painted after 1559, for they cease to show a concern with Siena and illustrate instead events which bore no real relationship to Sienese civic life. In consequence, they are empty, formless and lacking in any quality, reflecting the fact that political and civic life had become one empty and perpetual charade.

There remained, of course, religion, that traditional area in which Sienese corporate life found its most meaningful expression, and which was least amenable to domination from Florence. Much energy was, indeed, devoted to work of piety and to the celebration of religion, particularly by the ruling élite. An increasingly impoverished city still maintained a vast religious establishment and, even in the mid-eighteenth century, there were still some 2,000 religious in Siena. The noblewomen of Siena became famed throughout Europe for their religious devotion, and many of their husbands also shared their enthusiasm, carrying a new religious orthodoxy into every area of life. But the emphasis now was less on the joyful and charitable, more on the formal and morbid aspects of religion, and the piety of many Sienese aristocrats is epitomized by that of Fabio Chigi, subsequently Pope Alexander VII, who, throughout his adult life, slept with a coffin under his bed to remind him of the inevitability of his own death. Much of this religious piety did issue in works of exemplary charity, such as the medical services provided by the Misericordia, where an eighteenth-century ambulance is still preserved. Yet one cannot help sympathizing with the horror expressed by a British observer who visited the Academy of the Intronati in 1802 and found to his dismay that he was expected to sit through the delivery of dozens of sonnets. These were all written on the one theme of the Assumption of the Virgin as part of the annual mid-August civic celebrations.

The mediocre quality of these sonnets and of the countless other literary outpourings of the Sienese aristocrats in these centuries is suggestive; the ruling élite was declining not only in quantity but also in quality. Already, by the middle of the seventeenth century, a lack of qualified aristocratic candidates had made it necessary to modify the rules for appointing employees of the Monte dei Paschi—the financial and credit institution which lay at the heart of Sienese civic life in these centuries—and for admitting men to the General Council, and it even became difficult to find suitable candidates to fill the prestigious office of Captain of the People.

This qualitative decline in the ruling élite may most probably be related to its declining economic position. As we have seen, even before the loss of independence, the preferred noble way of life had become that of the *rentier*, living a cultivated existence on the basis of income from landed property. Few occupations were now felt to be worthy of a gentleman and in 1604 the Balìa was specifically asked to prevent:

noble splendour being obscured by the baseness and vileness of those who engage in dishonourable occupations.[4]

As the famous political economist Sallustio Bandini was to discover, the only respectable careers open to a young Sienese nobleman were in the army or the church. Since patronage in both of these areas lay largely with the Grand Dukes, this tended to bind the aristocracy more firmly to the new regime. Commerce and industry were worlds which social custom now debarred the aristocrats from entering, and the absence of both noble involvement and capital led to the continued decline of Sienese business activity, until by the mid-seventeenth century even the Sienese woollen industry had collapsed.

Land remained the major legitimate area of interest for the aristocracy and it was from land that their incomes were largely drawn. But the financial returns from this source were continually diminishing as Sienese agriculture declined. In what had once been a major grain-producing area the harvests were so poor that only in about one year in three were they sufficient to support the population of the old Sienese state, and in only one year in twenty was there ever any surplus for export. From the 1580s onwards the decline of Sienese agriculture was a major concern not only in Siena but also in Florence, and every commentator speaks of the extreme poverty of the Sienese state and particularly of the Maremma which by 1587 could be described as:

not only uncultivated but largely uninhabited, its estates once fruitful bearers of crops, now largely reduced to marshland . . .[5]

and by 1746 as 'almost abandoned and deserted'.[6] Some aristocrats, it is true, did try to remedy the situation, embarking on ambitious schemes of land-drainage and reform, but far more used their positions during the later years of Medici rule, to protect and encourage a brigandage from which they derived substantial profits.

Little time or energy was, therefore, devoted by Siena's aristocrats to profitable concerns, while much came to be expended on maintaining appearances and a way of life which involved increasing expenditure on such costly ephemera as games, festivals, dowries, weddings and funerals. Money spent on the arts went largely to provide a splendid setting for such events, with the result that even the best of Siena's eighteenth-century painters, Giuseppe Nasini, was really little more than an interior decorator. The nobility lived a pleasant, easy and undemanding kind of existence, as Grand Duke Pietro Leopold was to note when he remarked that the 'dedication of the Sienese nobility to a soft and easy life' made them totally unwilling to participate in the political life of the Grand Duchy of Tuscany. Even the poorest nobleman could surround himself with a host of servants, for the collapse of Sienese agriculture had driven whole armies of destitute peasants into the city in search of work. And, when ready cash was not available to maintain a sufficiently comfortable way of life, the aristocrats simply borrowed so that, by the mid-eighteenth century, many Sienese noble families had debts which amounted to more than twice their annual income.

In the process of social and cultural change which transformed the nature of the Sienese élite the existence of the grand-ducal court played a major contributory role. Successive Grand Dukes deliberately encouraged the Sienese aristocrats to think of themselves as a caste or class apart, and to bind their interests first to the Florentine court and only subsequently to the city of Siena. The most extraordinary and retrograde of the means devised to achieve this end was a partial refeudalization of the Sienese state with the creation of new fiefs, particularly in the Sienese Maremma. These were designed to tie to the new regime such ancient Sienese families as the Piccolomini, the D'Elci and the Tolomei. By acting in this manner the Grand Dukes may have ensured the loyalty of the beneficiaries of their policy, but they certainly also created a whole new series of barriers to improving the fortunes of an agricultural region which was already in full economic decline.

The masterly inactivity of the Sienese nobility in the economic sphere, symbolized in the change by which the Loggia della Mercanzia ceased to be a meeting-place for the business community of Siena and became 'the place where at midday in the summer the Sienese nobility meet to chat together',[7] was partially responsible for changing a once prosperous commercial centre into a run-down, agricultural market-town in which many of the poorest section of the community only survived because of the large number of charitable foundations dating from the middle ages. From the sixteenth century to the most recent past, when some attempt has been made, by means of industrial development, to produce an alternative non-agricultural economic base, Siena has been a place whose entire economy has been based upon the consumption in the city of profits created in the countryside. Siena has not lacked artisans, but they have been mainly engaged in the luxury trades—in the production of wrought-iron work, fine furniture, or expensive sweetmeats, like the famous *panforte* and *ricciarelli* of Siena. The only services offered to the countryside, in exchange for the profits the city has swallowed up, have been administrative ones. Even in the twentieth century, Siena long remained curiously innocent of the modern industrial world, and if blame is to be attached to that fact, then a large share must be borne by the city's traditional ruling-class.

Unable to provide economic leadership, the Sienese aristocrats were also incapable of providing that vigorous cultural leadership that once characterized their role in Siena. In the latter half of the sixteenth and early seventeenth centuries, among her leading painters Siena could still boast Arcangelo and Ventura Salimbeni, Francesco and Raffaello Vanni, Sebastiano Folli, Alessandro Casolano and Pietro Sorri, none of whom was an indifferent painter, and in Rutilio Manetti she produced one of the greatest of all seventeenth-century Italian artists. Other distinguished artists of the seventeenth and eighteenth centuries included Astolfo Petrazzi, Niccolò Torniolo, il Rustichino, Bernardino Mei and Francesco and Giuseppe Nasini. All of these were to some extent very dependent upon aristocratic patronage. Yet the fact that such artists are little known outside of Siena is significant. It indicates that Siena was no longer playing the leading role in the cultural life of Europe that she had in the past, and that her aristocratic patrons were increasingly more willing to look for the accepted and the acceptable than for innovation and radical change.

Such signs of cultural vitality, therefore, as are to be discerned in Siena, seem to have existed almost despite rather than because of her aristocracy, and emerged from completely new social structures. Thus, as we shall see in the following chapter, it was above all the *contrade* which, through the Palio, maintained the Sienese civic spirit after 1559, and among the earliest signs of cultural renewal in the early seventeenth century was the refounding of the Academy of the Rozzi. Despite a series of disagreements between those who wished the Rozzi to remain true to its original nature, and those who wished to turn its organization into a proper academy and to admit the nobility, the refounded Rozzi won immediate popular support and was immensely successful. Life in Siena became unthinkable without it and it even finally won a belated grand-ducal approval when in 1690 the Rozzi were given their first permanent theatre. Yet, in its very essence, the Academy of the Rozzi was anti-aristocratic for no nobleman was permitted to participate in its activities.

In various branches of science and learning Siena was to be distinguished in the seventeenth and eighteenth centuries. The Jesuit Collegio Tolomei, founded under the will of Celso Tolomei in 1628, and opened in 1676, rapidly earned a reputation as one of the best schools in Europe, attracting students from all over Italy; here some young Sienese noblemen were permitted to attend classes in the Humanities and in Italian. The Hospital of Santa Maria della Scala maintained its reputation and was enriched in the eighteenth century by the addition of a:

> beautiful Anatomy Theatre, built entirely with great magnificence and at no small cost.[8]

It had sufficient prestige to be able to attract numbers of aspiring young doctors to train and study

> under the instruction of most excellent professors who are employed to teach there and who also give their services free, always making the Hospital more celebrated not only in Siena but throughout all Italy . . .[9]

The doctors of Santa Maria della Scala were among the first in Europe to practise widespread vaccination against smallpox; by the 1750s Pompeio Neri could report to the Grand Duke that

> in Siena, which is a small city, many more experiments in inoculation have been made in proportion to the population than in any other place in Italy.[10]

One of the most important founders of modern economic theory, whose pioneering *Discorso Economico*, published in 1739, was based upon studies of the Sienese Maremma, was Sallustio Antonio Bandini. Although he was a Sienese aristocrat by birth, Bandini actually came from one of the most ardently republican and popular families, and was himself a younger son with a distaste for the principle of primogeniture and noble privilege. On his death Bandini made a particularly significant contribution to Sienese civic life by leaving to the city his valuable collection of books, amounting to some 2,900 volumes. This collection formed the nucleus of the first Sienese public library—the present Biblioteca Comunale—which was opened in 1759. It was a legacy of particular significance for it is clear that the intellectual life of the city had been seriously impoverished in the earlier eighteenth century by a grave shortage of books. It was precisely for this reason that, in 1737, L. A. Muratori advised a bright young Sienese scholar to leave his native city to study at Rome or Florence. Bandini was also largely responsible for reviving the Academy of the Fisiocritici which had originally been founded by Pirro Maria Gabbrielli as a scientific academy to demonstrate the 'modern philosophy'[11] to the Sienese. Gabbrielli had also been responsible for the creation of Siena's famous Botanic garden.

It would not, therefore, be correct to see Siena in the seventeenth and eighteenth centuries as a complete cultural backwater. In some areas, including in particular the applied sciences, there was a vigorous and lively intellectual development. Yet this development occurred without any very significant aristocratic participation. Indeed, for much of the eighteenth century, the really vital areas of Sienese cultural life were characterized by an ethos which was largely anti-aristocratic, hostile to noble exclusiveness and privilege. By the end of the century indeed most of the cultivated men in the city were Jacobin in their sympathies, including the majority of the University professors and the doctors of the Hospital, whereas the most reactionary of the counter-revolutionaries were all recruited from ancient aristocratic Sienese families: the Chigi, the Malavolti, the Piccolomini and the Bandini.

It is probable that the absence of aristocratic participation in the life of the city as a whole became a fundamental weakness. While in earlier centuries, as we have seen, the ruling-classes had controlled every area of civic life, they had remained in contact with all classes of society, and this was a constant source of vitality in civic life. Now this same ruling-class, while it continued to dominate the political life of the city, deliberately withdrew from all other social, cultural and civic contact, a withdrawal neatly symbolized by the decision of 1571 to close the Logge del Papa with strong iron gates, 'in order to keep out the poor and the animals that currently occupy it'.[12] Noble children received a separate and exclusive education at the Academy of the Arrischiati, where they were taught the arts most appropriate to noble life: rhetoric, philosophy, oratory, poetry, dancing, fencing and horseman-ship. The noble academies became more exclusive, dominated by routine, pomp, and formality, and more court-orientated. Less than a generation after the fall of the republic, it could already be argued that academies flourished best under princely rule since, 'only under the shadow of some great and good prince', could members pursue their intellectual interests, sheltered from all 'weighty and troublesome worries of the world'.[13] The one desire of the true nobleman was to withdraw from the troublesome urban world, preferably to an undemanding life in a villa in the nearby Tuscan countryside, where he might spend his time in the manner of the followers of Plato, who, in the words of Scipione Bargagli in 1569 pursued

> virtuous conversations for the comfort, utility, and recreation of our mortal life ... among peaceful woods and pleasant fields ... a mile away from the city of Athens.[14]

Such an ideal was the absolute antithesis of that involvement with, and pride in, civic life, which had once been expounded by Ambrogio Lorenzetti and which had epitomised Siena's ruling-class for so many centuries.

The most characteristic new institution of the Sienese nobility therefore must be their Casino, to which only they were admitted, and which effectively consisted of a series of public rooms for aristocratic reunions, meetings and entertainments, and for the display of conspicuous expenditure. Rarely did that expenditure involve the patronage of learning or the arts for these were now accorded a low priority. The aristocrat's cultural and intellectual horizons were normally bounded by his own family interests. He might employ a painter to decorate his family palace, or to paint family portraits; or he might expend money upon his family altar. If he was interested in learning at all it was, more often than not, genealogical research which fascinated him. Celso Cittadini's reputation in Siena was at least partially based on his historical research into the origins of Siena's noble families, and this clearly was a major reason for the success of Girolamo Gigli's *Diario*. Other typical compilations of genealogical material were made in 1724 by Abate Galgano Bichi and in 1738 by Giovanni Antonio Pecci. Such labours of family love have undoubtedly been of benefit to subsequent scholars, as has the family piety of the Piccolomini which led them to abstract from the archive, and so preserve, any of the *tavolette* which referred to their family. However, those families did not provide at the time either artistic inspiration or cultural leadership.

It is doubtful, in any case, whether Siena's aristocrats could have acted any longer as discerning patrons of art and learning within the Sienese tradition, for they had lost all real contact with their own past. Between 1500 and 1700, if we except the two great histories of Mala-volti and Tommasi, the Sienese seem, uncharacteristically, to have for-gotten their own history. When Uberto Benvoglienti addressed the Fisiocritici in 1699, on the subject of the antiquities of Siena, he felt bound to begin by remarking that:

I rather expect you will greet the new subject I have chosen with little applause.[15]

An ignorance of Sienese history was matched by an ignorance of the traditions of Sienese art and architecture, so that, in these areas, the Sienese aristocrats came slavishly to ape the tastes and fashions of the rest of Europe, even when these were hostile to the Sienese tradition. For it was predictable, if regrettable, that the Gothic splendours of Siena would be unlikely to engender enthusiasm in the true eighteenth-century man, long-trained to ignore all but the overtly classically-inspired. The vast majority of eighteenth-century travellers, if they had been sufficiently forewarned, followed the example of Smollett, and stopped in Siena only long enough to eat and sleep. Even if they permitted themselves the dubious pleasure of investigating the city, they were unlikely to enjoy themselves. Visiting the cathedral, des-cribed by Adam Walker in 1790 as 'a solemn sort of zebra, black and white',[16] they were most likely to share Addison's bewilderment:

When a man sees the prodigious pains and expense that our fore-fathers have been at in these barbarous buildings, one cannot but fancy to himself what miracles of architecture they would have left us had they only been instructed in the right way; for when the devotion of those ages was much warmer than it is at the present, and the riches of the people were more at the disposal of their priests, there was so much money consumed on these Gothic cathedrals as would have finished a greater variety of noble buildings than have been raised either before or since that time . . . nothing in the world can make a prettier show to those who prefer false beauties and affected ornaments to a noble and majestic simplicity.[17]

The Palazzo Pubblico was found to be equally uninspiring:

an old building with nothing to recommend it, or even to evoke curiosity, apart from a few paintings which are even more ancient and ugly than the palace itself . . .[18]

was the view of an eighteenth-century French traveller.

The triumphs of the Sienese renaissance were equally unsuccessful in evoking a favourable response. In 1770 Francesco di Giorgio's exquisite bronze angels on the high altar of the cathedral were described as:

> executed in a dry and arid manner such as one might expect from a sculptor to whom the sublime works of Michelangelo were as yet unknown.[19]

And even a hundred years later Crowe and Calvacaselle were to describe these same angels as:

> hard, dry and inelegant, of paltry type and form and draped in vestments of broken folds.[20]

Adopting and imitating such attitudes, the Sienese themselves while having the sense to decide in the early eighteenth century to erect the archbishop's palace in a Gothic style, spent far more time trying to impose some kind of neo-classical order upon their city. Although some attempt was made to regularize the façades of its palaces, the irregularity of the Campo remained a constant source of embarrassment, but, as we have seen, the interior of the cathedral was remodelled with carefully balanced altars in the side-aisles. Neoclassical façades were also added to San Martino in 1613 and by Giovanni Pietro Cremoni to San Vigilio and San Giorgio in the eighteenth century. Guide-books, whose main criterion of aesthetic values in discussing earlier works of art appears to have been a favourable mention of the painter or painting in question in Vasari's *Lives*, emphasized the contributions made by Siena to the art of the High Renaissance, but all the glories of Siena's Gothic past and of her early Renaissance were forgotten, misunderstood, or ignored. In Giovacchino Faluschi's *Cose Notabili della Città di Siena*, and in Gigli's *Diario*—that strange compilation of aristocratic Sienese self-congratulation—the city's medieval artists receive but scant attention, and their authors concentrate on the works of renaissance and post-renaissance painters: Sodoma, Francesco Vanni, Ventura Salimbeni, Alessandro Casolani and Rutilio Manetti. The illustrations to Faluschi's guide are carefully selected to give an impression of Siena as a neoclassical city: the Loggia della Mercanzia with its Gothic statuary shrunk to insignificance, the Piazza del Carmine, the Madonna del Provenzano portrayed with a classical simplicity which scarcely illustrates the reality, the Lizza, the Church of the Rifugio, the Logge del Papa combined with San Martino into a fine and regular neo-classical group, the renaissance Palazzo Spannocchi, the cathedral modified by the adjacent Royal Palace, whose classical credentials are quite unexceptional, and Palazzo Piccolomini d'Aragona. The sole Gothic intrusions in Faluschi's selection are a rather over-regularized Campo, and a somewhat romanticized Fontebranda. The only evidence in these and other works by Sienese authors of any independence of taste is a continued admiration for Beccafumi, at a time when mannerist artists were not favourably regarded. Ugurgieri, in his *Pompe Sanesi* of 1649, a work of great erudition, even went so far as to wonder why there was so little contemporary interest in Beccafumi compared with his Florentine contemporaries:

> as if his failure to be born in Florence meant that he could be permitted only a modest participation in the greatest and most important current of his age.

But it was not really until the very end of the eighteenth century that Guiglelmo della Valle dared to assert the value and autonomy of all medieval Sienese culture and, with a rare independence of judgement, the superiority of Sienese to Florentine painting in the fourteenth century.

In such a cultural context, it becomes easy to understand how, in the eighteenth and nineteenth centuries, so many Sienese works of art came to be destroyed, broken up, or sold to a few discriminating foreign collectors like the German Rambeaux who, in the 1840s, bought no less than thirty-five *tavolette* of the Gabella and Biccherna from street-vendors in Siena. For, if it was in the main the foreigner who condemned medieval Sienese culture, it was also the foreigner who, in the end, rehabilitated it. While the eighteenth century saw Siena 'as an old city of no great magnificence or extent',[21] with little to offer, save as the place where the best Italian might be learnt, to those influenced by the new spirit of romanticism it would be celebrated as part of their own re-discovery of the middle ages. Hence since the later eighteenth century Siena has appealed to the romantic imagination because, in the words of Manzoni, it is 'most singular for what remains of the Middles Ages, which to tell the truth is almost everything'.[22]

For literary figures, in particular, Siena became a popular place of resort. The Brownings, for instance, spent several summers at the Villa Alberti just outside the city and the William Wetmore Storys and Walter Savage Landor also spent much time in Siena. Many of these nineteenth-century visitors first arrived in the city after a stay in Florence, and, in consequence, found some difficulty in adjusting to the very different world. But, in the end, they were usually seduced, although they always tended to see Siena's charms in terms of her faded splendours. For William Dean Howells, for instance, the gardens, vineyards and olive-trees within the city's boundaries, which he delighted in, were still seen as symbols of the decline of the city's population, and of the ravages of the Black Death:

> generation after generation, the plough has gone over the dead streets, and the spade has been busy obliterating the decay, so that now there is no sign of them where the artichokes stretch their sharp lines, and the tops of the olives run tangling in the wind.[23]

For Henry James Siena's appeal also lay in its decline from an age of greater splendours and consequently in his descriptions of the city, it is above all a sense of decay which predominates:

> Everything is cracking, peeling, fading, crumbling, rotting. No young Sienese eyes rest upon anything youthful; they open into a world battered and befouled with long use. Everything has passed its meridian.[24]

Howeverr omantic such images of decay, they were not ones in which the Sienese themselves were able to take an unqualified pride. In fact, in the second half of the nineteenth century, when, for instance, the Lorenzetti frescoes had so deteriorated as to be virtually unintelligible, a number of leading citizens developed a sense of shame at the neglected heritage of their city. Their constant cry became, 'Conserve our monuments'.[25] One consequence was the development of a new kind of artistic patronage, one which sought, not to commission new works of art, but to pour resources into the restoration of the old, and it is indicative of the new cultural direction being taken by Siena that the Istituto delle Belle Arti, founded by the Governor of the city, Giulio Bianchi, in 1816, should have gained its international reputation not as a nursery of creative artists, but as a training school for first-class restorers of painting, architecture and sculpture.

Restoration became the great Sienese activity of the nineteenth century; work was carried out on San Francesco, the Fonte Gaia, the Palazzo Pubblico and the cathedral. On the Campo, Palazzo Chigi Zondadori was restored by Antonio Valeri in 1824, as was Palazzo Sansedoni and the Chapel by Enea Becheroni in 1848. In 1854 the Palace of the Captain of Justice, originally built in the thirteenth century and subsequently rebuilt in the renaissance style in 1449 by Luca di Bartolo da Bagnacavallo, was restored to its original Gothic form. Palazzo Spannocchi was restored and in fact actually completed for the first time in 1886 by Giuseppe Partini, who was also responsible for the restoration and enlargement of Palazzo Salimbeni.

In this process of urban restoration some members of the old Sienese aristocracy found a way of re-forging the traditional link between the aristocratic and the civic life. Siena came to owe a great deal to a few wealthy and enlightened aristocrats, such as Count Bernardo Tolomei who, as Sindaco of Siena, in 1868 first suggested the creation of a civic museum in the Palazzo Pubblico, or Count Scipione Borghesi who expended vast sums from his private fortune to pay for the restoration of sixteen severely damaged *tavolette* in the Archivio di Stato, or Count Niccolò Buonsignori, who, on his death in 1915, left his palace to the city for the foundation of a municipal art gallery. Most generous of all was Count Guido Saracini, who created the Chigiana Music Academy in 1930, and gave to the city his palace and private art collection.

More significant, however, than such isolated, individual acts of patronage was the corporate shift in attitude which they helped to bring about. The nineteenth- and early twentieth-century aristocrats, concerned for Siena's past which had given them their greatness, taught the Sienese to take once again a pride and an interest in their inheritance. One consequence was an almost absolute shift in interest from the city's present to its past. In 1870, for instance, the *Società delle Feste* celebrated the new Italy with a pageant performed in the old Fortress of Santa Barbara which, with the end of foreign rule, had become a large and embarrassing white elephant. This pageant simply re-enacted the expulsion of the Spanish from the city in 1552, and was quite unconcerned with Siena's more recent past, or, indeed, with her future. The same might be said of the event which was clearly the high-point of the whole movement to re-awaken an interest in Siena's past: the *Mostra dell'antico arte Senese* of 1904, organized in the Palazzo Pubblico by a committee of learned citizens under the chairmanship of the Sindaco Alessandro Lisini, and opened by Victor Emmanuel III on

8

his first visit to Siena as King. Accommodated in forty rooms, and divided into thirty sections, this exhibition presented the work of 160 Sienese artists. There is no doubt that for many of those who visited it, it revealed for the first time the real glories of Sienese civilization before 1555. Yet, as its title indicates, it showed no interest at all in Siena after the fall of the republic.

Increasingly all the civic institutions of Siena were becoming totally involved in the city's past. The commune financed the publication of civic records, the Monte dei Paschi works of scholarship dedicated to Sienese history and Sienese medieval art and architecture. Even the Academy of the Rozzi succumbed to the appeal of the past. Until the last quarter of the nineteenth century the Rozzi had still concerned themselves solely with the writing and the presentation of contemporary drama, and thus had served as an important nursery of dramatic talent within Siena. But they now began to broaden the scope of their interests to include the arts, literature, sciences, and natural history. Most significant of all was their publication of a journal, devoted not as might have been anticipated, to the drama, but to the history of Siena— the *Bullettino della Società Senese di Storia Patria*—a journal which, until recently, has been more inward than outward looking.

The *Bullettino* was but one version of a new-style Sienese *campanilismo*. Many other journals of a more or less scholarly nature devoted to Sienese history have followed it. One of the best of these was founded by Misciatelli and Lusini in 1926. Known as *La Diana*, it was a magazine devoted entirely to Sienese art and Sienese history, and was, in the words of one of its founders:

> inspired by . . . a great love of that Tuscan city, she who goes about her business, proud of her spiritual culture and of the beauty which irradiates her. . . .[26]

Another Sienese journal—*La Torre*— was founded in 1912 by two Tuscan writers, Domenico Giulotti and Federigo Tozzi. Tozzi, among the most important of modern Italian prose-writers, was himself a fine product of the new concern for Siena's ancient traditions. Much of his training as a writer came from a passionate and often scholarly study of Sienese prose writers of the thirteenth and fourteenth centuries, and particularly of St. Catherine who inspired his narrative poem—*La città della Vergine*—which is dedicated to the city of Siena. Significantly, however, after his move to Rome in 1914, Tozzi seems to have become aware of the dangers which lay in the Sienese attachment to their vanished past, a danger which he expressed with characteristic vehemence by declaring:

> We need to live and to recreate. The war (of 1914–18) must, in particular, be brought to bear on our libraries and on our schools.'[27]

In moving from Siena to Rome, Tozzi appeared to feel that he had moved from a world that was narrow and provincial to one that was vital, outward-looking, and concerned with universal values. He came in consequence to believe that the Sienese were too aware of their own history. Others have shared and share his concern. Certainly the intrepid few who laboured, somewhat fruitlessly, in the early twentieth century to create workers' organizations in Siena often had cause to regret the weight of history upon the city. In January 1919, for example, the organizers of the Popular Party confronted by the mass indifference of Sienese workers to the problems of industrial organization, were forced to confess that they had been able to achieve 'Nothing, absolutely nothing'.[28] Subsequently both the Fascist and the Communist party organizers came to the same conclusion. Sienese history has proved too powerful for all of them.

An enthusiasm for the city's past is, perhaps, preferable to total neglect. It is heartwarming to find a city whose citizens know so much of their own history, and whose children are so aware of the topography of that history. It would certainly be churlish on the part of the historian to deny that what has become the positive mania of the Sienese for their own past has done anything other than benefit serious scholarly study. Nevertheless even the historian may speculate whether excessive devotion to the past is always beneficial. Londonderry in Northern Ireland and Charleston in South Carolina could be cited as examples of towns ultimately imprisoned by the moments of high drama in their past.

The restoration of old works of art does not always lead to the creation of new ones. A dwelling with regret and nostalgia on the past does not always increase an ability to accommodate to the present; and, as Venice is bitterly learning, a city's vitality is not always increased if it is turned into a shrine of European culture. 'Siena', in the words of a recent commentator, 'is sustained by an overbearing taste for the archaic, for the decrepit, and for history, its own intimate history.'[29] Such over-concern for the past would not of itself be sufficient to sustain Sienese civilization. For the relationship between past and present to be a creative one in the city's life more is needed than a dedication, however passionate, to history. For the past to be the sustaining and dynamic context of urban life it must be seen to exist, not merely in museums, galleries and artistic monuments, but in the continuing renewal of the present. Twice a year the civic values of Siena are restated and reborn in the festival of the Palio with its permanent celebration and redefinition of traditional Sienese mores. It is, therefore, to a consideration of the Palio, as the principal source of vitality in modern Sienese civic life, that we must turn in our concluding chapter.

11

The Palio

Molti corrono al palio, ma uno è quello che'l prende.

IT IS the Autostrada del Palio that today carries most of the traffic between Florence and Siena. The new road's name must have taken little time in choosing, because it is for the Palio that Siena has long been best known; for those moments which occur twice in each summer, on 2 July to commemorate the miracles of the Madonna of Provenzano, and on 16 August to honour the Assumption of the Virgin, when, for approximately ninety seconds, ten horses race clockwise around the Campo, ridden bareback by hired jockeys, who wear the colours of Siena's *contrade*. It is the Palio which most visitors come to Siena to see, and it is through the Palio that the Sienese wish to be observed, hence their proverb 'He who has not seen the Palio does not know Siena'. Souvenir shops are filled with objects directly or loosely linked with the Palio; on Sundays and on holidays the Campo is filled with children playing games which are rooted in their experience of it; postcards sport the *contrada* flags; toy-horses and dolls are dressed in *contrada* colours; and you may even purchase bags of sweets wrapped in the same colours. Once a year *contradaioli*—the inhabitants of a *contrada*—parade the streets on their annual saint's day, displaying the virility of their *contrada* through their *alfieri* or flag-throwers and through the drums which still summon the people with the same compelling beat that has sounded through the city for centuries. In advertisement of the virtues of their *contrada* they press sheets printed with ballads into the hands of passers-by. From April until October the bill-hoardings of Siena are covered with old and new notices announcing events connected with the Palio or with *contrada* festivals.

All these things inevitably do appeal to tourists as, indeed, they are meant to do. The Sienese have preserved from the middle ages a strong commercial instinct as well as a Palio, and are not blind to the solid material advantages that it brings to their city. Even primary-school children are astute enough to get up early enough on the morning of the Palio in order to occupy one of the bollards that surround the Campo. This vantage-point they will subsequently sell for some 25,000 *lire* to some visitor to the city. Yet, even if they do fulfil the function of being a tourist attraction, these annual horse-races are not run solely nor even primarily for that purpose. Nor are they some modern, anachronistic imitation of a romantically-imagined medieval past. They are on the contrary a unique kind of reality, each individual Palio representing a point at which, within the Sienese imagination, past and present merge into one timeless moment, and at which Siena presents itself to the external observer as a city in complete equilibrium, both progressive and ancient, both serious and joyful. Through an imaginative appreciation of this equilibrium, it is possible to understand the continued value and the essential autonomy of Sienese culture.

The Palio creates a framework of life which is unique to Siena, and which, by means of a calendar of remarkable complexity, imposes its own rhythm upon the city. Like many festival cycles throughout the world, this calendar is of six months' duration, for the first important moment of the annual ritual occurs on the last Sunday in April, the festival of Valdimontone which coincides with the annual return of spring. The ritual then continues in a mounting crescendo, each *contrada* in turn as its annual saint's day arrives:

> Unfurling the symbol of ancient glory,
> And dreaming of the certain hour, of the return
> Of its own horse, laden with victory,[1]

until the great events of July and August, and the celebrations that follow them. These last until October when the rituals and events directly associated with the Palio end in a series of official banquets given by the *contrade*. Then for a terrible six months of the year there is a dead period in which there is little to do but to calculate in precisely how many months and days:

> there will be earth on the Piazza again and they'll be putting up the Judge's tribune; and if we are picked again and get a decent horse, there'll be no one to wrest that Palio away from us.[2]

Being so integral a part of the normal pattern of urban life, the Palio cannot, therefore, be separated from the rest of Sienese experience, and, for the man or woman, 'born in the shadow of the Torre del Mangia', life and the Palio are indeed synonymous. Thus the Sienese view of the world is most accurately reflected in the reply given to a group of entrepreneurs who offered vast sums to the poorer sections of the city if they would organize a kind of touring Palio in the rest of Italy: 'We do not play at the Palio. We live it.'[3] And the same view manifested itself in 1919 when there were serious riots and strikes throughout Italy, resulting from the confrontation of right and left-wing groups; in Siena it was decided to postpone all such activities until *after* the running of the Palio.

Without their Palio the Sienese are at a loss. Only on the rarest of occasions and for the most serious of reasons is it ever cancelled. In 1798 the city was struck by a terrible earthquake, which so damaged the fabric of Siena that it took decades for the city to recover. Scarcely a building in the city escaped unscathed, and the churches were so badly damaged that it was known as the 'Jacobin Earthquake'. Yet, although the July Palio was cancelled, that of August was run. And, as we have seen, the years between 1799 and 1815 were years of appalling disasters and of great deprivation for the Sienese, yet normally the Palio was still run. That of 1800 took place in particularly odd circumstances: the July Palio was to have been run under French auspices, and the Palio itself was painted as usual with the Madonna of Provenzano, but the counter-revolution and the occupation of Siena by the Aretines intervened. The July Palio was therefore delayed and run on 17 August, instead of the August Palio. It was won by the *contrada* of Nicchio who still possess the banner. The following years, Palî were also banned because of a French distaste in the uneasy political climate for 'drums, flags and gatherings of people',[4] but, apart from this, during the revolutionary and Napoleonic years the Palio was run annually and regularly with all the customary enthusiasm. Wars, both in the nineteenth and in the twentieth centuries, have occasioned the interruption of the normal Palio cycle, but the Sienese have eagerly returned to their traditional preoccupation immediately on the coming of peace.

Another indication of the importance of the Palio to the Sienese is that every possible pretext or excuse has always been taken for running extraordinary Palî, ones, that is, unconnected with the celebrations of the Madonna of Provenzano or of the Assumption. In the seventeenth and eighteenth centuries, for instance, every visit of a distinguished person to Siena was celebrated by the running of an extraordinary Palio; in 1673 one was run on the occasion of the visit of Cardinal Flavio Chigi, the nephew of Alexander VII, and one in 1680 for the

visit of Grand Duke Cosimo III. In 1722 Princess Violante Beatrice, a
most enthusiastic supporter of the Palio, gave an extraordinary one to
celebrate the visit of her brothers to Siena, and another was run in 1791
on the occasion of a visit by Grand Duke Francesco III. In the nineteenth and twentieth centuries this tradition has been maintained—an
extraordinary Palio celebrated the visit of Victor Emmanuel II in 1860
—but extraordinary Palî have also been used to honour major events
in the city's life: the completion of the Sienese railway-line in 1849, the
inauguration in 1893 of the monument to the young Sienese students
who fell in 1848 at Curtatone and Montanara, and the *Mostra dell'*
antico arte Senese in 1904.

The Palio is then the most important matter in the world to a
Sienese, an integral part both of his own and of his city's vitality. To
understand the reasons for this, it is necessary to look at the functions
which the Palio fulfills in Sienese society. Foremost among these must
be that found in all truly popular festivals—the provision of a time of
special licence when the natural order of things is temporarily reversed.
The festival thus becomes an outlet for the expression of all those inner
tensions and anxieties within society which cannot be overtly stated.

A good example of heterodox activity, sanctioned by the Palio, is
the blessing of the horse within each *contrada* church on the day of the
race. The Sienese, it is true, have a long tradition of including animals
in their corporate religious life; in the past animals were taken to be
blessed at the Church of San Martino on 17 January, and, as early as
the seventeenth century, the participating horses in the Palio were
blessed at the door of the cathedral before the race. Nevertheless, normally, a horse does not enter a church. On the day of the Palio, by
contrast, a horse is actually obliged to do so, for, in the early afternoon,
he will be escorted by the officials of the *contrada* to their church where,
once inside, he will be blessed by the *contrada* priest. The obligatory
nature of this ceremony is all the more significant in that manœuvring
a spirited race-horse into some of these churches requires both remarkable skill and pertinacity; the *contrada* church of Oca, the oratory of
St. Catherine, for instance, can only be entered down a steep flight of
steps. The aspect of licence here involved is emphasized by the popular
belief that if a horse defecates during the service of blessing, it is a sign
of good luck and thus to be positively welcomed.

Associated with this aspect of the Palio is the celebration of Fortune
or Chance, for Fortune has rightly been called the 'Queen of Palio'.[5]
Much energy and vast sums of money are devoted by participating

contrade to ensure that they will win the Palio. A great deal clearly can be achieved by careful planning, making cunning alliances, or by straightforward bribery. The *Partiti*—the arrangements by which this is done—are in fact the very foundation of the race, the essence of the Palio. They are the means by which the skill and the cleverness of a *contrada* can be employed to outwit or at least to limit the activities of Fortune. Yet, no amount of clever planning, no amount of expenditure, no number of *partiti*, can ever guarantee the result of a Palio for at three important moments Fortune rules supreme: in the choice of participating *contrade*, for only ten of a possible seventeen ever run, and three of these are chosen by lot; in the place allocated to the horses at the starting line, for these also are chosen by lot; and in the assignment of the horses to each *contrada*, again determined by lot. For the reason that Fortune must ultimately hold sway, once a horse has been assigned to a *contrada* it may never be substituted for any reason whatsoever—even death. Should such a terrible event occur the horse may only be present symbolically, in the flag of the *contrada* which is flown at half-mast in sign of mourning.

Another function of the Palio is also one normally found in popular festivals; it provides an opportunity for play for the community as a whole. In Siena this is particularly important in that, for as long as records exist, so too does evidence that games and ritualized play occupy a role of primary importance in civic life. The Sienese government was among the first in Western Europe to legislate in favour of the citizens' right to recreation; as early as 1314 regulations concerning the cleaning of the Campo were passed so that it might be kept clear 'for civic recreations'.[6] The earliest of recreational games which we know to have been played by the Sienese was Elmora or Emora, a kind of imitation battle in which fatalities were by no means uncommon. It was fought between Terzo di Città on one side, with the other two Terzi on the other. It was, in fact, so dangerous that by the end of the thirteenth century it had been made illegal, although for some years longer it was still played in defiance of the law. Its place was taken by Pugna, also a mock battle, but one in which, as its name suggests, the only permitted weapons were fists, and by another game called Pallone. Pallone, a kind of exceptionally vicious rugby football, was particularly dear to the Sienese heart, so dear in fact that the greatest homage that could be devised to honour Gregory XII in 1407, was to play a game of Pallone. Carnival, the period of licence which preceded Lent, was always celebrated throughout the city with countless games of

8*

Pallone, and the open square in front of San Agostino was especially reserved for play. Associated with both Pallone and Pugna was a children's game, known as Giorgiani, which was always played on 4 September to celebrate the victory of Montaperti. It also was a mock-battle and was fought with wooden weapons.

With the fall of the republic the play-principle became even more important in Sienese civic culture, for the only role left to the *contrade*, save that of maintaining order within their own boundaries, was to preserve the traditional structures of Sienese society through the organization of games and contests, based upon *contrada* rivalry. The willingness of the *contrade* to fulfil this role, in turn strengthened their capacity as units of social organization, so that, by the eighteenth century, virtually nothing of any importance could be done in Siena without consulting the *contrade*, and no ceremony of any significance was complete without their presence. In 1716, for instance, it was the *contrade* which erected a triumphal arch in honour of the city's new Archbishop; in 1717 it was the *contrade* which ceremonially greeted Princess Violante Beatrice, sending twenty persons bearing torches to greet her carriage at Porta Camollia; and in 1799 they participated in the festival of Liberty when the Tree of Liberty was planted on the Campo, the banners of Pantera and Oca winning particular applause, the one because its colours were those of the French tricolour, the other of the Cisalpine republic.* So important did the *contrade* become as social and political units that they were, on occasion, the only forces of social order in the city. It was the *contrada* of Oca, for example, that effectively kept order in Siena after the departure of the French in July 1799, and this continued to be true throughout the following period of short-lived regimes up until 1815. Again, at the end of the Second World War, at the time of the collapse of the Fascist regime, it was effectively the *contrade* that ran Siena and maintained a continuity of civic-life, until the arrival of Allied troops.

Throughout the history of Siena the vitality of the *contrade*, so essential to the civic health of the city, has clearly depended on the intense rivalry between these *contrade* and on the modes of expression chosen to resolve that rivalry. At first the outlet appears to have been bullfights which, from the fifteenth century onwards, were very popular in Siena and were encouraged by the commune because they attracted wealthy visitors to the city. Such bullfights continued to be

* The colours of the Cisalpine republic became, in due time, the colours of United Italy.

staged very regularly until 1597, despite the prohibition issued by the Council of Trent. It was from the ceremonies surrounding these bull-fights that the *contrade* probably acquired the traditional names by which they are now known. It became the custom to inaugurate each fight with processions to which the *contrade* contributed allegorical carts and machines in the form of animals. These machines were then drawn up on the Campo to act as refuges during the bullfights. It was these machine-animals which came, in the end, to embody the ethos of the different *contrade*, and to give them the names which survived even after the bullfights were abolished in 1599, replaced first by buffalo-races and, after 1650, by horse-races.

These horse-races have a long history. Some form of horse-race in which the prize was a banner of special material—the *pallium* or Palio—was already being run in Siena in the twelfth century, and one has been run in honour of the Assumption on 16 August since at least 1232. From the thirteenth to the eighteenth centuries, as we have seen, a Palio was run annually in honour of the Blessed Ambrogio Sansedoni. In the fifteenth and sixteenth centuries we read also of Palî run for S. Pietro Alessandrino and for St. James, and of one run in honour of the Magdalen, instituted by the Petrucci to celebrate their return to the city in 1487. It became a Sienese custom always to allow a Petrucci horse to win this particular Palio.

In earlier centuries, however, the Palio was not run as it is today in the Campo—*alla tonda*. It was held in many different places and along many different routes, but the race normally began outside the city and ended either in Piazza del Duomo or at some other point in the centre. Such races were thus essentially linear, entailing movement from one point to another, and the significance of the difference be-tween these and the modern Palio run in the Campo, is clearly ex-plained by two modern commentators:

> The modern *palio alla tonda* . . . is confined to Piazza del Campo, and the race is circular, not linear. In order to win, one must return (or arrive again) at the starting point. Also the focus is entirely in the centre of the city which is by definition the farthest point from the world outside . . . the fall of the Republic in 1555 may well have led to a shifting of emphasis from a concern with events occurring out-side the walls of the city to those taking place in the city.[7]

In fact, the earliest reference we have to a *Palio alla tonda* is in the year 1632 or 1633, but the race in this form was clearly an immediate success. It was followed by others in 1641, 1643, when it was run to celebrate the birthday of Prince Matthias, then governor of Siena, 1645, 1647, and 1650, when it was run in honour of Grand Duke Ferdinand II and his wife who, 'having driven three times around the Campo in their superb carriages, retired to watch the race'[8] from Palazzo Chigi Zondadori. Thereafter the *Palio alla tonda* became increasingly the accepted form of the Sienese Palio.

A similar process to that of the change from the *Palio alla lunga* to the *Palio alla tonda* was the transformation of the Palio from an aristocratic festival to a *contrada* festival. Before the fall of the republic, the Palio run as a part of the celebrations of mid-August was a noble preserve, a kind of tournament in which the aristocrats could win renown for their horses, and it was an event in which the *contrade* took no part. Although the Palio of mid-August did remain an aristocratic concern, and was not completely taken over by the public until 1802, after the fall of the republic the *contrade* began increasingly to participate in it. Ultimately, in 1656, the *contrade* instituted their own Palio, that of 2 July, which thus boasts an entirely popular origin.

The Palio is a city at play; an assertion of the right of humans to play together and so to liberate themselves from boredom and indifference. But it is, of course, at the same time, far more than a game. It is an important religious festival, one of the most important acts of corporate religious worship in the Sienese calendar. The preparations of each *contrada* take place in a religious context; the banner which is the prize—the Palio itself—is decorated with a representation of the Blessed Virgin, in whose honour the race is run; and the patron saints of each *contrada* are intimately concerned with the outcome of every Palio. On the morning of the race itself, mass is said once more in the Chapel on the Campo, as if to consecrate the event and render the Campo a sacred place. After the event the winning *contrada* is obliged to give thanks, in the Church of Provenzano in July, in the Cathedral in August.

Because the Palio is both a corporate game and a corporate act of worship, all Siena is present at it. In one sense, then, it can be seen as the supreme democratic moment in the life of the city, since here the collective responses of the Sienese over a whole range of topics are expressed without the possibility of control or reprisal. It is not entirely surprising, therefore, that the first public expression of Jacobinism in Siena should have occurred at the July Palio of 1797; that the cancelled Palio of 1799 should have provided the occasion for the Sienese counter-revolutionaries to attack the French-held fortress in Siena and to sack the ghetto; nor that Palî of the first half of the nineteenth century should have provided opportunities for the expression of support for the ideals of the Risorgimento.

It is not, however, normally great international or national issues which are on trial in the Palio. It is true that each Palio is, through an expression of ritualized violence, turned into a conflict or battle. It is in its way a violent and bloody festival; the riders seek to dismount each other and are armed with helmets to protect their heads from the shower of blows which will be rained upon them by other jockeys. The only obstructive measures actually forbidden to the jockeys are seizing hold of another jockey or another horse's reins. The true miracle of Sienese history is that no jockey has ever yet actually been killed during the Palio. But what is at issue here is a localized Sienese conflict, the acting out of the rivalry of the *contrade*, each of which is represented in the race by his *fantino* or jockey, and this rivalry is as significant to the life of the city as its twice-yearly resolution in the Palio.

The Palio is essential to the life of the *contrade*. The *contrade*, in turn, are essential to the life of Siena. Palio, *contrade*, Siena, thus compose a virtually inter-dependent trinity. The number of *contrade* varied over the centuries but, in 1675, they were fixed at the present seventeen: Aquilà, Bruco, Chiocciola, Civetta, Drago, Giraffa, Istrice, Leocorno, Lupa, Nicchio, Oca, Onda, Pantera, Selva, Tartuca, Torre, and Val di Montone. To each of these, by royal decree, Princess Violante Beatrice assigned a specific territory on 7 January 1729, thus creating the boundaries which, ever since, have divided the Sienese against themselves, while uniting them against the rest of an uncomprehending world.

Membership of a *contrada* then is not elective but a fact of birth. The *contrada* itself is a territory, a city. That it is seen in such terms is suggested by the twentieth-century practice of twinning a *contrada* with another town, rather than with a part of another town, and by the fact that inter-*contrada* relationships are conceived of in terms of 'alliances'. The *contrada* is also a tribe which seems almost to have an existence external to the collectivity of its members. Thus, inhabitants of different *contrade* are often assumed to have the characteristics associated with the animal symbol by which they are known. In the early nineteenth century, for instance, because the colours of the Austrian flag were the same as those of the *contrada* of Tartuca, the inhabitants of that *contrada* were believed to be opposed to the cause of Italian nationalism, while the inhabitants of Oca whose colours were, as we have seen, red, white and green, were believed to be its most ardent supporters.

A Sienese, then, is not just born into a family, but also into the extended family of his *contrada*, which he may indeed refer to as his 'mother'. The *contrada* will be concerned for his social well-being throughout his life. He will receive not only a Christian baptism, but also a baptism into his *contrada*, at one of the fountains which have been built, for the most part, only in this century; the fountain of Bruco, for example, was completed as recently as 1978. Some of these fountains are extremely fine examples of modern sculpture; that of Lupa, for instance, designed by Emilio Montagnani, or that of Giraffa, designed in 1970 by Salvatore Bocci. Again, if a member of a *contrada* graduates from the University he is sent formal congratulations by his *contrada*. When he marries, the *contrada* herald is obliged to attend his wedding, presenting a bouquet to the bride, made up of flowers in the *contrada* colours, and bound with matching ribbons. When he dies he may well be buried with the *contrada* flag, and, even after death he will be remembered by other *contradaioli* in prayers on 4 November, 'the day of the dead'.

The *contrada* is an ideal form of social control. It preserves within itself many of the most ancient social structures of Siena including that of a dominating élite. Since the fall of the republic, the role of the aristocrats within the *contrade* has been recognized in that it is they who have been and are nominated official Protectors of the *contrade*. The *contrada* also preserves the traditional authority of the old over the young. Within the *contrada* the old must be valued because they are the transmitters of all the traditions which make the *contrada* unique. The *contrada* is thus also an excellent method of curbing adolescent turbulence. Not only does the *contrada* authorize a form of ritualized violence in the form of *contrada* rivalry, consummated on the days of the Palio, it also provides a role for the young men to play in relation to younger adolescents and boys. For it is the young men who make up the *comparsa*—the public image of the *contrada*—the drummers, flag-throwers, and heralds. They are therefore possessors of vital skills which only they can transmit to a younger generation of *contradaioli* who will eventually succeed them. Thus an ideal bond is created between the older and the younger males of the *contrada*, since only the older can initiate the younger into the mysteries of a group which all desire to join.

Each *contrada* also serves as a social club and as a means of social assistance. Any member of a *contrada* in need will be assisted with *contrada* funds, often without his having to request such assistance. The *contrada* also above all gives an identity to every man and woman who belongs to it. Each is small enough for all the inhabitants to be known to one another. Within his *contrada*, therefore, a man's anonymity is denied; here he is recognized and known, whether he is hated or loved, popular or unpopular. In return each member of a *contrada* must identify completely with it; he will rejoice when it rejoices, grieve when it grieves. The enemies of the *contrada* are his enemies, its friends are his friends. When the *contrada* is humiliated he will share that humiliation, and when it is successful he will partake in its success. The *contrada* church is a particularly sacred place to him and the *contrada* saint is his own saint. Bellesort, in 1919, recalled the *contrada* feast of Selva at which the local parish priest tried to explain the peculiar nature of *contrada* loyalty by pointing out a free-thinking socialist and militant anti-clerical who, according to Bellesort's informant, 'would like the government to pull down all the churches, except, of course, that of San Sebastiano', the *contrada* church of Selva. The priest continued:

> You must understand . . . that when I take the catechism in the church close by, I scarcely get ten children from the district. But, when I hold the catechism here, all the free-thinkers of the *contrada* send me their children. The Christ of San Sebastiano died specially for the people of Selva, and their Madonna is not the same as the Madonna of Torre or of Giraffa.[9]

Each *contrada* is a self-governing community with its own general council and a Seggia or Sedia of officials who are elected annually on the second Sunday in May. The supreme head of the *contrada* is the Prior, Rector or Governor, and he or she has a deputy or vicar to represent him in his absence. He is also assisted by councillors who number between two and four. Other *contrada* officials are the Captain, who publicly represents the *contrada* during the Palio, the Treasurer and the Chancellor, the *contrada* priest, and the custodian of the *contrada* church or oratory.

The oratories are a focus of considerable pride and are of great significance since so much of the ceremonial life of the *contrada* is centred upon them. It is here that the communion between the living and dead inhabitants of the *contrada* is maintained, through services for the dead. It is here that the *contrada* worships together on its annual feast-day; here that it prays for victory before the Palio; and here, if it is victorious, that it subsequently gives thanks. The origins of such oratories are diverse. Some in fact were built by the *contradaioli* themselves, including that of Oca, begun in 1465 and dedicated to St. Catherine. The symbol of Oca—the goose—together with that of the commune, appears on the very beautiful renaissance façade. Most of the oratories date, however, from the seventeenth and eighteenth centuries. In 1680 Bruco's church, dedicated to the Most Holy Name of Jesus, was built by the *contrada*; in 1684 Tartuca, which had previously gathered in the oratory of the Carceri di San Ansano, erected its own church, dedicated to St. Anthony of Padua, and designed by Giacomo Franchini. Tartuca commissioned the Sienese sculptor, Giovan Antonio Mazzuoli, to make a statue of St. Anthony, and the painters Antonio and Giuseppe Nasini, Antonio Buonfigli and Annibale Mazzuoli, to decorate the ceilings. Montone met originally in the church of San Clemente ai Servi and subsequently, until 1741, in the oratory of the Trinity. It then transferred to the Church of St. Leonard, which had previously belonged to the Knights of St. John, and completely rebuilt it at the expense of the *contrada*. The church of Nicchio which has recently been restored to all of its original prettiness, was also built by the *contrada* in 1680. It was dedicated to St. Gaetano da Thiene and was decorated by the distinguished Sienese stuccoist, Giacomo Franchini, and by the painters Giuseppe Nasini and Tommaso Bonechi. Chiocciola also built their own oratory in the seventeenth century, dedicated to the Madonna del Rosario, but they subsequently moved in 1814 to the church of the suppressed convent of Saints Peter and Paul.

It was about this time that the majority of the *contrade* acquired their own oratories usually from the suppressed guilds and confraternities. The oratory of San Giovanni Battista dei Tredicini was given, for instance, to Aquilà in 1778, and Selva obtained their oratory of San Sebastiano at about the same time. Pantera, in 1813, acquired the Church of the Carmine; however, in 1958, they transferred to the church of San Quirico. Onda in 1787 obtained the Oratory of St. Joseph from the suppressed Guild of Carpenters; Giraffa in 1824 the Oratory of the Suffragio; and Istrice in 1788 the church of S. Vincenzio and S. Anastasio. Torre have met since 1526 in the church of St. James the Apostle, a church built at communal expense in celebration of the victory of Porta Camollia. Civetta originally met in the church of S. Pietro in Banchi, but since 1787 they have gathered in the famous church of San Cristoforo in Piazza Tolomei; the Tolomei have been associated with Civetta for many centuries. Drago transferred from its original home in San Domenico to the church of the Paradiso in 1789. Lupa's church is the Oratory of San Rocco, in front of which in 1584 the *contrada* built a column surmounted by a statue of the She-Wolf and her twins. The church of Leocorno is San Giorgio, formerly the Archbishop's seminary, which the *contrada* was given in 1869.

These oratories are the heart of each *contrada* and are normally near or attached to the secular seat of the *contrada* which also serves as a social centre. They therefore also lie at the centre of the intense rivalries between them which are played out in the Palio. The very nature of these rivalries indicates how deeply the experience of the Palio is embedded in the traditional structures of Sienese society. For what we have in the Palio is not some recently created conflict or rivalries like the antagonisms often displayed by modern football crowds. The conflicts are rather the product of ancient antipathies, which the modern participants in the drama of the Palio may not even know they have inherited. In the Palio the question is not one of equally intense rivalries between all the *contrade*, but rather of particular and acute rivalries between two *contrade* who are sworn enemies. Most *contrade* will therefore be found to have their own direct, acknowledged rivals, with enmities occurring in reciprocal pairs; so Montone is Nicchio's enemy, Nicchio's Montone, and so on for fourteen out of the seventeen. Such paired rivalries must inevitably recall the old dyadic family feuds of the middle ages with, for example, the Tolomei opposed to the Salimbeni, Piccolomini to Malavolti. There seems little doubt that the modern antagonisms between certain *contrade* in fact continue to enshrine such traditional rivalries when we consider to how great an extent the medieval clan was territorially based within the city, and how similar these clans were in their structure to the modern *contrade*.

Equally medieval in its origin is that tradition by which within the context of the Palio we still find an institutionalized form of the *vendetta*. The Christian tradition of forgiveness has no place here. Events which occur during the Palio, especially betrayals, are never forgiven or forgotten by the injured parties who clearly have not only the right but the obligation to take appropriate revenge in the future. Whatever the underlying reasons, *contrada* rivalry is real, bitter and intense, and occasionally causes real scandal in Siena. In the early nineteenth century, for instance, the peace of the city was so frequently shattered by running street-battles between Tartuca and Chiocciola that, in the end, public opinion forced the pair to make a solemn if uneasy peace in 1847 in a *Festa* at which a *Te Deum* was sung at the Chapel on the Campo. And, even today, fighting and violence over *contrada* matters is tolerated during the Palio festival by a society which accepts no other expression of public lawlessness.

The ritualization of the violence, within the context of the Palio, is probably related to the Palio's earliest history when such races were normally associated with war and battles. In the thirteenth and four-teenth centuries when Palî were run not only in Siena but in many other cities, we hear of them most frequently as a form of insult to a besieged city. The army, encamped outside, would run a Palio as a form of triumph. In 1264, for instance, the Pisans ran a Palio beneath the walls of Lucca and, in the summer of 1289, when the Florentines laid siege to Arezzo, 'they caused a Palio to be run there for the festival of St. John'.[10] In 1325 the Lucchesi, by way of revenge, ran three Palî under the walls of Florence, while, in the same year, the Modenese ran one at the gates of besieged Bologna. This custom, was probably meant to demonstrate that a city under attack had lost control not only over its territories but also over its peculiarly urban pre-rogatives.

Such Palî of the past are inevitably recalled by the Palio of the present, for each Palio is, in a sense, a re-enactment of Siena's history. To understand the Palio it is essential to understand Sienese history, but to understand Sienese history it is also necessary to understand the Palio. This truth is particularly emphasized by the parade—*the corteo storico*—which precedes the actual race and in which the golden age of Sienese civilization, from Montaperti in 1260 until the fall of the republic in 1555, comes alive again. The *corteo storico* thus lends manifest substance to a common view of the Palio which was vividly expressed in 1977 by a member of the victorious *contrada* of Val di Montone when he explained that:

> ... for me, to return to the Palio is to recover a lost past—one never actually known but always dreamed of—an age in which my city stood free and alone, capital of a state which differed from every other state in the world.[11]

Thus, for all those who witness it, the Palio certainly recreates the past, but it does so in no antiquarian spirit. It is entirely creative. The past it describes so carefully, and with such meticulous attention to detail, never actually existed. Thus, even the traditional costumes of the *contrade*, for all their picturesque quality, are not actual copies of real medieval costumes. They are rather inspired and original works of art, designed by the best contemporary artists to give an aesthetically satisfying impression of Sienese history.

In the *corteo storico*, which asserts the essential paradox that despite its death in 1555, the Sienese republic still lives in the heart of each citizen, the first group represents Siena itself. It includes the standard-bearer who carries the *balzana* and who is preceded by six macebearers and followed by four parade marshals. The standard-bearer's horse is led by a footman. The procession also includes characters who represent the ancient republican officers: the Captain of the People, the *podestà*, the Biccherna officials. There are also twelve trumpeters and a number of musicians who play the familiar nineteenth-century march, the Marcia del Palio composed by Piero Formichi.

Some of the ancient towns and communes over which Siena once held sway no longer exist, but these also are resurrected in the historic parade, for the Sienese officials are followed by some thirty other standard-bearers who represent the former dependencies, led by Montalcino. Montalcino occupies this special place of honour in recognition of the debt that Siena incurred to the Montalcinesi, first by their heroic resistance to the imperialists in 1552–53, and second by the sanctuary they offered to the Sienese exiles who fled the imperialists in 1555. At the very rear of the procession comes the *carroccio*, first introduced into the *corteo storico* in 1813, on which is hoisted the actual Palio, the prize which awaits the winning *contrada*. Besides these elements the *corteo storico* also includes the officials and the *comparse* of all the *contrade*, whose flag-throwers perform their characteristic, athletic, balletic displays, at fixed points around the Campo, as well as the horses of the participating *contrade*.

Thus, momentarily, the former glories of Siena live once more in the city's beloved Piazza del Campo, and for the few minutes that the horse race will take, past and present are held together in a timeless equilibrium. All the characteristics of this unique city are born again for another year. Thus it is the celebration of the Palio simultaneously polarizing and uniting every section of the city, which ensures the maintenance of a distinct Sienese cultural identity. Whatever deep divisions may rend their society, and the Sienese are no more immune to current political, social and economic difficulties than are other Italians, in the Palio they become one people. In the Palio they find a unity of being. The Palio preserves them from that sense of alienation,

so markedly prevalent among the inhabitants of many other modern
European cities. By an act of dedication to his *contrada* and his city,
through the Palio, the Sienese discovers both a personal and a corporate
identity. This is the secret of Siena's unique success as a twentieth-
century city where, despite all the difficulties of urban living encountered by a modern community occupying a congested medieval town,
something approaching an ideal urban community seems to have
evolved. This most civilized of cities has a crime rate which is among
the lowest in the western world. Among its adolescent population,
drug-addiction, alcoholism, and delinquency are virtually unknown,
as is that most characteristic of Italian vices—political violence. The
secret of this success lies in the maintenance of the city's corporate
identity, symbolized both by the Palio and by the uniquely beautiful
fabric of this lovely city to which each citizen lays claim as his own
personal birthright in one of the most famous of countless Palio songs:

> In the Piazza del Campo
> There verbena grows.
> Long live Siena!
> The most beautiful of cities.
>
> Long live our square
> The tower and the chapel!
> Long live Siena
> The most beautiful of cities :

ABBREVIATIONS

A.S.I.	Archivio Storico Italiano
A.S.S.	Archivio di Stato di Siena
B.C.S.	Biblioteca Comunale di Siena
B.S.S.P.	Bullettino Senese di Storia Patria
J.W.C.I.	Journal of the Warburg and Courtauld Institutes
R.I.S.	Rerum Italicorum Scriptores
R.S.I.	Rivista Storica Italiana

NOTES

Chapter 1

1. Dante, *Purgatorio*, v. 34.
2. G. Milanesi, ed., *Documenti per la Storia dell'Arte Senese,* i (Siena, 1854), 160–1.

Chapter 2

1. *Chroniques Siennoises*, ed. Duc de Dino (Siena, 1846), 116.
2. G. Balestracci and G. Piccini, *Siena nel Trecento: Assetto Urbano e Strutture Edilizie* (Florence, 1977), 56.
3. Dante, *Inferno*, x, 85–6.
4. Balestracci and Piccini, op. cit., 147.
5. Dante, *Purgatorio*, xiii, 151–4.
6. Balestracci and Piccini, op. cit., 145.
7. D. Waley, *The Italian City-Republics* (London, 1978), 48.
8. G. Piccini, 'I "Villani Incittadinati" nella Siena del xiv secolo', *BSSP*, lxxxii–lxxxiii (1975–6), 207.
9. Ibid.
10. Ibid.

Chapter 3

1. W. M. Bowsky, *The Finance of the Commune of Siena 1287–1355* (Oxford, 1970), 259.
2. 'Chronicon Senese Italice Scriptum ab Andrea Dei et ab Angelo Turae continuatum, 1186–1352,' in L. Muratori, *Rerum Italicorum Scriptores*, xv (Milan, 1729), 40.
3. Bowsky, *Finance*, op. cit., 253.
4. Ibid., 231.
5. S. Tortoli, 'Per la storia della produzione laniera a Siena nel Trecento e nei primi anni del Quattrocento,' *BSSP*, lxxxii–lxxxiii (1975–6), 228.
6. A. Cairola and E. Carli, *Il Palazzo Pubblico di Siena* (Siena, 1967), 18.
7. Bowsky, *Finance*, op. cit., 20.
8. W. M. Bowsky, 'Medieval Citizenship: The Individual and the State in the Commune of Siena, 1287–1355', *Studies in Medieval and Renaissance History*, iv (1967), 214.
9. 'Chronicon', op. cit., 54.
10. Ibid., 116.

11. Ibid., 555–7. See also W. M. Bowsky, 'The Impact of the Black Death upon Sienese Government and Society', *Speculum*, xxxix (1964).
12. G. Piccini, op. cit., 212.
13. Ibid.
14. W. M. Bowsky, 'The Medieval Commune and Internal Violence: Police Power and Public Safety in Siena, 1287–1355', *American Historical Review*, lxxiii (1967), 16.

Chapter 4

1. G. Gigli, *Diario Senese, in cui si veggono alla giornata tutti gli avvenimenti più ragguardevoli spettanti si allo Spirituale sì al Temporale della Città e Stato di Siena* (Lucca, 1723), i, 362.
2. For this section, see the perceptive comments in J. Larner, *Culture and Society in Italy, 1290–1420* (London, 1971), 67.
3. G. Della Valle, *Lettere Sanesi* (Venice, 1782), i, 192.
4. S. Borghesi and L. Banchi, *Nuovi Documenti per la Storia dell'Arte Senese* (Siena, 1898), 98.
5. See Larner, op. cit., 67.
6. Milanesi, op. cit., ii, 177, 201.
7. Ibid., i, 157.
8. Borghesi and Banchi, op. cit., 98.
9. Milanesi, op. cit., ii, 166–7.
10. Milanesi, ii, 198.
11. Milanesi, i, 332.
12. Milanesi, ii, 39.
13. Milanesi, i, 142.
14. Milanesi, i, 186–8.
15. Milanesi, i, 251–2.
16. Milanesi, i, 251–2.
17. Borghesi and Banchi, op. cit., 629.
18. Ibid.
19. Milanesi, op. cit., iii, 266.
20. Ibid., iii, 37.
21. Della Valle, op. cit., i, 177.

Chapter 5

1. Gigli, op. cit., ii, pt. 1, 222.
2. A. Marinoni, 'Popular feasts and legends in Italy', *The Sewanee Review*, xxiv (1916), 69.
3. G. Sermini, *Novelle* (Lanciano, 1911), 54.
4. See W. Heywood, *Palio and Ponte* (New York, 1969), 34.
5. Gigli, op. cit., i, 71.
6. 'Diarii scritti da Allegretto Allegretti delle cose senesi del suo tempo', in L. A. Muratori, *Rerum Italicorum Scriptores*, xxiii, 768–860.
7. Gigli, op. cit., i, 138–9.
8. 'Diarii scritti da Allegretto Allegretti', op. cit., 833.
9. M. D'Ercole, *Un Biennio di Storia Senese* (Siena, 1914) has an account of the famine.

10. Borghesi and Banchi, op. cit., 76.
11. 'Chronicon', op. cit., 38.
12. For this see A. Cairola and E. Carli, *Il Palazzo Pubblico di Siena* (Siena, 1967), 25.
13. San Bernardino, *Le Prediche Volgari*, 991.
14. Milanesi, op. cit., i, 180.
15. Ibid., i, 1.
16. *Revelation*, iv, 2.
17. Ibid., iv, 5.
18. Ibid., iv, 6.
19. San Bernardino, *Le Prediche Volgari*, 861.
20. Ibid., 991.
21. For a full exposition of the allegory and significance of these frescoes and for those of Lorenzetti see N. Rubinstein, 'Political ideas in Sienese art: the frescoes by Ambrogio Lorenzetti and Taddeo di Bartolo in the Palazzo Pubblico', *J.W.C.I.* (1958), 178–207.
22. G. Sermini, *Novelle* (Lanciano, 1911), 52.
23. W. D. Howells, *Tuscan Cities* (Leipzig, 1911), 152.
24. Ibid.
25. Milanesi, op. cit., iii, 127.
26. C. Falletti-Fossati, *Costumi Senesi nella seconda metà del secolo xiv* (Siena, 1881), 80.

Chapter 6

1. Milanesi, op. cit., ii, 120.
2. Ibid., 280.
3. Ibid., 283.
4. Ibid., 236–8.
5. Borghesi and Banchi, op. cit., 453.
6. Milanesi, op. cit, ii., 236–8. See also A. Coffin Hanson, *Jacopo della Quercia's Fonte Gaia* (Oxford, 1965), 237.
7. Borghesi and Banchi, op. cit., 91.
8. Ibid., 29.
9. 'Diarii . . . da Allegretto Allegretti', op. cit., 776.
10. Milanesi, op. cit., ii, 326–7.
11. Ibid., iii, 12. See also Borghesi and Banchi, op. cit., 354–5.
12. Borghesi and Banchi, op. cit., 234–5.
13. ASS Balìa n., 100.
14. Borghesi and Banchi, op. cit., 356.
15. Ibid., 357.
16. Milanesi, op. cit., iii, 139.

Chapter 7

1. Milanesi, op. cit., i, 1.
2. W. Heywood, *Palio and Ponte* (New York, 1969), 42.
3. ASS, Consiglio Generale, n. 246, f. 34.
4. Ibid., f. 34v.

5. M. D'Ercole, *Un Biennio di Storia Senese 1799–1800* (Siena, 1914), 140.
6. A. Touletti, 'Cronistoria del Palio dal 1938 al 1972', in V. Grassi, *Le contrade de Siena e le loro feste Siena,* 1973, ii, 80.
7. *The Dialogue of the Seraphic Virgin Catherine of Siena* (London, 1896), Transl. A. Thorold, 49.
8. San Bernardino, op. cit., 42.
9. I. Origo, *The World of San Bernardino* (London, 1963), 74–5.
10. BCS, A VI 21, f. 35*v*.
11. San Bernardino, op. cit., 640–1.
12. Milanesi, op. cit., i, 108.
13. Ibid., i, 188.
14. W. M. Bowsky, 'The Anatomy of Rebellion in Fourteenth Century Siena: From Commune to Signory?' in L. Martines ed. *Violence and Civil Disorder in Italian Cities 1200–1500* (Los Angeles and London, 1972), 231.
15. ASS, Balìa, n. 100, f. 3.
16. BCS, Cod. A VI 21, f. 60.
17. ASS, Consiglio Generale, n. 246, f. 110.
18. Thorold, op. cit., 254–5.
19. Origo, op. cit., 151.
20. San Bernardino, op. cit., 90.
21. ASS, Consiglio Generale, n. 246, f. 164*v*.
22. Balestracci and Piccini, op. cit., 62.
23. Bowsky, 'Anatomy', op. cit., 231.
24. Balestracci and Piccini, op. cit., 28.
25. San Bernardino, op. cit., 809.
26. P. Misciatelli, *The Mystics of Siena*, transl. M. Peters-Roberts (Cambridge, 1929), 75.
27. Ibid., 61.
28. V. Marchetti, *Gruppi Ereticali Senesi del Cinquecento* (Florence, 1975), 43.
29. Gigli, op. cit., i (1854), 63.
30. *Saint Catherine of Siena as seen in her letters* (London, 1905), V. D. Scudder, transl. and ed., 63.
31. Thorold, op. cit., 106–7.
32. Ibid., 32–3.
33. Ibid., 79.
34. Ibid., 79.
35. Scudder, op. cit., 107.
36. Thorold, op. cit., 64.
37. I. Origo, op. cit., 16.
38. Ibid., 73.
39. San Bernardino, op. cit., 888.
40. Ibid., 950.
41. Ibid., 341.
42. ASS, Balìa n. 102, f, 36*v*. See also ibid., n. 1033 ff. 5–6, for a list of beneficiaries in January 1554 when the state could least afford it.
43. ASS, Balìa n. 82, f. 21.
44. Ibid., n. 41, f. 125.
45. Ibid., n. 469, ff. 241–241*v*. See also ibid., f. 107.

Chapter 8

1. M. Meiss, *Painting in Florence and Siena after the Black Death* (New York, 1973), 27.
2. A. Cairola and E. Carli, *Il Palazzo Pubblico di Siena* (Siena, 1967), 204.
3. Milanesi, op. cit., ii, 364–5.
4. Balestracci and Piccini, op. cit., 35.
5. Ibid.
6. S. Torcelli, 'Per la Storia della Produzione Laniera a Siena nel Trecento e nei primi anni del Quattrocento', *BSSP*, lxxxii–lxxxiii, (1975–6), 238.
7. Milanesi, op. cit., iii, 446–7.
8. Balestracci and Piccini, op. cit., 59.
9. Borghesi and Banchi, op. cit., 76.
10. Balestracci and Piccini, op. cit., 17.
11. Borghesi and Banchi, op. cit., 222.
12. Ibid., 88.
13. Ibid., 91.
14. Ibid., 91.
15. Ibid., 91.
16. G. Faluschi, *Breve Relazione delle Cose Notabili della Città di Siena* (Siena, 1784), 151.
17. Milanesi, op. cit., ii, 353.
18. Borghesi and Banchi, op. cit., 220.
19. Milanesi, op. cit., iii, 9.
20. B. Varchi, *Storia Fiorentina*, Book VI, ch. 30.
21. A. K. Chiancone Isaacs, 'Popolo e Monti nella Siena del Primo Cinquecento', *RSI*, lxxxii, pt. 1 (1970), 63.
22. C. Falletti-Fossati, *Costumi Senesi nella seconda metà del secolo xiv* (Siena, 1881), 48.
23. Della Valle, op. cit., ii, 25.
24. M. S. Maylender, *Storie delle Accademie d'Italia* (Bologna, 1926), iii, 355–6.
25. Milanesi, op. cit., ii, 358–60.
26. P. Misciatelli, *Studi Senesi* (Siena, 1931), 56.
27. Borghesi and Banchi, op. cit., 206.
28. Ibid., 201.
29. Milanesi, op. cit., iii, 9.
30. Ibid., 20.
31. Thorold, op. cit., *passim*.

Chapter 9

1. A. K. Chiancone Isaacs, 'Popolo e Monti nella Siena del Primo Cinquento', *R.S.I.* lxxxii, pt I (1970), 34.
2. ASS, Balìa n. 601, f. 18. See also ff. 21, 26.
3. Ibid., n. 607, f. 32.
4. ASS, Consiglio generale, n. 246, f. 132*v*.
5. Ibid., f. 141*v*.
6. San Bernardino, *Prediche Volgari*, op. cit., 347–8.
7. Milanesi, op. cit., ii, 148.
8. V. Marchetti, *Gruppi Ereticali del Cinquecento* (Florence, 1975), 8.

9. ASS, Balìa, n. 601, f. 20. See also, ibid., f. 41.
10. Ibid., n. 608, f. 27.
11. Ibid., n. 600, f. 55. See also ff. 43, 52.
12. Ibid., n. 607, f. 4. See also ibid., n. 608, ff. 45, 57, 64.
13. Ibid., n. 608, f. 21.
14. Ibid., n. 609, f. 10.
15. Sozzini, op. cit., 303.
16. Ibid., 288.
17. Ibid., 288.
18. Ibid., 277.
19. Ibid., 235.
20. Ibid., 275.
21. Ibid., 275.

Chapter 10

1. A. Zobi, Storia Civile della Toscana (Florence, 1860), i, 99. See also Gigli, op. cit., ii, 720–3.
2. G. R. F. Baker, 'Nobiltà in declino: il caso di Siena sotto i Medici e gli Asburgo-Lorena', Rivista Storica Italiana (1972), 587.
3. S. Whatley, A Short Account of a late journey to Tuscany, Rome and other parts of Italy (London, 1741), 13.
4. Baker, 'Nobiltà', op. cit.
5. I. Fosi Polverini, 'Un programma di politica-economica: le infeudazioni nel Senese durante il principato mediceo', Critica Storica (1976), 85.
6. A. Zobi, op. cit., i, 248.
7. Gigli, op. cit., i, 41.
8. G. Faluschi, Breve Relazione delle Cose Notabili della Città di Siena (Siena, 1784), 47.
9. Ibid.
10. E. W. Cochrane, Tradition and Enlightenment in the Tuscan Academies (1690–1800) (Chicago, 1961), 141.
11. G. R. F. Baker, Sallustio Bandini (Florence, 1978), passim.
12. Borghesi and Banchi, op. cit., 578.
13. Cochrane, op. cit., 22.
14. Ibid., 23.
15. Ibid., 159.
16. A. Walker, Ideas suggested in an excursion through Flanders, Germany, Italy and France (London, 1790), 334.
17. J. A. Addison, Remarks on several parts of Italy etc. in the Years 1701, 1702, 1703 (London, 1718), 299–300.
18. P. Misciatelli, Studi Senesi (Siena, 1931), 213.
19. A. McComb, 'The Life and Works of Francesco di Giorgio', Art Studies (1924), 11.
20. Ibid., 12.
21. Ed. E. Gosse, Gray's Works (London, 1884), ii, 64–5.
22. P. Merisio and R. Barzanti, Siena; a Territory, a Festival (Siena, 1972), n.p.
23. W. D. Howells, Tuscan Cities (Leipzig, 1911), 162.
24. H. James, Italian Hours (London, 1909), 249–50.

25. Ed. A. Cairola, *Il Museo Civico nel Palazzo Pubblico di Siena* (Siena, n.d.), *passim*.
26. P. Misciatelli, *Studi Senesi* (Siena, 1931), ix–x.
27. N. F. Cimmino, *Il mondo e l'arte di Federigo Tozzi* (Rome, 1966), 53.
28. T. Gaspari, *La Resistenza in Provincia di Siena* (Florence, 1976), 9.
29. P. Merisio and R. Barzanti, op. cit.

Chapter 11

1. From an anonymous poem offered to the Protectors of the Noble *Contrada* of Aquilà in 1978.
2. G. Cecchini and D. Neri, *The Palio and the contrade: Historical Evolution* (Siena, 1958), 327.
3. A. Bellesort, 'La Joie de Sienne', *Revue des Deux Mondes*, vol. 53 (1919), 403.
4. Grassi, op. cit., 199.
5. Cecchini and Neri, op. cit., 275.
6. R. Rocchigiani, 'Urbanistica ed Igiene negli Statuti Senesi del XIII e XIV secolo', *Studi Senesi*, lxx (1958), 387.
7. A. Dundes and A. Falassi, *La Terra in Piazza* (Berkeley, Los Angeles and London, 1975), 7.
8. Grassi, op. cit., 134.
9. A. Bellesort, op. cit., 398.
10. G. Villani, *Cronica*, Book vii, Chapter 132.
11. M. Bussagli, 'Il Palio è un'altrà realtà' in *Apoteosi ai Servi* (Siena, 1977), n.p.

BIBLIOGRAPHY

This bibliography cannot be exhaustive. I have, therefore, listed only those works to which I am especially indebted and those which are cited in the footnotes to each chapter.

1. ARCHIVAL AND MANUSCRIPT SOURCES

Archivio di Stato di Siena: Balìa 41
      ,,   82
      ,,   86
      ,,   94
      ,,   99–102
      ,,   145–146
      ,,   433–434
      ,,   460–469
      ,,   472
      ,,   581
      ,,   600–601
      ,,   604
      ,,   606–609
      ,,   742
      ,,   755–756
      ,,   1033
      Consiglio Generale, 246
      Patrimonii Restii, 804 bis.
Archivio General de Simancas, M.S. 878
Biblioteca Comunale di Siena, Cod. A VI 21
Biblioteca Nazionale Centrale di Firenze, M.S. II. III, Cod. 128

2. PRINTED SOURCE MATERIAL

J. Addison, *Remarks on Several Parts of Italy in the Years 1701, 1702, 1703* (London, 1718).

'Diarii di Allegretto Allegretti delle cose senesi del suo tempo', in L. Muratori, *Rerum Italicorum Scriptores*, xxiii (Milan, 1733).

Le Prediche Volgari di San Bernardino da Siena, ed. Pargellini (Milan—Rome, 1936).

S. Borghesi and L. Banchi, *Nuovi Documenti per la Storia dell'Arte Senese* (Siena, 1898).

'Breve degli Speziali 1356–1542', ed. G. Cecchini and G. Prunai, *Statuti Volgari Senese*, i (1942).

G. Canestrini and A. Desjardins, *Négociations Diplomatiques de la France avec la Toscane* (Paris, 1861).

'Carlo Quinto in Siena, nell'Aprile del 1536', ed. P. Vigo, in *Scelta di Curiosità Letterarie inedite o rare*, vol. lxix (Bologna, 1968).

The Dialogue of the Seraphic Virgin Catherine of Siena, transl. A. Thorold (London, 1896).

Saint Catherine of Siena as seen in her Letters, transl. and ed. V. D. Scudder (London, 1905).

G. Cecchini, ed. *Il Caleffo vecchio del comune di Siena* (Siena 1934).

'Chronicon Senese Italice Scriptum ab Andrea Dei et ab Angelo Turae continuatum 1186–1252' in L. Muratori, *Rerum Italicorum Scriptores*, xv (Milan, 1729).

Duc de Dino, *Chroniques Siennoises* (Siena, 1846).

G. Faluschi, *Cose Notabili della Città di Siena* (Siena, 1754).

G. Gigli, *Diario Senese* (Siena, 1854).

Gray's Works ed. E. Gosse (London, 1884).

N. Hawthorne, *Passages from the French and Italian Notebooks* (London, 1871).

W. D. Howells, *Tuscan Cities* (Leipzig, 1911).

Il Campo Imperiale sotto Montalcino nel MDv III eds. L. Banchi and A. Lisini (Siena, 1885).

'Il Memoriale delle offese' ed. L. Banchi, *Archivio Storico Italiano*, ser. iii, vol. 22 (1875), 197–234.

Indicatore della città di Siena: almanacco storico morale per gli anni 1834–5 (Siena, 1834).

H. James, *Italian Hours* (London, 1909).

J. Luchaire, *Documenti per la storia dei rivolgimenti politici del comune di Siena dal 1354–1369* (Lyons, 1906).

O. Malavolti, *Historia de fatti e guerre de'Senesi, così esterne come civili* (Venice, 1899).

G. Milanesi, *Documenti per la Storia dell'Arte Senese* (Siena, 1856).

Commentaires de Blaise de Montluc, Maréchal de France, ed. P. Courteault (Paris, 1911).

A. Piccolomini, *L'Alessandro*, ed. F. Cerreta (Siena, 1966).

A. Piccolomini, *La Raffaela* (Florence, 1944).

'Ricordi di una famiglia Senese del secolo decimoterzo', *Archivio Storico Italiano* (1847), Appendix 5, No. 20.

G. Sermini, *Novelle* (Lanciano, 1911).

A. Sozzini, 'Diario delle cose avvenute in Siena dal 20 Luglio 1550 al 28 Giugno 1555', *Archivio Storico Italiano*, ii (1842), 1–434.

G. Tommasi. *Dell'Historie di Siena* (Venice, 1625–6).

G. della Valle, *Lettere Sanesi* (Venice, 1782).

B. Varchi, *Storia Fiorentina* (Florence, 1963).

G. Villani, *Cronica Fiorentina*, ed. F. Dragomanni (Florence, 1844–5).

A. Walker, *Ideas Suggested in an excursion through Flanders, Germany, Italy and France* (London, 1790).

S. Whatley. *A short account of a late journey to Tuscany, Rome and other parts of Italy* (London, 1741).

3. SECONDARY WORKS

A. D'Addario, *Il problema Senese nella Storia Italiana della prima metà del Cinque-cento* (Florence, 1958).

Apoteosi ai Servi (Siena, 1977).

Archivio di Stato di Siena: *Archivio di Balìa: Inventario* (Rome, 1957).

Archivio di Stato di Siena, *Archivio di Concistoro del Comune di Siena: Inventario* (Rome, 1972).

E. Armstrong, 'The Sienese Statutes of 1262', *English Historical Review*, xv, (1900).

P. A. Bacci, *Fonti e Commenti per la Storia dell'Arte Senese* (Siena, 1944).

G. R. F. Baker, 'Nobiltà in declino: il caso di Siena sotto i Medici e gli Asburgo-Lorena', *Rivista Storica Italiana* lxxxiv (1972), 584–616.

G. R. F. Baker, *Sallustio Bandini* (Florence, 1978).

D. Balestracci, ' "Li lavoranti non cognosciuti"; il salariato in una città medievale (Siena, 1340–1344)', *Bullettino Senese di Storia Patria*, lxxxii–lxxxiii (1975–6), 65–157.

D. Balestracci and G. Piccini, *Siena nel Trecento: Assetto Urbano e Strutture Edilizie* (Florence, 1977).

F. Bargagli-Petrucci, *Le Fonte di Siena ed i Loro Aquedotti* (Siena: Florence: Rome, 1906).

R. Belladonna, 'Cenni biografici su B. Carli Piccolomini', *Critica Storica* (1974), 507–516.

R. Belladonna, 'Pontanus, Machiavelli and a case of religious dissimulation in early sixteenth century Siena', *Bibliothèque d'Humanisme et Renaissance* (1975), xxxvii, 377–385.

B. Berenson, *Italian Painters of the Renaissance: Central Italian and North Italian Schools* (London, 1968).

B. Berenson, *Essays in the Study of Sienese Painting* (New York, 1918).

D. Bizarri, *Studi di Storia del Diritto Italiano* (Turin, 1937).

E. Borsook, *The Mural Painters of Tuscany from Cimabue to Andrea del Sarto* (London, 1960).

W. M. Bowsky, 'The anatomy of rebellion in fourteenth century Siena: from commune to signory?', in *Violence and Civil Disorder in Italian Cities, 1200–1500*, L. Martines ed. (Berkeley and Los Angeles, 1972), 229–272.

W. M. Bowsky, 'The *Buon Governo* of Siena (1287–1355): a medieval Italian oligarchy', *Speculum*, xxxvii (1962), 368–381.

W. M. Bowsky, 'City and *contado*: military relationships and communal bonds in fourteenth century Siena', *Renaissance Studies in Honour of Hans Baron*, ed. A. Molho and J. A. Tedeschi (Florence, 1971), 75–98.

W. M. Bowsky, *The Finance of the Commune of Siena, 1287–1355* (Oxford, 1970).

W. M. Bowsky, 'The Impact of the Black Death upon Sienese Government and Society', *Speculum*, xxxix (1964), 1–34.

W. M. Bowsky, 'Medieval citizenship: The individual and the state in the commune of Siena 1287–1355', *Studies in Medieval and Renaissance History*, iv, (1967), 193–243.

W. M. Bowsky, 'The medieval commune and internal violence: police power and public safety in Siena 1287–1355', *American Historical Review*, lxxiii (1967), 1–17.

9

C. Brandi, *Giovanni di Paolo* (Florence, 1947).

C. Brandi, *Quattrocentisti Senesi* (Milan, 1949).

C. del Bravo, *Scultura Senese del Quattrocento* (Florence, 1970).

E. A. Brigidi, *Giacobini e Realisti e il Viva Maria* (Siena, 1882).

V. Buonsignori, *Storia della Repubblica di Siena* (Siena, 1856).

V. Buonsignori, *Sulla Condizione Civile ed Economica della Città di Siena al 1857* (Siena, 1857).

T. Burckhardt, *Siena* (London, 1960).

A. Cairola, ed. *Il Museo Civico del Palazzo Pubblico di Siena* (Siena, 1962).

A. Cairola and E. Carli, *Il Palazzo Pubblico di Siena* (Siena, 1967).

P. Cammaresano, *La Famiglia dei Berardenghi* (Spoleto, 1974).

R. Cantagalli, *La Guerra di Siena* (Siena, 1962).

E. Carli, *Sienese Painting* (New York, 1956).

E. Carli, *Le Tavolette di Biccherna e di altri ufficii dello stato di Siena* (Florence, 1950).

G. Catoni, 'Genesi e ordinamento della Sapienza di Siena', *Studi Senesi*, lxxv (3 ser. xxii), 1973, fasc. 2, 155–176.

G. Cecchini and D. Neri, *The Palio and the Contrade: Historical Evolution* (Siena, 1958).

F. Cerreta, *Alessandro Piccolomini: Letterato e Filosofo Senese del Cinquecento* (Siena, 1960).

N. F. Cimmino, *Il Mondo e l'arte di Federigo Tozzi* (Rome, 1966).

E. W. Cochrane, *Tradition and Enlightenment in the Tuscan Academies (1690–1800)* (Chicago, 1961).

A. Coffin Hanson, *Jacopo della Quercia's Fonte Gaia* (Oxford, 1965).

M. D'Ercole, *Un Biennio di Storia Senese 1799–1800* (Siena, 1914).

Langton Douglas, *A History of Siena* (London, 1902).

A. Dundes and A. Falassi, *La Terra in Piazza* (Berkeley, Los Angeles, London, 1975).

G. H. Edgell, *A History of Sienese Painting* (New York, 1932).

C. Falletti-Fossati, *Costumi Senese nella seconda metà del secolo xiv* (Siena, 1881).

C. Falletti-Fossati, 'Principali Cause della caduta della repubblica senese', in *Atti dell'academia dei Fisiocritici*, ser. iii, vol. II (Siena, 1879).

U. Feldges-Henning, 'The Pictorial Programme of the Sala della Pace: a new interpretation', *Journal of the Warburg and Courtauld Institutes*, xxxv (1972), 145–162.

L. Frati, 'Una novella amorosa del 1500', *Bullettino Senese di Storia Patria*, xii (1905), 308–317.

R. Galluzi, *Istoria del Granducato di Toscana sotto il governo della Casa Medici* (Florence, 1781).

E. G. Gardner, *The Story of Siena and San Gimignano* (London, 1904).

A. Garosi, *Siena nella Storia della Medicina 1250–1555* (Florence, 1948).

T. Gaspari, *La Resistenza in Provincia di Siena* (Florence, 1976).

A. Geffroy, 'Tables inédites de la Biccherna e de la Gabella de Sienne' in *Mélanges d'Archeologie et d'Histoire de l'École Française a Rome*, ii (1882), 401–434.

S. Gigli, *The Palio of Siena* (Siena, 1960).

V. Grassi, *Le contrade di Siena e le loro feste: il Palio attuale* (Siena, 1973).

P. Grendler, *Critics of the Italian World* (London, 1969).

E. Guidoni, *Il Campo di Siena* (Rome, 1971).

W. Heywood and L. Olcott, *Guide to Siena* (Siena, 1904).

W. Heywood, *Palio and Ponte* (New York, 1969).

W. Heywood, *A Pictorial Chronicle of Siena* (Siena, 1902).

D. Hicks, 'Sienese Society in the Renaissance', *Comparative Studies in Society and History*, xi, 4 (July 1960), 412–420.

D. Hicks, 'The Sienese State in the Renaissance', in ed. C. H. Carter, *From the Renaissance to the Counter-Reformation* (London, 1966).

A. K. Chiancone Isaacs, 'Popoli e monti nella Siena del primo cinquecento', *Rivista Storica Italiana*, lxxxvi, 1 (1970), 32–80.

P. J. Jones, 'Communes and Despots: the city-state in late medieval Italy', *Transactions of the Royal Historical Society* (1965), 71–96.

P. F. Kirby, *The Grand Tour in Italy 1700–1800* (New York, 1972).

Leo Kosuta, 'Siena nella vita e nella opera di Marino Darsa', *Ricerche Slavistiche*, ix (1961), 67–121.

J. Larner, *Culture and Society in Italy 1290–1420* (London, 1970).

M. C. di Franco Lilli, *La Biblioteca Manoscritta di Celso Cittadini* (Vatican, 1970).

A. Lisini and S. Chierichetti, *Siena. An Illustrated Guidebook* (Siena n.d.).

A. Lisini, *Le Tavolette dipinte di Biccherna e di Gabella del R. Archivio di Siena* (Florence, 1904).

A. McComb, 'The Life and Works of Francesco di Giorgio', *Art Studies* (1924), 3–30.

M. Mallory, *The Sienese Painter Paolo di Giovanni Fei* (New York and London, 1976).

V. Marchetti, *Gruppi Ereticali Senesi del Cinquecento* (Florence, 1975).

A. Marinoni, 'Popular feasts and legends in Italy', *The Sewanee Review*, xxiv (1916), 69–80.

V. M. Maylender, *Storia delle Accademie d'Italia* (Bologna, 1926).

M. Meiss, *Painting in Florence and Siena after the Black Death* (New York, 1973).

P. Merisio and R. Barzanti, *Siena: a territory, a history, a festival* (Siena, 1972).

P. Misciatelli, *The Mystics of Siena*, transl. M. Peters-Roberts (Cambridge, 1929).

P. Misciatelli, *Studi Senesi* (Siena, 1931).

R. J. Mitchell, *The Laurels and the Tiara: Pope Pius II 1458–1464* (London, 1962).

P. Nardi, 'Note sulla scuola giuridica senese negli anni della caduta della repubblica', *Studi Senesi*, lxxxvii (Siena, 1975), 195–220.

P. Nardi, 'I Borghi di San Donato e di San Pietro a Ovile. "Populi", contrade e compagnie d'armi nella società senese dei secoli xi-xiii', *Bullettino Senese di Storia Patria*, lxxiii–lxxv (1966–1968), 7–59.

P. Nardi, 'Recenti studi di storia dell'eresia in Siena nel Cinquecento', *Archivio Storico Italiano*, vol. 128 (1970), 345–360.

I. Origo, *The World of San Bernardino* (London, 1963).

G. Pardi, 'Perchè cadde la repubblica di Siena', *Nuova Rivista Storica* anno VI. (1922), fasc. 3–4.

G. Pardi, 'La popolazione di Siena attraverso i secoli', *Bullettino Senese di Storia Patria*, xxx (1922), xxxii (1924).

G. Parenti, *Prezzo e mercato di Grano a Siena (1546–1765)* (Florence, 1942).

G. A. Pecci, *Storia del Vescovado della città di Siena unita alla serie cronologia dei suoi vescovi ed arcivescovi* (Lucca, 1748).

G. A. Piccini, ' "I villani incittadinati" nella Siena del xiv secolo', *Bullettino Senese di Storia Patria*, lxxxii–lxxxiii (1975–6), 158–220.

I. Fosi Polverini, 'Un programma di politica economica; le infeudazioni nel senese durante il principato mediceo', *Critica Storica* (1976), 76–88.

J. Pope-Hennessy, *Italian Gothic Sculpture* (London, 1955).

J. Pope-Hennessy, *A Sienese Codex of the Divine Comedy* (London, 1947).

G. C. Pratilli, *L'Università ed il Principe* (Florence, 1975).

R. Rocchigiani, 'Urbanistica ed Igiene negli Statuti Senesi del xiii e xiv secolo', *Studi Senesi*, lxx (1958), 369–419.

G. Rondoni, *Sena Vetus e Il Comune di Siena* (Turin, 1892).

N. Rubinstein, 'Political Ideas in Sienese Art: the frescoes by Ambrogio Lorenzetti and Taddeo di Bartolo in the Palazzo Pubblico', *Journal of the Warburg and Courtauld Institutes*, xxi (1958), 179–207.

V. Rutenberg, *Popolo e movimenti popolari nell'Italia del '300 e '400* (Bologna, 1971).

E. Sandburg-Vavala, *Sienese Studies. The Development of the School of Painting of Siena* (Florence, 1953).

D. Sanminiatelli, *Domenico Beccafumi* (Milan, 1967).

L. Santi, *Quelli del Mangia* (Siena, 1948).

F. Schevill, *Siena. The History of a Medieval Commune* (New York, 1937).

G. Simoncini, *Architetti e architettura nella cultura del Rinascimento* (Bologna, 1967).

O. di Simplicio, 'Due secoli di produzione agraria in una fattoria del Senese 1550–1751', *Quaderni Storici*, vii (1972), 781–826.

G. Sinibaldi, *I Lorenzetti* (Siena, 1933).

P. Torriti, *La Pinacoteca Nazionale di Siena: I Dipinti dal xii al xv secolo* (Siena, 1977).

S. Tortoli, 'Per la storia della produzione laniera a Siena nel trecento e nei primi anni del quattrocento', *Bullettino Senese di Storia Patria*, lxxxii–lxxxiii (1975–6), 220–239.

G. Valsecchi, *Le contrade di Siena* (Orvieto, 1889).

V. de Vecchi, 'L'architettura gotica civile senese', *Bullettino Senese di Storia Patria*, lvi (1949), 3–52.

G. Vigni, *Lorenzo di Pietro, detto il Vecchietta* (Florence, 1937).

A. S. Weller, *Francesco di Giorgio 1439–1501* (Chicago, 1943).

J. White, *Art and Architecture in Italy 1250–1400* (London, 1966).

H. Wieruszowski, 'Art and the Commune in the time of Dante', *Speculum*, xix (1944), 14–33.

L. Zdekauer, *La Vita Privata dei Senesi nel Dugento* (Siena, 1896).

L. Zdekauer, *La Vita Pubblica dei Senesi nel Dugento* (Siena, 1897).

L. Zdekauer, *Lo Studio di Siena nel Rinascimento* (Milan, 1894).

A. Zobi, *Storia Civile della Toscana* (Florence, 1860).

INDEX